Through Mama's Eyes

Through Mama's Eyes

Unique Perspectives in Southern Matriarchy

Edited by Cheylon K. Woods
and Kiwana T. McClung

2021
University of Louisiana at Lafayette Press

ISBN 13 (paper): 978-1-946160-74-4

http://ulpress.org
University of Louisiana at Lafayette Press
P.O. Box 43558
Lafayette, LA 70504-3558

Printed on acid-free paper in the United States
Library of Congress Cataloging-in-Publication Data

Names: Woods, Cheylon, 1987- editor. | McClung, Kiwana Tiffany, 1983- editor.
Title: Through mama's eyes : unique perspectives in Southern matriarchy / edited by Cheylon Woods and Kiwana Tiffany McClung.
Description: Lafayette, LA : University of Louisiana at Lafayette Press, 2021. | Includes bibliographical references.
Identifiers: LCCN 2021004020 | ISBN 9781946160744 (paperback ; alk. paper)
Subjects: LCSH: Women--Southern States--History. | Matriarchy--Southern States--History. | Matriarchy in literature.
Classification: LCC HQ1438.S63 T47 2021 | DDC 305.40975--dc23
LC record available at https://lccn.loc.gov/2021004020

To the women who made me who and what I am:
Linda Alex-Woods
Gladys Thomas
Corrine Woods
Georgia Merrit
Thank you for shaping me. I love you.

—Cheylon K. Woods

This book is dedicated to the memory of the Matriarchs
who have been the most influential in my life:

Ola Mae Cérf
Victoria Gibson Stewart
Pearline Young Veal
Sylvia Bryant McClung

Rest in Peace.

—Kiwana T. McClung

Table of Contents

Acknowledgments

As a person raised in California by a mother from Shreveport, Louisiana, I had a very interesting intersection of culture and worldviews that made the novels of Ernest J. Gaines incredibly fascinating and relatable. Dr. Gaines's migration intensified his love for his home of Oscar, Louisiana, his culture, and, most importantly, his community. His novels are powerful and have played an important role in personifying incredibly southern traits and experiences that provide a richness to rural Louisiana that move it beyond the southern catchall—the *Gone with the Wind* antebellum trope—and exposes the world to its beautiful complexities that mirror the best and worst of humanity. There is something about his work that echoed so many lessons from my own childhood—traits my very southern mother was determined to instill in me, although we were hundreds of miles away from the landscape and culture. Nonetheless, her determination to raise a GRITS (Girl Raised in the South) was assisted by the imagery of strong, determined women created in Dr. Gaines's novels. On the topic of mothers, this book would have never been possible without my mother, Linda Alex-Woods. My mother has supported me in every activity in which I showed an interest. From baton twirling to candle making, my mother has always shown a level of encouragement and motivation that allowed me to flow from one idea to another until I finally found my path in life. Without her, this book is not possible.

I will forever be grateful and thankful for Ernest J. Gaines. His work and his friendship pushed me to stay focused on my purpose, which was also his purpose: to preserve and share the history and culture of rural Black southern communities. I am thankful to Mrs. Dianne Gaines, who has always been my biggest supporter and advocate. If not for that opportunity and the friendships I built with Dr. Gaines and his family, this book could not have come to fruition. I am grateful to Lois Yong and Norbert Collar, Dr. Gaines's brother and sister, who took the time to tell me about their Aunt Augusteen and Mama Zuma.

This book was inspired by a collaborative project between the Ernest J. Gaines Center and the University of Louisiana at Lafayette's chapter of the

National Organization of Minority Architecture Students. This project gave students the opportunity to engage with the concept of southern matriarchy through their own perspectives and participate in an intergenerational dialogue with the audience and presenters on the concept of matriarchy and the impact it has played in developing their identities and worldviews. I am grateful to UL Lafayette's NOMAS chapter and their excitement on the topic—their work was the spark of so many conversations.

Thank you to all of the contributors to this book. You are all wonderful! Your work is amazing, and I am glad we have gone on this journey together. Thank you to those who could not contribute but listened to me think out ideas for months on end. I appreciate you and thank you for being my friend. Thank you to the staff of UL Press for having faith in this project and patience with me.

—Cheylon Woods

This unique collection of essays has been such a joy to conceive and collaborate on, leaving me with so many people to thank and acknowledge. I want to thank my husband Glenn T. McClung II for his unwavering support and understanding. A sincere thank you goes to my amazing co-editor Cheylon Woods, director of the Ernest J. Gaines Center, for her consultation work on the H.E.R. House installation and for embarking on this incredible journey with me into the intricacies of southern matriarchy.

I offer a heartfelt thanks to Associate Professor Thomas J. Cline, PhD, for his direction and assistance with the concept, design, and construction of the H.E.R. House installation. To the members of the UL Lafayette chapter of the National Organization of Minority Architecture Students who worked on the design and construction of the H.E.R. House installation: David Allen, Breanna Booker, Mark Jones, Darrell Landry, William Molock, Shaela Nelson, Theron Page, Chloe Reyes, and Seth Roy. Thank you for your earnest engagement, dedication, and physical efforts. Thank you to the UL Lafayette Undergraduate Research Committee for believing in the project and granting us the funds to conduct research and purchase the materials for the H.E.R. House installation. I also want to give a special thanks to Dean H. Gordon Brooks II, FAIA, and Associate Dean and Professor Michael McClure, AIA, FAAR, for facilitating the use of Fletcher Hall's unfinished classrooms spaces and shop facilities for the construction of the H.E.R. House installation.

Finally, I offer a big thanks to Lynda Frese for the fantastic cover art, to all of the wonderful, engaging authors of the essays in this work, and to Devon Lord of the UL Press; without you, this book wouldn't be possible. Thank you all.

—Kiwana McClung

Introduction

The idea of women and the role they play in society has been contemplated and researched time and again. With so much scholarship on topics like women in politics, women in activism and other humanities-based fields, and women in STEM, it can feel like all possible themes related to how women have contributed to developing the world we now inhabit have been completely exhausted. A theory regarding the volume of research on women is that a) there are many outstanding women in the world whose stories have not been told yet, and b) there are so many concepts wrapped in the idea of womanness, such as femininity, softness, quiet strength, determination and, of course, motherhood. Every concept associated with womanness is influenced by many factors, such as race, regionality, and location, and can be unpacked and evaluated on its own merit and plays its own role in how we understand gender roles in our society.

This book looks at the concept of southern matriarchy and how it has influenced American society. In 2016, the Ernest J. Gaines Center hosted a public program that explored the way women use physical space in literature. This program included the creation of a "house" based on how architecture students interpreted the needs of the matriarchs in *The Autobiography of Miss Jane Pittman*, *A Raisin in the Sun*, and *The Color Purple*. That program created many discussions of how the term *matriarch* is understood and applied, especially in the southern regions of the United States. Those conversations quickly dovetailed into topics not related to literature and served as a springboard for this book. Southern matriarchy is something that has been idolized and parodied in popular formats such as movies and film, and the purpose of this book is to explore the multifaceted interpretations of southern matriarchy and its impact on our society. This book contains seventeen interdisciplinary essays that each look at the way standard tropes of southern matriarchy are interpreted and challenged through literature, history, and the sciences. Every contributor has a fascinating perspective on the topic, and each writer has spent innumerous hours carefully crafting their essays to illuminate different aspects of southern matriarchy as they perceive it. A brief biographical note, which includes the authors' specific scholarly areas of interest, is included at the end of each essay.

Like the program that inspired the book, each essay can be used as an invitation to engage in deeper conversations and research about southern matriarchy and its perceptions as a whole. No one essay completely answers the question "what is southern matriarchy?" nor was that ever the intent. The sheer vastness of these multidimensional and ever-evolving topics of matriarchy and, specifically, southern matriarchy, ensure their continued study, contemplation, and unique consumption by scholars and the general public alike. This book is a compilation of curiosity and intrigue surrounding a societal structure that has influenced so many aspects of so many cultures across the United States: the southern matriarch.

Part I

Representation of the Black Domestic Figure

Between Two Families
The Mammy and the Matriarch

Adam Nemmers

In a 1912 letter to the *Independent,* a "Negro Nurse" of the South made a startling claim regarding Black domestic workers: "Tho today we are enjoying nominal freedom, we are literally slaves."[1] After establishing her bona fides as a house-girl, chambermaid, cook, and nurse serving White families for the past thirty years, the author went on to detail a litany of indignities and abuses she and others had suffered: long hours and low salary; a grueling medley of menial tasks; being called "nigger" instead of her given name; and how she lost her place for refusing the advances of her madam's husband. Perhaps the cruelest condition of her employment, however, was the stipulated separation from her family. As she stated: "I am compelled by my contract, which is oral only, to sleep in the house. I am allowed to go home to my own children, the oldest of whom is a girl of 18 years, only once in two weeks, every other Sunday afternoon—even then I'm not permitted to stay all night."[2] In the absence of her own kin, she was required to serve as surrogate mother to her employer's White children: "I not only have to nurse a little White child, now eleven months old, but I have to act as playmate or 'handy-andy,' not to say governess, to three other children in the home, the oldest of whom is only nine years of age."[3] Her experience was not an outlier, but sadly common for African American women, the majority of whom "were so rigidly excluded from good jobs that 60% of those who were employed in

1. A Negro Nurse, "More Slavery at the South," *Independent* (New York), January 25, 1912, http://historymatters.gmu.edu/d/80/.

2. A Negro Nurse, "More Slavery."

3. A Negro Nurse, "More Slavery."

1940 worked as maids."[4] Someday, she concluded, "a monument of brass or stone will be erected to the Old Black Mammies of the South, but what we need is present help, present sympathy, better wages, better hours, more protection, and a chance to breathe for once while alive as free women."[5]

As this testimony evinces, the oral accounts of domestic workers' experiences were drastically different from the public propaganda and beliefs of the time. Composed at the midpoint between emancipation and the civil rights movement, her letter, titled "More Slavery at the South," serves as a broadside to the romanticized figure of the happy Mammy that had been popularized and propagandized as part of the Lost Cause movement. In the White southern imagination, the Black female domestic was a sort of adjunct aunt who nursed, reared, and loved White children—as or in lieu of her own—supplying human evidence that slaves and servants were well treated and happy with their masters and employers.

In reality, the Mammy was and always had been overworked and underpaid, forced to entertain the capricious and degrading whims of her masters and employers with little recourse in the face of physical and sexual abuse. At the same time, these women were not weak and passive victims but strong, dignified, and resolute, acting with determined agency to provide for themselves and their Black kin. When returning home, Black women served as matriarchs of their own families, responsible for education, moral training, and religious instruction, to say nothing of the discipline and diligence required to raise African American children in the racially stratified South. The Janus-like duality of the Mammy—who often wore opposing faces when looking after her two families—makes for a strange contradiction and has served as a proxy in the battle over ownership of Black and female bodies across southern history and literature. Her experience is reflected in figures such as Dilsey (*The Sound and the Fury*), Calpurnia (*Go Set a Watchman*), Roxy (*Pudd'nhead Wilson*), Mama Lena (*Raisin in the Sun*), and Mammy Barracuda (*Flight to Canada*). These texts demonstrate that the Mammy had not only a mind but also a family of her own; and that though figuratively and literally positioned as a servant at the margins of White texts and spaces, the Mammy takes center stage as a matriarch in her own sphere. Yet to reduce the experience of the Black domestic to either of these tropes does a disservice to her full humanity, the remedy to which is only now being introduced to American society.

4. "The Help, Updated," *The Economist*, August 30, 2014, https://www.economist.com/united-states/2014/08/30/the-help-updated.

5. A Negro Nurse, "More Slavery."

The Mammy

The "Mammy" figure is not an artifact of historical reality but was rather reconstructed in service of the Confederate Lost Cause in the early twentieth century. Indeed, as Catherine Clinton reports, "in primary records from before the Civil War, hard evidence for [the Mammy] does not appear."[6] During that time period, only the very rich could afford to keep a servant exclusively in the kitchen. Slaves who worked in this capacity were most often teen-aged girls or elderly women ill-suited for arduous fieldwork. Further, "house slaves" tended to be either skinny or sickly and of mixed race—sometimes they were given a domestic position on account of a direct relation to the master of the house. It was only after the Civil War that Black women began to be commonly hired as domestic servants, and that the caricature of the Mammy, like the Sambo, was disseminated within and beyond the South. In order to understand how the "Mammy" caricature came to exist, one must first understand why it was so useful as White southern propaganda.

To begin, the Mammy, who "recognizes her place," "is paid next to nothing, and yet "cheerfully accepts her inferior status,"[7] served as a ready rebuttal to the charge that slaves had been unhappy or mistreated under the "peculiar institution" of the South. Instead, the caricature demonstrated that Blacks were not subjugated chattels but instead warm-hearted and parafamilial—the faithful, devoted domestic servant who cares for her White family as if they were her own. The notion of the slave as a grateful and loyal servant was the seed of apocryphal stories circulating after the Civil War: the nurse who refused to leave her master after emancipation; the field hand who fought against invading Yankees; the particularly beloved servant buried in the family plantation plot. Through such methods, "the image of Mammy was used to illustrate the closeness of the slave to the master and his family,"[8] and thereby legitimize the supposedly beneficent system of sharecropping and paternalism even after emancipation.

At the same time, the Mammy figure was used for a concurrent purpose—to demonstrate that female slaves had not become *too* close with their

6. Catherine Clinton, *The Plantation Mistress: Woman's World in the Old South* (New York: Pantheon, 1984), 202.

7. Patricia Hill Collins, "The Meaning of Motherhood in Black Culture and Black Mother-Daughter Relationships," in *Gender Through the Prism of Difference,* ed. Maxine Baca Zinn, et al. (Oxford: Oxford University Press, 2015), 315.

8. Venetria K. Patton, *Women in Chains: The Legacy of Slavery in Black Women's Fiction* (Albany: State University of New York Press, 1999), 33.

masters. Commonly portrayed as a middle-aged, homely, and portly woman, the Mammy was established as an asexual being, often called Aunt or Auntie with the implication that she was unwed and childless. Even after emancipation, Rebecca Sharpless reports, "employers tried to disregard the fact that their cooks had lives outside the boundaries of the employers' homes, preferring to view their cooks as workers rather than as wives, mothers, or daughters. Expecting their employees to leave behind their own homes and children to care for those who paid their wages, they considered unmarried cooks to be a boon and actively discriminated against women with children."[9] Thus the image of a large-boned, dark-skinned woman cooking and cleaning in the Big House was diametrically at odds with lurid accounts of rape, sexual assault, and adultery that resulted in miscegenated offspring. In this way, Clinton observes, the Mammy served as "a counterpart to the octoroon concubine [or Jezebel], the light-skinned product of a 'White man's lust' who was habitually victimized by slaveowners' sexual appetites."[10] In reality, "Mammies" of all ages, slave and servant both, were frequently sexually harassed and assaulted by their owners and employers. Jacqueline Jones reports that many house servants were even required to "sleep on the floor at the foot of a mistress's bed (increasing the chances that they would sooner or later be bribed, seduced, or forced into sexual relations with the master)."[11] Few would imagine the de-eroticized Mammy (such as Aunt Jemima) as the victim of sexual advances, thereby burying such associations in the popular imagination.

Though she might sleep in the same room as her mistress, the Mammy served as a stark contrast to the White woman, who principally derived her self-value from virtuous membership in the Cult of True Womanhood. Paradoxically it was the labor of the Mammy that enabled the plantation mistress to achieve domestic ease and bliss, as the White woman could spend more of her time on crafting, socializing, charity, religious study, and moral edification rather than housework or childcare. A large component of the Mammy's work involved the rearing and nursing of White children, and many Mammies, even into the mid-twentieth century, were expected to breastfeed their wards. This intimate form of labor both alleviated the physical distress

9. Rebecca Sharpless, *Cooking in Other Women's Kitchens: Domestic Workers in the South, 1865–1960* (Chapel Hill: University of North Carolina Press, 2010), 110.

10. Clinton, *The Plantation Mistress,* 202.

11. Jacqueline Jones, *Labor of Love, Labor of Sorrow: Black Women, Work, and the Family, from Slavery to the Present* (New York: Vintage, 1985), 27.

of upper-class White women[12] and fed into common stereotypes of Blacks as bestial or animal—in this case, with the Mammy serving as a milk cow, a "warm bod[y] to serve white needs."[13] In keeping with southern standards of propriety, the Mammy's Black family was not spoken of publicly; yet the fact that a wet nurse was able to lactate meant she must have had young children of her own, whose feeding she was forced to subordinate in deference to the privilege of her "White" family. Patton writes that the "Mammy is seen as the ideal mother figure, yet ironically, in breastfeeding the White mistress's children, she is often unable to perform the same duties for her own children, which is what keeps her from attaining the title of 'mother' within the rubrics of the cult of true womanhood."[14] The Negro Nurse claimed that "during my lifetime I myself have served as 'wet nurse' to more than a dozen white children," and further that "perhaps a million of us are introduced daily to the privacy of a million chambers throughout the South, and hold in our arms a million white children, thousands of whom, as infants, are suckled at our breasts."[15] The irony of this arrangement, of course, is that in other circumstances Black women were prohibited from the most glancing physical contact with Whites, both inside the home (most were denied access to White bathrooms or tableware) and in public (whether water fountains, restaurants, or theaters). Yet somehow southern politicians could boast about being "suckled at the black breast" in an attempt to "establish a tender family feeling" and exhibit the warm and natural race relations inherent to the South.[16]

In sum, as Deborah Gray White states, "As the personification of the ideal slave, and the ideal woman, Mammy was an ideal symbol of the patriarchal tradition," created and disseminated by southern Whites in service of the idealized image of itself.[17] It comes as no surprise that a similar image was promulgated across southern literature, chiefly during the Jim Crow era in which the Lost Cause narrative found footing. The most famous literary Mammy is the selfsame character from Margaret Mitchell's *Gone with the Wind* (1936), who appears as a happy, loyal, and devoted servant who refuses to leave her mistress's side, even after emancipation. Mammy, who is such a cipher that

12. Patton, *Women in Chains,* 32.

13. Clinton, *The Plantation Mistress,* 202.

14. Patton, *Women in Chains,* 33.

15. A Negro Nurse, "More Slavery."

16. Clinton, *The Plantation Mistress,* 202.

17. Deborah Gray White, *Ar'n't I a Woman?: Female Slaves in the Plantation South* (New York: W. W. Norton, 1999), 58.

she is identified only by her pet name, has no personal agency, and lives only to support Scarlett, as in the iconic scene where she cinches Scarlett's corset. This Mammy caricature is buttressed by such characters as Dilsey from *The Sound and the Fury,* Calpurnia from *To Kill a Mockingbird*, and Berenice Sadie Brown from *The Member of the Wedding,* who were modeled after the authors' real-life mammies. Certainly, these domestic servants were beloved by their wards and tremendously dear to the authors into adulthood—Faulkner even dedicated *Go Down, Moses* to his "Mammy Callie." Yet the fictional characters are given the idealized characteristics of their real-life analogs, with a similar function in the text as reality: feeding, advising, and caretaking for White people and especially their children. The lives of these women are seen only through a White narrative prism, with their characterization no more complex than the inchoate understanding of a child. Susan Tucker writes that "for white girls who happened to be motherless, like Frankie and Jean Louise, the Black domestic was often the main interpreter of race, gender, and a host of other human conditions."[18] That is, on top of her duties cooking, cleaning, and caretaking for a White family, in the novels, these Mammies have the additional role of "race whisperer," serving as the locus of understanding about "the human condition." Across southern literature, these Mammies could play only the consummate supporting actress—as evinced by Hattie McDaniel's 1939 Oscar award—allowing White characters to pursue their dreams while subordinating or silencing their own. Especially for those who did not grow up in the South during this era, these works of literature helped establish the Mammy caricature and a lasting impression about the nature and state of the Black domestic woman.

The Matriarch

These accounts, of course, were only half of the story, and White stories at that. Southern literature has historically been written by White authors, situated in White spaces, and told from the perspective of White characters, establishing the stereotype of the Mammy according to the motives outlined above. By shifting focus away from a White perspective, however, we may encounter a very different person and character: a Black woman torn between work responsibilities to her White "family" and the needs of her own blood and kin, for whom she serves as a strong and resourceful matriarch. This

18. Susan Tucker, *Telling Memories Among Southern Women: Domestic Workers and Their Employers in the Segregated South* (Baton Rouge: Louisiana State University Press, 1988), 242.

tug-of-war between "work" and "home" lives was particularly fraught for the Mammy, who was enslaved or employed at-will and had no recourse through a union or the legal system. Even if a particular grievance was to be recognized, there were few if any protections for Black slaves or domestic workers, who might suffer corporal punishment or termination if their responsibilities to their own family proved troublesome. Sharpless writes that for in-home cooks, "putting the needs of their families foremost had major ramifications . . . Primarily, it meant that cooks constantly risked conflict with their employers, for the best interests of the cook's family often were diametrically opposed to those of the employer."[19] While these women negotiated for shorter hours, higher wages, and more flexible work duties, every loss or gain came at the expense of one family or the other. Every dollar in their salaries had to come from a White pocket; every hour spent caring for White children was an hour Black children lost with their mothers. Jones adds that "the welfare of a black family (as defined by its own members) could have explicitly negative implications for white landowners and housewives," as when Black domestic workers returning home at night "deprived white women of a servant 'on call' twenty-four hours a day."[20] Such was the fraught ambivalence of the Black domestic, who must simultaneously please her White owners/employers and utilize resourceful strategies to provide for and mother her own children.

The work of a Black domestic was a far cry from the romanticized valet service of Mammy in *Gone with the Wind.* For instance, the enslaved mother of Mingo White from Alabama, who "served as personal maid to the master's daughter," had the following responsibilities: "cooked for all the hands on the plantation, carded cotton, spun a daily quota of thread, wove and dyed cloth. Every Wednesday she carried the White family's laundry three-quarters of a mile to a creek, where she beat each garment with a wooden panel. Ironing consumed the rest of her day. Like the lowliest field hand, she felt the lash if any tasks went undone."[21] Of course, this unpaid, abusive labor was conducted in addition to her usual motherly duties for her own family, which had to be performed during "breaks" or the end of her work day. Another domestic slave mother:

> milked fourteen cows . . . in addition to caring for the children of mothers who worked in the fields. She also cooked for the slaves on the plantation,

19. Sharpless, *Cooking in Other Women's Kitchens,* 110.
20. Jones, *Labor of Love, Labor of Sorrow,* 4.
21. Jones, *Labor of Love, Labor of Sorrow,* 23.

> and did all the ironing and washing for the master's household as well as for her own husband and seven children (including three orphans she had adopted). At night she "would find one boy with his knee out, a patch wanting here, and a stitch there, and she would sit down by her lightwood fire, and sew and sleep alternately."[22]

Servant mothers only had it a little better than slave mothers; they often lived a long distance from their employers and had to make taxing trade-offs in order to fulfill their expected duties. Sharpless reports that "most employers expected their cooks to arrive at their houses early to prepare and serve them breakfast. The cooks might have to roust their own children out of bed in the wee hours and try to feed them before they left between five and six o'clock."[23] Such sacrifices were incumbent upon the Black matriarch if she wished to remain in good standing with her employer while ensuring her children were fed and ready for school.

As these accounts reveal, family time was the most precious and inelastic quantity for the Black domestic mother. Catherine Marquis reports that during slavery "most babies spent a very limited time with their natural mothers. . . . Three or four [visits a day] became the standard during the nineteenth century" and "many women only saw their children for a few minutes at night and on weekends."[24] Slave mothers compensated for these restrictions by bringing their children to the field, whether strapped to their backs or left on pallets at the end of rows[25] and "caused themselves no little trouble by lying or trying to maneuver the overseer into giving them more time" with their children.[26] Many domestic servants engaged in similar efforts, attempting to bring their children to work ("usually with the employer's permission") or even to house their children on employers' properties.[27] As the Matriarch of her Black family, the domestic made the best of an impossible predicament, at once working full-time for Whites and struggling to devote sufficient quality time to the development of her own children.

22. Jones, *Labor of Love, Labor of Sorrow,* 42.

23. Sharpless, *Cooking in Other Women's Kitchens,* 124.

24. Catherine Marquis, "The Rearing of Slave Children and Their Parental Relationships Before and After Emancipation," *The Sloping Halls Review* vol. 3 (1996): 102.

25. Wilma King, *More than Chattel: Black Women and Slavery in the Americas* (Bloomington: Indiana University Press, 1998), 153.

26. Marquis, "The Rearing of Slave Children," 102.

27. Sharpless, *Cooking in Other Women's Kitchens,* 126, 121.

With regard to payment, domestics were often subjected to the whims of their employers. Slaves received no wages, obviously, but even contracted domestic workers garnered an intermittent and/or paltry salary. One domestic servant recalled, "In those days, us colored people had to take what we could get to try to make a living. You never know if you'd get paid or not. Sometimes they pay us in clothes. You could take it and go; they wasn't gonna give you no money anyway."[28] Another explained that "if we got any money for what they call 'domestic work,' it would be like fifty cents for all daywork."[29] In the face of this instability, Mammies had to find a way to pay rent and to satisfy their children's hunger, both of which were stable and perennial. One way to provide for one's family was through the "service pan"—a supply of leftover food brought home to a Black family after hours or on the weekend. In her letter, the Negro Nurse claimed that

> with all of us poor people, the service pan is a great institution; it is a great help to us, as we wag along the weary way of life. And then most of the white folks expect their cooks to avail themselves of these perquisites; they allow it; they expect it. I do not deny that the cooks find opportunity to hide away at times, along with the cold "grub," a little sugar, a little flour, a little meal, or a little piece of soap; but I indignantly deny that we are thieves. We don't steal; we just "take" things—they are a part of the oral contract, expressed or implied.[30]

Here the Negro Nurse writes against the grain of a narrative which denounced the service pan as "support[ing] idle negroes," contending that providing food or charity, no matter how small, caused Blacks to become lazy and overly dependent on the largesse of Whites. On the contrary, this tactic exemplifies not sloth and theft but the industry and resourcefulness of Black Matriarchs who were often unmarried, widowed, or deserted and had the responsibility of feeding children squarely upon their own shoulders.

In the same vein, given the onerous requirements of their work, many Black mothers looked to networks of kin and community for childcare. While mothers labored on plantations, "child care sometimes rested in the hands of slaves who were either too infirm, too old, or too young to work

28. Katherine S. Van Wormer, David W. Jackson III, and Charletta Sudduth, *The Maid Narratives: Black Domestic and White Families in the Jim Crow South* (Baton Rouge: Louisiana State University Press, 2010), 104.

29. Van Wormer, Jackson, and Sudduth, *The Maid Narratives*, 97.

30. A Negro Nurse, "More Slavery."

elsewhere."[31] Such arrangements were not a temporary fix, but rather part of a larger network of kin-care with roots in African culture heightened by the necessity of physical female labor. Patricia Hill Collins explains that "African and African-American communities have [long] recognized that vesting one person with full responsibility for mothering a child may not be wise or possible. As a result, *othermothers*—women who assist blood mothers by sharing mothering responsibilities—traditionally have been central to the institution of Black motherhood."[32] These othermothers, including aunts, friends, and grandmothers, were essential for child-rearing, especially during the domestic era when biological mothers were forced to live a distance away from their children. Irene Williams and her siblings, whose mother was a "live-in maid," were routinely left "with our grandmother so she could go off to work. And I remember her coming home, and I was so glad to see my mother. She stayed with us Saturday and Sunday, and she told me, she said, 'Baby, Mamma got to leave again.' And I would cry. I didn't want my mother to leave, but she did. And my grandmother took me into the kitchen as she didn't want my mother to see me crying and feel sorry because she had to leave me."[33] Many Mammies did treat White children as more than employers or clients, forming close and warm bonds with their wards. But this duty was still heavy-hearted, conducted with full knowledge of the despair of their sons and daughters left at home. Such was the dilemma of the Matriarch, who had to simultaneously provide childcare for her employer while being forced to arrange childcare for her own children.

In these and other ways, Black domestics not only served as a Mammy for White employers, but as the Matriarch of their own family. Portrayals of this stereotype appear across southern literature as well, though usually in a brief interlude or aside that returns to the main narrative. In *The Sound and the Fury*'s fourth section, for example, the narrative shifts from the White Compsons to the Black Gibsons as they complete their domestic tasks on Easter Sunday and then attend church. In this light, Dilsey becomes not just the servant of a White family in decline but also the mother hen of her own clan, responsible for raising her Black children alongside the White Benjy. In *A Member of the Wedding*, Frankie pauses her own worrying to ask Berenice about her Mammy's four husbands, all of whom are deceased. After Berenice recounts her misery on the night her favorite husband died, Frankie becomes

31. Collins, "The Meaning of Motherhood in Black Culture," 152.

32. Collins, "The Meaning of Motherhood in Black Culture," 153.

33. Van Wormer, Jackson, and Sudduth, *The Maid Narratives*, 109–110.

"sadder about Ludie than any other dead person" including her own mother and grandmother.[34] Perhaps the best example arrives in Harper Lee's *Go Set a Watchman* when the adult Jean Louise travels to visit Calpurnia in the "colored" part of Maycomb. There she discovers that her childhood recollection of "Cal" is sepia-toned and errant. Her Mammy is in reality old and bony, "sitting in a haughty dignity that appeared on state occasions."[35] Scout no longer, Jean Louise realizes "how small [Calpurnia] looks," how she "never knew exactly" how old Calpurnia was, how much she had sacrificed to raise Scout and Jem, at times to the detriment of her own Black family which is now imperiled.[36] In reference to the persecution inflicted upon Blacks by Whites during the civil rights movement, Calpurnia asks her one-time ward, "What are you all doing to us?" Jean Louise, who has grown up considering her Mammy to be part of her family, is horrified by her use of the word *us*, but Cal has "no hint of compassion" and repeats the word.[37] She asks whether Calpurnia hated the Finch family, to which her Mammy, "bearing the burden of her years," finally shakes her head, a transparent gesture of kindness if not truth that gives Jean Louise no consolation. It is clear that Jean Louise has for the first time seen her Mammy as fully human, with a life, family, and belief system of her own.

Such passages paint the southern domestic in an entirely new light, and in taking characters like Jean Louise and Frankie as surrogates, invite White readers to reconsider characters they (and we) always took for granted. Indeed, once one begins to look for the Black Matriarch, she is present in a number of places. Consider Roxy in Mark Twain's *Pudd'nhead Wilson* (1894) who rescues her child at birth to prevent his enslavement, then spends the next eighteen years lying, cheating, threatening, flattering, and working on his behalf. Or Mammy Barracuda, the Black domestic in Ishmael Reed's novel *Flight to Canada* (1976), whose exaggerated speech and appearance satirize the romanticized figure of the Mammy. Though in a supposedly subservient position vis-à-vis the Swill family, Barracuda exercises surreptitious power and comedic violence to dominate the entire plantation household. These are strong Black women who must work for Whites but do not wholly exist to satisfy the needs of their employers and masters. Rather, these matriarchs cast aside

34. Carson McCullers, *The Member of the Wedding: A Play* (New York: New Directions, 2006), 75.

35. Harper Lee, *Go Set a Watchman* (New York: HarperCollins, 2015), 159.

36. Lee, *Go Set a Watchman,* 160.

37. Lee, *Go Set a Watchman,* 160.

the grinning complaisance of the Mammy in order to make rational decisions on behalf of themselves and their families. To regard the Black domestic as a Matriarch, then, is to see beyond the performative role the Mammy was forced to play for White audiences (owners, employers, and readers).

Beyond Mammies and Matriarchs

Southern literature is full of submissive Mammies and strong Matriarchs—sometimes within the very same text. Yet even the construction presented herein proves problematic, paralleling either/or dichotomies like the good Negro/bad nigger and Madonna/whore. From the White perspective, as Collins writes in "The Meaning of Motherhood," even though "Black women were forced to become domestic servants and be strong figures in Black households, labeling them Mammies and matriarchs denigrates Black women" by placing them in a "no-win situation."[38] On the other hand, Tucker claims, "in the writings of blacks . . . it is the black domestic who mothered white children who is most attacked for making alliances with whites. She is stereotyped as mammy, mistrusted for what strength she does have, and despised for her weakness in conforming with what whites wanted."[39] Put simply, the dual caricature of Mammy and Matriarch denies the full reality of the Black woman's humanity. We do receive a sympathetic, if partial, picture of the Black woman in texts written by White authors, and a more vibrant version in texts written by Black men. But our understanding of the Black domestic's experience is stymied by an overall lack of texts written by Black women on the subject, especially by those who actually lived the lives in question. Much of this paucity, of course, is due to long-standing inequities for women and people of color, who have historically had limited access to literacy, materials, and time to write, and the publishing infrastructure. For this reason, the recording of oral histories is of paramount importance. As-told-tos like *Cooking in Other Women's Kitchens, Telling Memories Among Southern Women*, and *The Maid Narratives* allow Black women to tell their own stories (often though the medium of a White interviewer), offering an anthology of unfiltered lives that would otherwise be unrecognized.

Recently, several efforts have been made to market the stories of Black domestics to a broader popular audience. Yet too often these are significant missteps, as with the controversy surrounding the 2011 film *The Help*, which was itself adapted from the 2009 novel of the same name by White

38. Collins, "The Meaning of Motherhood in Black Culture," 317.

39. Tucker, *Telling Memories Among Southern Women,* 17.

author Kathryn Stockett. Though the story attempts to chronicle the lives of two Black maids during the civil rights movement, the narrative is framed through the plot trajectory of a young White woman, "Skeeter," who uses their stores to establish herself as a journalist. Thus, the experience of Black domestic is again filtered through a White prism and used for White agency. Critics like Melissa Harris-Perry argued that "the African American domestic workers become props" for the White protagonist, and that the film "reduced the struggles of laborers in the South to light Hollywood fare."[40] Such a construction is all too common in popular films which appropriate the labor of chauffeurs (*Driving Miss Daisy*), caddies, (*The Legend of Bagger Vance*), and cooks (*Mr. Church*) for the profit and pleasure of White employers. To be fair, a number of authors and auteurs have countervailed the usual depiction of Black domestics in southern literature. In *Ruth's Journey* (2015) Donald McCaig offers a necessary correction to the portrayal of Mammy in *Gone with the Wind*, giving the character both a name and three-dimensional character, as well as agency enough to serve as a protagonist. (This, after a previous novel, *The Wind Done Gone* by Alice Randall, invented a character that was Scarlett's half-sister and Mammy's daughter.) Lee Daniels's *The Butler* (2011) foregrounds the experience of long-serving White House butler Eugene Allen instead of the succession of White presidents he served. Scholars and educators have similarly revisited narratives that push back against tropes of Black women, from Harriet Jacobs's *Incidents in the Life of a Slave Girl* to Lorraine Hansberry's *A Raisin in the Sun* to Sherley Anne Williams's *Dessa Rose.* (All three, notably, are texts written by Black women).

The danger of looking backward, however, is that retrospection may ignore the present plight of domestic workers, who are still chiefly women of color and remain one of the only classes of American workers exempt from basic working protections. A 2017 report by *Al Jazeera* illuminated the lives of these "invisible women," detailing an all-too-familiar situation: low and irregular pay, casual racism, onerous and capricious scheduling, sexual harassment, and unsafe working conditions. The stories of two women, in particular, seemed to duplicate the Mammy's: "Camille," a fifty-two-year-old domestic in Massachusetts who "sometimes leaves her home in the middle of the night to answer her employer's call. . . . 'When she asks me to sleep over [with

40. "Film Reviews of *The Help*" in *Chicken Bones: A Journal for Literary & Artistic African-American Themes,* http://www.nathanielturner.com/filmreviewsofthehelp.htm.

her children], I leave my children to sleep there with them.'"[41] Her compatriot, a Brazilian house-cleaner named Lucimara Rodrigues, was once fired from an employment agency on account of her pregnancy and later had her wages withheld "because, after having a child, she wanted to work at houses closer to her own home."[42] There are over two million domestic workers in the United States and tens of millions worldwide, many of whom still face slave-like working conditions without protections one hundred years after the Negro Nurse wrote her letter. The "monument of brass or stone" she sought may not come to fruition. Yet her call for "present help, present sympathy, better wages, better hours, more protection, and a chance to breathe for once while alive as free women" is more imperative than ever.

Bibliography

A Negro Nurse. "More Slavery at the South." *Independent* (New York), January 25, 1912. http://historymatters.gmu.edu/d/80/.

Bick, Carolyn. "Invisible Women: Domestic Workers Underpaid and Abused." *Al Jazeera News.* Published October 21, 2017. https://www.aljazeera.com/news/2017/10/invisible-women-domestic-workers-underpaid-abused-171019104144316.html.

Clinton, Catherine. *The Plantation Mistress: Woman's World in the Old South.* New York: Pantheon, 1984.

Collins, Patricia Hill. "The Meaning of Motherhood in Black Culture and Black Mother-Daughter Relationships." In *Gender Through the Prism of Difference* 5th ed., edited by Maxine Baca Zinn, et al., 315–324. Oxford: Oxford University Press, 2015.

"Film Reviews of *The Help*." *Chicken Bones: A Journal for Literary & Artistic African-American Themes.* Accessed September 8, 2018. http://www.nathanielturner.com/filmreviewsofthehelp.htm.

Jones, Jacqueline. *Labor of Love, Labor of Sorrow: Black Women, Work, and the Family, from Slavery to the Present.* New York: Vintage, 1985.

41. Carolyn Bick, "Invisible Women: Domestic Workers Underpaid and Abused," *Al Jazeera News,* October 21, 2017, https://www.aljazeera.com/news/2017/10/invisible-women-domestic-workers-underpaid-abused-171019104144316.html.

42. Bick, "Invisible Women."

King, Wilma. *More than Chattel: Black Women and Slavery in the Americas.* Bloomington: Indiana University Press, 1998.

Lee, Harper. *Go Set a Watchman.* New York: HarperCollins, 2015.

Marquis, Catherine. "The Rearing of Slave Children and Their Parental Relationships Before and After Emancipation." *The Sloping Halls Review* vol. 3 (1996): 99–110.

McCullers, Carson. *The Member of the Wedding: A Play.* New York: New Directions, 2006.

Patton, Venetria K. *Women in Chains: The Legacy of Slavery in Black Women's Fiction.* Albany: State University of New York Press, 1999.

Sharpless, Rebecca. *Cooking in Other Women's Kitchens: Domestic Workers in the South, 1865–1960.* Chapel Hill: University of North Carolina Press, 2010.

Tucker, Susan. *Telling Memories Among Southern Women: Domestic Workers and Their Employers in the Segregated South.* Baton Rouge: Louisiana State University Press, 1988.

Van Wormer, Katherine S, David W. Jackson III, and Charletta Sudduth. *The Maid Narratives: Black Domestic and White Families in the Jim Crow South.* Baton Rouge: Louisiana State University Press, 2010.

White, Deborah Gray. *Ar'n't I a Woman: Female Slaves in the Plantation South.* New York: W. W. Norton, 1999.

Adam Nemmers is an assistant professor of English at Lamar University in Beaumont, Texas, where he teaches courses in American literature. His research focuses on modernism and multiethnic American literature, including recent essays and articles on *Passing,* Richard Wright, Faulkner, and radio drama. His forthcoming published work will include essays on American protest literature and the Harlem Renaissance; an anthology on Transatlantic literature across the long nineteenth century; and a monograph on American modernism and the epic. He is pleased to offer a contribution to this volume and would like to dedicate his essay to his own mother, who is neither Southern nor Black, but nevertheless the matriarch of his family.

The Darker Side of (White) Southern Matriarchy

Charity Gibson

Southern culture has long carried an affinity with a specific type of femininity. While the nostalgic image of a White woman wearing a billowing plantation-era gown may have finally been abandoned, there is a definitive imprint on southern culture even today of how motherhood intersects with the proper enactment of femininity. The American South has been largely impacted by Victorian culture's concept of the cult of domesticity. W. D. White of St. Andrews Presbyterian College examines the veneration of southern women, saying, "Southern life has been dominated by the Victorian notion of the patriarchal family, centered on a deference to the father and an idealization of the mother."[1] The belief that good women were associated with domesticity, which typically tied them to motherhood, adheres strongly to the concept of the Angel in the House. This ideology is an extension of the principles of the cult of domesticity, an enactment that was only possible for White, middle-class women. Although living on a pedestal provides a small radius in which to enact autonomy, southern mothers, while valued in their society, have struggled with the demands of remaining within its favor. As African American literature scholar Nagueyalti Warren and southern literature scholar Sally Wolff have noted, "If the southern mother has been idealized, she has also been held hostage by the societal expectations of her as ideal."[2] The position is both desirable and detrimental.

1. W. D. White, "Victorianism," in *The New Encyclopedia of Southern Culture: Volume 4: Myth, Manners, and Memory* (Chapel Hill: The University of North Carolina Press, 2006), 186.

2. Nagueyalti Warren and Sally Wolff, "Introduction," in *Southern Mothers: Fact and Fictions in Southern Women's Writing* (Baton Rouge: Louisiana State University Press, 1999), 1.

While southern White women have been impeded by their position, they have certainly also assisted in the inhibition of others. Though White women did not institute the enslavement of African Americans, they aided in its maintenance. Even after slavery, White women continued to obstruct Black women's agency, employing them as poorly compensated domestics and enforcing a culture of segregation. While some could reductively interpret these historical realities as simply evidence of racism, a careful reading will show that White women's maintenance of White supremacy is closely linked to their belief in the importance of flawlessly enacting femininity, specifically motherhood. Black bodies have enabled White women to reach an idealized standard that no woman could achieve on her own. "The southern ideal was the belle, and the lady-mother. The black woman and others of similarly lowly status were the other-mothers—the caregivers."[3] The idea of the mammy figure during slavery who is expected to happily care for White children still largely relates to the domestic work Black women of the 1950s and '60s, performed as a means for White women to enact proper femininity and motherhood.

Most research focusing on women of color's contribution to White families emphasizes how children and families of color are deprived of the presence and energy of the mother because that woman is mothering elsewhere. While this is an important dynamic to recognize, there has been less emphasis on how White women's reliance on Black women to help raise their children impacted their role as mothers as well as their relationships with their children. Readers must recognize that domestic workers were both underappreciated and exploited influences on the White family unit, while also recognizing that although many White southern women were privileged due to race and socioeconomic status, they were victims of a patriarchal society in which the enactment of motherhood required women to adhere to the cult of domesticity. Southern matriarchy suggests limited agency when White mothers perform according to a sanctioned script.

Two works that address the ways that southern White motherhood in the 1950s depended upon the labor of Black women are Rebecca Wells's *Divine Secrets of the Ya-Ya Sisterhood* (1996) and Kathryn Stockett's *The Help* (2009). In both works, a tense mother-daughter relationship is set against the daughters' close relationships with their African American caregiver during their childhood. Stockett's text critiques a mother for being unwilling to stand up against racial injustice (though, ironically, Stockett overlooks many racial

3. Warren and Wolff, *Southern Mothers,* 5.

issues herself), and Wells's text oscillates between celebrating and berating mothers who veer from the concept of a good mother and a good southern lady (though Wells addresses race only in simplistic ways). In both texts, as has been true historically, the Black women who have continuously assisted White families are inextricably bound to White women in their role as southern matriarchs. Although in several scenes Stockett and Wells portray White mothers as racist, the exaggeration of these women's thoughts and actions makes it too easy for White readers to distance themselves from any association with racism.

White culture's long-standing tradition of falling into mother blame is at work in these texts. The belief that mothers are responsible for "virtually anything that goes wrong with their young or adult offspring" is a belief that society pervasively holds and which creates much guilt and apprehension for women.[4] Feminist author and journalist Susan Maushart argues that we must unmask motherhood.[5] English professor Elizabeth Podnieks and feminist and maternal scholar Andrea O'Reilly advocate in their co-written article that "the mask of motherhood confers an idealized and hence unattainable image of motherhood" from which mother blame arises when the impossible standard is unmet.[6] This condition allows imperfect southern mothers to serve as scapegoats for collective White guilt, preventing readers from exploring the deeper ways that racism subtly works, and it also hinders readers from viewing White mothers empathetically, especially in southern culture, and recognizing the legitimate obstacles they faced. However, as Thomas Vander Ven and Marikay Vander Ven explain, mother blame is connected to "proper ideas about social roles for women" and is less likely to be applied to women who "show an embracement of patriarchal proscriptions for what a woman should be."[7] Therefore, texts that highlight mother blame for White southern women must be analyzed in light of the racial and gendered dimensions of

4. Paula J. Caplan, "Mother Blame," in *Encyclopedia of Motherhood,* vol. 2, ed. Andrea O'Reilly (London: Sage Publications, 2010), 803–804.

5. Susan Maushart, *The Mask of Motherhood: How Becoming a Mother Changes Our Lives and Why We Never Talk About It* (London: Penguin Books, 2000).

6. Elizabeth Podnieks and Andrea O'Reilly, *Textual Mothers/Maternal Texts: Motherhood in Contemporary Women's Literatures* (Waterloo: Wilfrid Laurier University Press, 2011), 3.

7. Thomas Vander Ven and Marikay Vander Ven, "Exploring Patterns of Mother-Blaming in Anorexia Scholarship: A Study in the Sociology of Knowledge," *Human Studies* 26, no. 7 (2003): 97.

motherhood that simultaneously influence the text and the readers' perception of it.

It is noteworthy that both Wells and Stockett position their fictional narratives within close proximity to their own historical reality. Wells was born in Rapides Parish, Louisiana, and likewise sets her novel in Louisiana, though in the fictional town of Thornton. Wells's family employed a Black woman, and she says in an interview that she is still learning "what it is to have grown up as a woman in the South where the black hands that touched me from the time I was born were also hands that forgave me enough to keep on loving me. I see that I have tried and still try to accept the way I was shaped by the cult of southern ladyhood."[8] Stockett grew up in Jackson, Mississippi, and similarly sets her story there. Stockett also grew up under the influence of a Black domestic worker. She says in the afterword that she wrote her novel because she never asked her own childhood maid her story: "It never occurred to us to ask . . . I have wished for many years, that I'd been old enough and thoughtful enough to ask Demetrie that question . . . I've spent years imagining what her answer would be. And that is why I wrote this book."[9] Thus, both authors' motivation in writing their stories seems to be somewhat entwined in their own experience receiving care from Black women. However, although they attempt to recognize the racist structure that influenced their upbringing, they reduce the complexities of the situation due to their inability to deconstruct Whiteness as a concept as well as their inability to fully deconstruct the intersection of patriarchy with Whiteness. The main concept that I will explore in this paper is the latter issue. White mothers in southern literature are often presented as flawed characters due to their racist and narcissistic natures; however, a close reading will reveal that it is traditional southern culture itself that typically mandates problematic enactments of White maternity. Because Wells's and Stockett's works have been extremely successful, both appearing on the best sellers list (aided by serving as Oprah's Book Club selections) and both having been made into successful films, it is important to critique the explorations of Whiteness and Blackness in order to help educate mainstream culture on how to navigate this complicated issue.

Beginning chronologically with *Divine Secrets*, Wells is very careful to give credit to the work that is done by the Black bodies in the characters' households. The central plotline focuses on Vivi Abbot Walker and her three

8. Erin Z. Bass, "Rebecca Wells Comes Home," *Deep South Magazine*, October 14, 2016, www.deepsouthmag.com/2016/10/14/Rebecca-wells-comes-home/.

9. Kathryn Stockett, *The Help* (New York: Penguin Group, 2009), 451.

girlfriends, who call themselves the Ya-Yas, as the narrative spans their friendship from childhood to old age. The narrative also focuses on the maternal line and Vivi's own relationship with her mother, Buggy, as well as her relationship with her daughter, Sidda. Domestic laborers are central to the way the Ya-Yas are mothered, as well as how they mother once they have their own families. Growing up, Vivi feels close to her family's maid Ginger; then, once Vivi is herself a mother, she employs Willetta, to whom Sidda feels close. Vivi also periodically employs Melinda as a caregiver.

As an adult reflecting back on her childhood, Sidda recognizes the complicated relationship her family had with the Black women they employed: "Of the countless cruelties of racism, Sidda thought, one is the unspoken rule that white children, once we reach a certain age, are supposed to renounce the passionate love we feel for the black women who raised us. We're supposed to replace it with a sentimental, patronizing affection. We're supposed to let the thinly veiled jealousy of our own mothers obscure what we feel for the women they hired as maids."[10] Sidda still feels love for Willetta though she believes she should instead simply be nostalgic toward her. She acknowledges, "My mother's life, my own life, would not have been possible without Willetta. What we owe her is so complex I'll never figure it out."[11]

Sidda's and her mother's lives would not have been possible without the extensive support of Willetta. Their lives and relationship help demonstrate that in order to perform southern matriarchy properly, the White mother must be largely absent or preoccupied. The "stereotypical ideal mother" in southern culture is one "who transfers the actual care of her children to someone else."[12] This transfer took place so that women were available to adhere to patriarchal standards of the proper activities for the lady of the house, including charity work, entertainment of guests, socialization with the community, and the list goes on. Of course, it is reductive to turn a domestic caregiver into a stereotypical mammy figure who sacrificially embraces her role and holds no ambivalence regarding her subjugated position. The Black caregiver is exploited through her cheap labor and the expectation of not only physical but also emotional care. Nonetheless, Sidda "ached for this woman who had been a mother to her."[13] However, it is problematic to think of a Black caregiver as

10. Rebecca Wells, *Divine Secrets of the Ya-Ya Sisterhood* (New York: Harper Collins, 1996), 258.

11. Wells, *Divine Secrets of the Ya-Ya Sisterhood,* 258.

12. Warren and Wolff, *Southern Mothers*, 5.

13. Wells, *Divine Secrets of the Ya-Ya Sisterhood,* 258.

a mother to the White child. In her work *Skin Trade,* Anne duCille explains that this claiming of "my Black mother" allows an African American woman no "identity of her own and, in fact, does not exist beyond the nurture she gave."[14] In reality, Sidda's maid "is not her black mother, but a laborer whose role as mammy is also constructed."[15]

Despite the errors of categorizing a domestic worker as a White child's Black mother, as archival consultant Susan Tucker explains, "in literature and in the popular imagination, for example, the black domestic is cast as . . . mother surrogate to white children."[16] However, the expectation that a domestic should function as a Black mother to White children is not only harmful for the African American community; it also has negative impacts for the White mother-child relationship. Undoubtedly, the image of an absent mother, replaced by a watchful Black caregiver, could lead to a White child-viewed stigma of the mother. Though southern literature academic Joan Wylie Hall specifically writes of the antebellum mammy, the expectations of White and Black women regarding the enforcement of White maternity connect to a domestic worker as well. This mammy is "the Angel in the Big House. . . . Her chief concern is to assure a child that she will never be abandoned. Though 'lady mamma' may leave for the ball, mammy will remain."[17] The White mother is also burdened with the expectation to outwardly perform her femininity to the world, forging a rift between her and her child that will undoubtedly arise as a dichotomy in the child's mind between her good Black mother and her absent White one. English professor Kathryn Lee Seidel comments, "The mammy's role is that of a mother substitute to the usually motherless belle."[18] Although Sidda certainly has a mother, she often feels un-mothered, perhaps due southern culture's

14. Ann duCille, "Domesticity and the Demon Mother," *Burning Down the House: Recycling Domesticity* (London: Westview Press, 1998), 107.

15. duCille, "Domesticity and the Demon Mother," 193.

16. Susan Tucker, *Telling Memories Among Southern Women: Domestic Workers and Their Employers in the Segregated South* (Baton Rouge: Louisiana State University Press, 2002), 5.

17. Joan Wylie Hall, "'White mamma . . . black mammy': Replacing the Absent Mother in the Works of Ruth McEnery Stuart," in *Southern Mothers: Fact and Fictions in Southern Women's Writing* (Baton Rouge: Louisiana State University Press, 1999), 67.

18. Kathryn Lee Seidel, *The Southern Belle in the American Novel* (Gainesville: University Press of Florida, 1985), 21.

maintenance of a performative femininity that must rely on others to care for the children. Sidda's colleague comforts her feelings of motherlessness, urging her to find refuge in her career, "It creates family for all kinds of orphans."[19] While it is easy for readers to blame Vivi for her shortcomings, and she certainly has them, it is important to recognize that, in part, her rift with Sidda has been sparked by her adherence to southern expectations of motherhood, in which there is an often-absent White mother while the surrogate Black mother appropriates the situation.

Throughout the narrative, Sidda espouses large displays of mother blame and even hate toward Vivi: "Mama, you bitch, she thought. You devouring, melodramatic bitch."[20] These feelings could be rooted in the lack of relationship southern mother and daughter were able to form, due to their duty to adhere to "southern ladyhood." During her children's upbringing, Vivi often seeks respite from her mothering duties. Reflecting on her days with young children, she admits, "I longed for someone to swoop down and take them off my hands for long enough to think one single thought without interruption."[21] She becomes dependent on Black women's assistance in an unhealthy way: "I did not want to beg a colored person to help me, but I couldn't help myself."[22] Vivi does not have the parenting strategies she needs to effectively and manageably mother her own children because the cultural expectation is that a Black woman should largely bear the load. As Professor of Africa Studies Paula Marie Seniors says, "[T]he Southern belle could not exist without her oppression of the black subject."[23] Ironically, Vivi's oppression of Black women simultaneously results in her own self-inflicted (but societally influenced) lack of agency as a competent mother. Vivi is ill-equipped to know how to serve as the primary maternal figure because she has grown accustomed to transferring maternal energy to another.

Vivi is often self-focused and even jealous of her daughter when Sidda achieves dreams Vivi will never see actualized in her own life. Sidda recognizes

19. Wells, *Divine Secrets of the Ya-Ya Sisterhood,* 182.

20. Wells, *Divine Secrets of the Ya-Ya Sisterhood,* 3.

21. Wells, *Divine Secrets of the Ya-Ya Sisterhood,* 261.

22. Wells, *Divine Secrets of the Ya-Ya Sisterhood,* 262.

23. Paula Marie Seniors, "Mae Mallory and 'The Southern Belle Fantasy Trope' at the Cuyahoga County Jail, 21st and Payne/Pain," in *From* Uncle Tom's Cabin *to* The Help*: Critical Perspectives on White-Authored Narratives of Black Life,* eds. Claire Oberon Garcia, Vershawn Ashanti Young, and Charise Pimentel (New York: Palgrave Macmillan, 2014), 103.

this, asking, "Was there a viscous glue of jealousy passed down from mother to daughter in our lineage, invisible and life-threatening as cancer?"[24] However, rather than falling into simplistic mother blame of Vivi, readers should note that she is a product of southern femininity. Seidel explains that "society's emphasis on the beauty of the belle can produce a selfishness and narcissism that cause her to ignore the development of positive aspects of her personality."[25] For traditional southern womanhood, White motherhood means leaving the mundane and labor-intensive aspects of raising children to a Black woman. It is then no surprise if the mothers are narcissistic. Sidda has learned that "[m]y mother lived in a world that could not or would not acknowledge her radiance, her pull on the earth—at least not as much as she needed."[26] However, Vivi is a product of her culture and its gendered social mandates. This does not mean she could not have risen above it, but if she is to be critiqued, so also must be the system.

Perhaps Wells is trying to make amends for her own complicity in southern culture's oppression of Black women. In an effort to right the wrongs, she draws attention to the complexity and injustices of Black women's societal place, showing times when the maids are cruelly treated or looked upon with racial diffidence. However, popular culture critic Lori Robinson argues that Wells only addresses racism in superficial ways in order to show the kindheartedness of the Ya-Yas when they defend their maids. Robinson argues that the domestic worker's "true function here is to show us that life is hard for the white girls because they will have to become white, southern, bourgeois 'ladies.'"[27] Wells's text, therefore, continues to use Black women in exploitative ways. While Wells's attempts to show the injustice of Black women having no other options but to serve as domestics shows progress of a sort, as Robinson notes, Wells rather simplistically shows wronged Black women in order to celebrate enlightened White girls and women who are able to function as heroines when they question the system. Furthermore, because the White mothers have organized the Black women's employment, they become easy targets to blame. However, while Robinson rather dismissively addresses the concept of becoming "white,

24. Wells, *Divine Secrets of the Ya-Ya Sisterhood,* 178.

25. Seidel, *The Southern Belle in the American Novel,* 32.

26. Wells, *Divine Secrets of the Ya-Ya Sisterhood,* 33.

27. Lori Robinson, "Bodies, Southern Nostalgia, and the Construction of Whiteness in *Divine Secrets of the Ya-Ya Sisterhood,*" *Journal of Popular Culture* 42, no. 6 (2009): 1127.

southern, bourgeois 'ladies,'" this concept deserves more consideration. Wells seems to suffer, like many, from White guilt. Certainly, there is a place and time for such feelings. However, many too simplistically create a binary between oppressed Blacks and oppressive Whites. In this narrow categorization, the double bind in which White southern women inhabited the place of both oppressor and oppressed is overlooked. This often results in mother blame. Southern White mothers such as Vivi should be critiqued for their shortcomings, but they should also receive some grace, as they had to navigate a patriarchal institution that afforded little agency.

Kathryn Stockett seems to have been motivated, like Wells, by at least some degree of White guilt. She rightly emphasizes the humanity and ill treatment of domestic women but is only able to do so by ignoring the ways in which White women are subjected. She is unable to simultaneously critique racism and White patriarchy. Stockett's story is essentially about a White young woman, Eugenia "Skeeter" Phelan, and her journey of repudiating traditional, southern, White norms as she interviews Black maids and anonymously publishes their stories of what it is really like to serve in White households. Stockett focuses on two Black women, Minny Jackson and Aibileen Clark. However, ironically, she falls into very reductive portrayals, categorizing Aibileen as a mammy figure whose primary identity is found through the nurturance of White children, and Minny as an Aunt Jemima figure, whose primary identity is found through cooking for the White family. As I have shown with Sidda's sentimentalized memories of her caregiver, this strips Black women of autonomy outside of a White-enforced laborer role. While popular culture has revered Stockett and praised her for her appropriate treatment of race relations, academia has largely challenged Stockett for her portrayal of a historically absent White savior as well as for ignoring Black people's own activism in fighting for their rightful freedoms.

Stockett falls into romantic racialism with her portrayal of stereotypical Black characters, and she ultimately, though probably unknowingly, seeks to protect Whiteness. However, in moving past this well-tread territory, I seek to focus on a little-explored aspect of her work, which is the way that southern expectations of motherhood influence the text. While Stockett naively presents Skeeter as a White woman who has the ability and bravery to transcend the racism of her time in a way that history does not support, I am interested in the way that Stockett, similarly to Wells, creates a neat binary in which Whites are oppressors and Blacks are oppressed (save for Skeeter who works to change the situation.) Due to her desire to renounce the South's sordid past with segregation and racism, Stockett portrays Skeeter's mother as part of the system that she must work against. While southern womanhood undoubtedly made deals with the devil, supporting atrocities toward people of color in order to maintain some semblance of power in their culture, mothers in particular bear the brunt of culpability in superficial explorations of race relations. Unmarried or childless White women and White men are portrayed much more sympathetically.

In Stockett's account, Skeeter and her mother are constantly at odds, while her father, the truly privileged person within White patriarchy, is presented as the loving parent, often serving as the mediator between mother and daughter. The very first time Skeeter's mother, typically referenced simply as "Mama" or "Mother" but actually named Charlotte Phelan, is introduced, it is as an oppositional force: "Mother would be furious."[28] Charlotte is portrayed as a superficial character who focuses only on the enforcement of feminine tropes: "My own mother is looking at me as if I completely baffle her mind with my looks, my height, my hair."[29] Charlotte wants to enforce traditional femininity upon Skeeter: "Mother berates me about finding a husband every other day."[30] While self-proclaimed, enlightened feminist readers can easily dismiss Charlotte for her narrow-mindedness, historically, White women were only able to achieve even a semblance of authority by navigating the social system and choosing limited power via domesticity.

Bonnie Thornton Dill, whose scholarship focuses on the intersection of race and gender, explains the value placed on domestic women in eighteenth and nineteenth-century America: "[P]reservation and protection of families . . . was seen as crucial to the growth and development of American society. . . . Thus while women had few legal rights as women, they were protected through public forms of patriarchy that acknowledged and supported their family role of wives, mothers, and daughters because they were vital for building American society."[31] This trade-off White women made of sacrificing public autonomy for societally celebrated domestic power is one that has largely impacted southern culture and the psyche of southern womanhood.

Stockett portrays Charlotte as a flawed character but draws no attention to the structure that created the mindset of her and other southern mothers like her. As antebellum South historian Elizabeth Fox-Genovese says regarding

28. Stockett, *The Help*, 54.

29. Stockett, *The Help*, 56.

30. Stockett, *The Help*, 58.

31. Bonnie Thornton Dill, "Our Mothers' Grief: Racial Ethnic Women and the Maintenance of Families," *Journal of Family History* 13, no. 4 (1988): 415–16.

mothers and daughters, "[W]omen's social situation as well as their specific national and cultural traditions—and, sometimes, their race—have influenced their perceptions of and relations to one another."[32] Charlotte is passing on expectations of femininity to her daughter because she sees them as essential for the maintenance of their way of life. Though Skeeter interprets her mother's view only negatively, "I was longing for Mother not to be disappointed in me,"[33] Charlotte's disappointment is a reflection of society's disappointment in a southern belle gone wrong. This aligns her with a long tradition of flawed literary mothers. African American and women's literature scholar Elizabeth J. West notes, "Skeeter's mother is little more than the stock melodramatic, superficial, whining, and weakly matron of so many Southern novels."[34] This vilification of mothers without noting the rationale behind their actions is essentially a way of punishing mothers while maintaining patriarchal White mandates.

Stockett starkly contrasts Charlotte with the character Constantine, who serves as the Phelan family's maid. She distinguishes them from one another the moment Constantine enters the narrative. Constantine works in the kitchen, and Charlotte physically distances herself from both Constantine and her children: "Mother ate her breakfast early in the dining room, then moved to the relaxing room to do needlepoint or write letters to missionaries in Africa. From her green wing chair, she could see everyone going almost anywhere in the house."[35] Charlotte enacts femininity through her needlework and social duties through her letters. She sees her role to be overseeing her home but not actually attending to her children. Whereas Constantine greets Skeeter with "Good morning, beautiful, girl!," Charlotte greets Skeeter with a list of reprimands or directions. From all this, Skeeter says she learned many things, "But mostly, I learned to just stay in the kitchen,"[36] which is, of course, where Constantine resides.

32. Elizabeth Fox-Genovese, "Mothers and Daughters: The Tie that Binds," in *Southern Mothers: Fact and Fictions in Southern Women's Writing*, ed. Nagueyalti Warren and Sally Wolff (Baton Rouge: Louisiana State University Press, 1999), xviii.

33. Stockett, *The Help*, 360.

34. Elizabeth J. West, "Blackness as Medium: Envisioning White Southern Womanhood in Eudora Welty's 'A Worn Path' and *Delta Wedding* and Kathryn Stockett's *The Help*," in *From* Uncle Tom's Cabin *to* The Help*: Critical Perspectives on White-Authored Narratives of Black Life*, eds. Claire Oberon Garcia, Vershawn Ashanti Young, and Charise Pimentel (New York: Palgrave Macmillan, 2014), 53.

35. Stockett, *The Help*, 63.

36. Stockett, *The Help*, 64.

This negative portrayal of southern motherhood moves from showing Charlotte as trivial to ultimately cruel. In what could be argued as the climax of the novel, Skeeter learns that the reason Constantine left town is not, as she has been told, unknown. Rather, her mother dismissed her on account of rude treatment she received from Constantine's daughter Lulabelle, who is light-skinned enough to pass as White, though Charlotte made sure that did not happen. Skeeter is sickened by learning of her mother's actions, to which Charlotte replies, "It's time you learned, Eugenia, how things really are. You idolize Constantine too much. You always have."[37] This suggestion that Charlotte is jealous of the way her daughter views the hired help is similar to Wells's description of how White mothers begrudge their Black servants the relationship they have with their children: "Sidda remembered how resentful Buggy was about the way Vivi and Ginger carried on."[38] Certainly, White women placed themselves in a situation in which they were estranged from their children by allocating care to domestic workers. Employing a maid was an outward sign of economic security, and leisure was an expectation of femininity. As Mary Beth Haralovitch says of the White 1950s homemaker, "she was promised leisure and freedom from housework."[39] However, in their pursuit of leisure, these White mothers were compelled by an unhealthy internalization of social mores to propitiate a system that put them in competition with another woman for the love and respect of their own children.

Critiquing the subjugation of mothers would require a critique of patriarchy. In her book *Young, White, and Miserable: Growing Up Female in the Fifties,* sociologist and anthropologist Wini Breines explains that this critique is usually sidestepped: "The mother appears in social science and popular literature as a more powerful figure than she was."[40] Stockett does not challenge the double bind of the southern White mother, but her text does subtly suggest the reality of these women's limited world. In doing the necessary social justice work to dismantle White superiority, Whites' reliance on Black labor has been and must continue to be deconstructed. Black families suffered immeasurably from the thankless work Black women performed in White families. However, perhaps out of a reticence to repeat the mistakes

37. Stockett, *The Help*, 364.

38. Stockett, *The Help*, 133.

39. Mary Beth Haralovitch, "Sitcoms and Suburbs: Positioning the 1950s Housemaker," *Female Representation and Consumer Culture* 11, no. 1 (1989): 61.

40. Wini Breines, *Young, White, and Miserable: Growing Up Female in the Fifties* (Chicago: University of Chicago Press, 2001), 45.

of the past, society often simplistically views southern White women as cut-and-dried perpetrators. This allows the White mothers to be blamed as opposed to criticizing the patriarchal dominant culture that encouraged these women's desperate grasps of power. Acknowledging the complexity of the patriarchal/racial caste system which bound both White and Black women is antithetical to preserving the patriarchy itself, which is why most views on the issue are so simplistic. Almost no scholarship has emerged exploring how the employer/domestic relationship harmed White women's relationship with their own children. After interviewing White women of their experience employing Black domestics, Tucker notes that often women "protest[ed] that the paternalistic system had worked well."[41] This shows a continued lack of awareness amongst Whites of both the insidious racism and sexism inherent in the expectation that White women need assistance in managing their lives and families.

Regarding Stockett's work, much of the scholarship assumes that White women maintained total agency. For example, historian Katrina Dyonne Thompson unequivocally claims, "*The Help* alters a tumultuous time of gender and racial inequality into an era in which white country club women have the most power in society."[42] While Thompson is correct in noting that historically, gender inequality did exist, she is incorrect to assume that women in Stockett's work hold the most power. Because southern White mothers are portrayed so un-redeemingly in the work, it is easy to overlook their precarious grasping for authority as something that only exists when they play by patriarchy's rules. Mother blame abounds in Stockett's creation of her characters as well as in audiences' interpretations. Charlotte alludes to this when she confesses why she has not told Skeeter the truth about Constantine, "Because I knew you'd blame me when—it wasn't my fault."[43] Stockett's intended message is that it is indeed Charlotte's fault. I would suggest, however, that, yes, it is Charlotte's fault, but it is also the fault of the society that shaped her.

Stockett's ultimate message seems rather sinister when focused on southern motherhood. Skeeter, the most "progressive" character, moves to New

41. Tucker, *Telling Memories Among Southern Women,* 4.

42. Katrina Dyonne Thompson, "'Taking Care a White Babies, That's What I Do': *The Help* and American's Obsession with the Mammy," in *From* Uncle Tom's Cabin *to* The Help*: Critical Perspectives on White-Authored Narratives of Black Life,* eds. Claire Oberon Garcia, Vershawn Ashanti Young, and Charise Pimentel (New York: Palgrave Macmillan, 2014), 64.

43. Stockett, *The Help*, 365.

York, possibly turning her back on the traditional roles of marriage and motherhood. Celia Foote, the other White character who does not succumb to prejudice, is unable to have children. Something similar occurs in Wells's *Divine Secrets*: Sidda, like Skeeter, moves away from the South; she chooses not to have children though she acknowledges a longing for them, suggesting that the only way she knows to avoid becoming a narcissistic woman from the South, blameless of oppressing Blacks and children, or perhaps both, is by avoiding the situation altogether. This leaves readers wondering if southern motherhood can even be compatible with social justice regarding racial issues.

Although Wells and Stockett have many shortcomings in their understanding of both race relations and patriarchy, they have initiated important conversations and should be lauded for their willingness to engage, even superficially, in difficult topics. However, scholarship should seek to find a balance that many fictional works have not yet achieved in which White mothers are held accountable but not pitted against domestic workers to debate who was more abused in the system. While the travesty of racism must be addressed, additionally, the detriment of a society that puts women on pedestals for performing maternity according to White, bourgeois, patriarchal mandates must be deconstructed.

Bibliography

Bass, Erin Z. "Rebecca Wells Comes Home." *Deep South Magazine*. October 14, 2016. www.deepsouthmag.com/2016/10/14/Rebecca-wells-comes-home/.

Breines, Wini. *Young, White, and Miserable: Growing Up Female in the Fifties*. Chicago: University of Chicago Press, 2001.

Caplan, Paula J. "Mother Blame." In *Encyclopedia of Motherhood,* vol. 2, edited by Andrea O'Reilly. London: Sage Publications, 2010.

Dill, Bonnie Thornton. "Our Mothers' Grief: Racial Ethnic Women and the Maintenance of Families." *Journal of Family History,* 13, no. 4 (1988): 415–31. *Sage Journals,* https://doi.org/10.1177/036319908801300125.

duCille, Ann. "Domesticity and the Demon Mother." In *Burning Down the House: Recycling Domesticity,* edited by Rosemary Marangoly George, 279–300. London: Westview Press, 1998.

Fox-Genovese, Elizabeth. "Mothers and Daughters: The Tie that Binds." In *Southern Mothers: Fact and Fictions in Southern Women's Writing*, edited by Nagueyalti Warren and Sally Wolff, xv–xviii. Baton Rouge: Louisiana State University Press, 1999.

Hall, Joan Wylie. "'White mamma . . . black mammy': Replacing the Absent Mother in the Works of Ruth McEnery Stuart." In *Southern Mothers: Fact and Fictions in Southern Women's Writing*, edited by Nagueyalti Warren and Sally Wolff, 64–80. Baton Rouge: Louisiana State University Press, 1999.

Haralovitch, Mary Beth. "Sitcoms and Suburbs: Positioning the 1950s Housemaker." *Female Representation and Consumer Culture* 11, no. 1 (1989): 61–83.

Maushart, Susan. *The Mask of Motherhood: How Becoming a Mother Changes Our Lives and Why We Never Talk About It.* London: Penguin Books, 2000.

Podnieks, Elizabeth and Andrea O'Reilly. *Textual Mothers/Maternal Texts: Motherhood in Contemporary Women's Literatures.* Waterloo: Wilfrid Laurier University Press, 2011.

Robinson, Lori. "Bodies, Southern Nostalgia, and the Construction of Whiteness in *Divine Secrets of the Ya-Ya Sisterhood.*" *Journal of Popular Culture,* 42, no. 6 (2009): 1115–33. https://doi.org/10.1111/j.1540-5931.2009.00725.x.

Seniors, Paula Marie. "Mae Mallory and 'The Southern Belle Fantasy Trope' at the Cuyahoga County Jail, 21st and Payne/Pain." In *From* Uncle Tom's Cabin *to* The Help*: Critical Perspectives on White-Authored Narratives of Black Life*, edited by Claire Oberon Garcia, Vershawn Ashanti Young, and Charise Pimentel, 101–31. New York: Palgrave Macmillan, 2014.

Seidel, Kathryn Lee. *The Southern Belle in the American Novel.* Gainesville: University Press of Florida, 1985.

Stockett, Kathryn. *The Help.* New York: Penguin Group, 2009.

Strother-Adams, Pearlie. "'Savior,' Good Mother, Jezebel, Tom, Trickster: *The Blind Side* Myth." In *From* Uncle Tom's Cabin *to* The Help*: Critical Perspectives on White-Authored Narratives of Black Life*, edited by Claire Oberon Garcia, Vershawn Ashanti Young, and Charise Pimentel, 171–95. New York: Palgrave Macmillan, 2014.

Thompson, Katrina Dyonne. "'Taking Care a White Babies, That's What I Do': *The Help* and American's Obsession with the Mammy." In *From* Uncle Tom's Cabin *to* The Help*: Critical Perspectives on White-Authored Narratives of Black Life*, edited by Claire Oberon Garcia, Vershawn Ashanti Young, and Charise Pimentel, 57–72. New York: Palgrave Macmillan, 2014.

Tucker, Susan. *Telling Memories Among Southern Women: Domestic Workers and Their Employers in the Segregated South*. Baton Rouge: Louisiana State University Press, 2002.

Vander Ven, Thomas, and Marikay Vander Ven. "Exploring Patterns of Mother-Blaming in Anorexia Scholarship: A Study in the Sociology of Knowledge," *Human Studies* 26, no. 7 (2003): 97–119 Accessed Jan 5, 2019. https://doi.org/10.1023/A:1022527631743.

Warren, Nagueyalti, and Sally Wolff. "Introduction." In *Southern Mothers: Fact and Fictions in Southern Women's Writing,* edited by Nagueyalti Warren and Sally Wolff, 1–12. Baton Rouge: Louisiana State University Press, 1999.

Wells, Rebecca. *Divine Secrets of the Ya-Ya Sisterhood.* New York: HarperCollins, 1996.

West, Elizabeth J. "Blackness as Medium: Envisioning White Southern Womanhood in Eudora Welty's 'A Worn Path' and *Delta Wedding* and Kathryn Stockett's *The Help*." In *From* Uncle Tom's Cabin *to* The Help*: Critical Perspectives on White-Authored Narratives of Black Life*, edited by Claire Oberon Garcia, Vershawn Ashanti Young, and Charise Pimentel, 39–56. New York: Palgrave Macmillan, 2014.

White, W. D. "Victorianism." In *Myth, Manners, and Memory,* 184–8. Vol. 4 of *The New Encyclopedia of Southern Culture*, edited by Charles Reagan Wilson. Chapel Hill: University of North Carolina Press, 2006.

Charity Gibson, PhD, is an associate professor of English in southwest Missouri where she teaches undergraduate courses in literature and composition. Her doctoral and teaching area of specialization is contemporary American literature. In much of her research, she explores issues related to motherhood, the mother-daughter relationship, and parenting in contemporary culture. She is raising her children with her husband. She enjoys walking outside, playing the piano, traveling, and reading.

QUEERING THE MAMMY

Southern Black Domestics and Revolutionary Mothering as Social Practice

Joanna Davis-McElligatt

In 2011, when the film adaptation of Kathryn Stockett's 2009 novel *The Help* arrived in theaters, I received a pastel pink invitation from a group of White women requesting my attendance at a cocktail party and screening of the film. I strongly considered going along, if only for the mint juleps and Sazeracs, when a proviso caught my eye: all attendees were required to dress in period attire as mid-century southern women. I was a new mother and the first Black woman ever hired to the tenure track in my department, at the very end of a bewildering and difficult first year in the Deep South—and so I initially felt as though I was missing something. Surely, they understood that asking me, a Black woman, to accompany them, a group of White women happily pretending to be in the Jim Crow South, put me a position to filter myself through the lens of an imagined Black womanness and motherhood intimately associated with servitude and indebtedness to White folks. Even if I sported a fancy cocktail dress to the screening, I did not see how I could fail to bring to mind the image of the Black domestics in *The Help*—Aibileen Clark and Minny Jackson—in their perfectly pressed gray and white uniforms. As Trudier Harris explains in *From Mammies to Militants: Domestics in Black American Literature*, uniforms were designed to disembody and dehumanize Black domestics: "When the black woman takes off the clothes in which she has ridden the train or bus to her job and puts on that uniform, she becomes THE MAID, not somebody's mother or sister or wife. Her primary function is to serve the needs of the family which has thus defined her."[1] Were they hoping I would transform myself into a maid with infant in tow in order to make the experience feel more authentic for them? Perhaps they

1. Trudier Harris, *From Mammies to Militants: Domestics in American Literature* (Philadelphia: Temple University Press, 1982), 12. Emphasis in original.

expected that I would model myself after Aibileen, a mammy who lovingly and repeatedly reminds her White charge that she is smart, she is kind, she is important. Or was I being invited to perform as Minny Jackson, exacting my revenge with a shit pie to complement the cocktails? Of one thing I felt certain: given the context of the film, my Blackness, my womanness, and my being motherful, I'd been invited to pretend to be their domestic help.

I entertained the idea that the invitation was intended to put me in my place. But even if that wasn't the intent, it was nevertheless the effect. Yet because the novel and film seek to rewrite recent history for White women, it was entirely possible that the women who invited me thought of themselves as descendants of Skeeter Phelan, the White, upper-middle-class protagonist who graduated from Ole Miss one year after a racist mob ran James Meredith off of its campus. Upon noticing the maltreatment of Black domestic laborers, Skeeter decides to translate their experiences of oppression into narratives intended for White audiences. Ultimately, her project is successful. In Stockett's version of US history, it is the mysteriously radicalized White daughter of conventional racists who becomes, at the height of the civil rights movement, the sole arbiter of the help's racial liberation. I argue that Stockett's most deceptive and appealing historical revision is her construction of White southern women as necessary allies to Black women in the struggle for freedom. If the White women who invited me to the film screening saw themselves as Skeeters, then they may have conceived of themselves as aligned with me in the struggle against oppression—perhaps even working *on my behalf.* Because the film and novel invite White women to see themselves as vital supports for Black women—even as *The Help* offers an exploration of the ways White women denigrated and brutalized Black women—it was conceivable that the women who invited me thought of our positions as somewhat homologous.

I declined the invitation, explaining that I could not see any other role I could fill in their charade than that of their mammy or maid. Over the years, however, I've periodically returned to my decision to my refusal to play a Black domestic. Though I didn't want to play the role of mammy or maid alongside White women, I wasn't ashamed to be associated with the Black women who labored in the homes of White families. Black domestic workers were and continue to be underutilized experts not only on mothering and the art of survival, but on balancing the demands of motherhood and working outside the home, a requirement for generations of Black women well before White feminists began to do the same. Black women have raised multiple generations of children, both Black and White; thus, Black mothering has shaped the American psyche in profound and complex (yet largely ignored) ways. Black domestics dealt with unreasonable demands and mistreatment from their often physically and emotionally abusive employers, and were grossly underpaid—if they were paid at all. Although Black women working as domestics had no lobbying support and were second-class citizens without access to the vote, they organized and formed unions. As Harris notes, in the 1920s there were ten local unions of domestic laborers across southern cities, and in 1936, "the most ambitious organizing effort was that headed by Dora Jones, the black executive secretary of the Domestic Workers' Union. . . . Five years later the organization had 350 members, 75 percent of them black women."[2] Despite the misconception that mammies were completely loyal to their White families, perpetuated by texts such as *To Kill A Mockingbird* and *Gone with the Wind*, Black women were resentful and disdainful of their White employers, emotions they were required to outwardly suppress under threat of death. Black women's personal lives were generally unknown by their White employers, who often did not know their servants' surnames. Nevertheless, Black women maintained active lives mothering their children, shaping the social and ethical lives of their communities, and maintaining relationships with partners, friends, and family. In spite of their complexity, Black women have been systemically and structurally typecast. Maya Angelou, in the following passage, catalogs many of the contradictory ways Black women are regarded in the United States: "Called Matriarch, Emasculator and Hot Momma. Sometimes Sister, Pretty Baby, Auntie, Mammy and Girl. Called Unwed Mother, Welfare Recipient and Inner City Consumer. The Black American Woman has had to admit that while nobody knows the troubles she saw, everybody, his brother and his dog, felt qualified to explain her, even to herself."[3] As Susan Tucker explains in her oral history *Telling Memories Among Southern Women: Domestic Workers and Their Employers in the Segregated South*, "Interpreting and reinterpreting the past is crucial for survival, strength, and carrying on."[4] To this end, I argue that if we wish to understand the ideology that undergirds misrepresentations of Black women in films such as *The Help*, then we must reinterpret and reimagine the role Black mothering has played in the United States.

In this essay I want to approach Black domestics—specifically those women who cared for and raised generations of White and Black children—through

2. Harris, *From Mammies to Militants,* 10–11.

3. Harris, *From Mammies to Militants,* 4.

4. Susan Tucker, *Telling Memories Among Southern Women: Domestic Workers and Their Employers in the Segregated South* (Baton Rouge: Louisiana State University Press, 1988), 4.

the lens of "revolutionary mothering," as described by Alexis Pauline Gumbs in *Revolutionary Mothering: Love on the Front Lines*. To that end, I briefly explore critical scholarship about and select interviews with Black domestics, and read Black domestic labor—as Gumbs has suggested—as an inherently "queer thing":

> To name oneself "mother" in a moment where representatives of the state conscripted "Black" and "mother" into vile epithets is a queer thing. To insist upon Black motherhood despite . . . white feminist attempts to use the maternal labor of Black women as domestic servants to buy their own freedom (and to implicitly support the use of Black women as guinea pigs in their fight to perfect the privilege of sterilization) is an almost illegible thing, an outlawed practice, a queer thing.[5]

I work to reimagine the labor and lives of Black domestic workers away from regularizing terms established by the US nationalist-capitalist framework that renders Black women's labor, bodies, and humanity invisible, and instead place Black women who worked as domestics within a framework of radical queer mothering. By queering the mammy, which I will explain in great depth later in this essay, I read Black women's mothering as a necessary disruption of the normative conception of motherhood as a sacred White women's institution. I argue that Black domestics who cared for children are progenitors of radical mothering, and I ask us to reevaluate Black mothers as integral to the survival of both Black and White communities—and worlds beyond them, as well.

Any reflection on the radical love-labor of Black domestics would have to take into consideration the ways in which popular representations of "the help," as they were commonly described from Calpurnia to Aunt Jemima, have shaped US American conceptions of motherhood. My desire to rethink their contributions to US American life, therefore, must begin with a (re) consideration of the function of motherhood in US American popular memory, and our historical and present understanding of both White and Black women as mothers. Katherine Van Wormer, David Jackson III, and Charletta Suddeth argue in their book *The Maid Narratives: Black Domestics and White Families in the Jim Crow South* that though most interpret the dynamics

5. Alexis Pauline Gumbs, "m/other ourselves: a Black queer feminist genealogy for radical mothering," in *Revolutionary Mothering: Love on the Front Lines*, eds. Alexis Pauline Gumbs, China Martens, and Mai'a Williams (Oakland, CA: PM Press, 2016), 21.

between Black and White southerners as decidedly paternalist, "the sociologist Judith Rollins suggests that the term 'maternalism' is far more relevant to the description of the mistress-servant relationship. . . . The character of the mistress-servant relationship, Rollins argues, is distinctly female. In contrast to paternalism, which stems from the tradition of patriarchal authority, maternalism 'is a concept related to women's supportive intrafamilial roles of nurturing, loving, and attending to affective needs.'"[6] Though the description of the relationship between White women and Black women in domestic relations as "female" is dated and inaccurate, it is true that their interactions were governed by complex dynamics of race, class, and gender, among other things. Van Wormer, Jackson, and Suddeth suggest that "women of both races . . . lived under the dominance of southern white men,"[7] yet I argue that southern women's engagements in the close space of the home were overtly shaped by the psycho-sexual dynamics of White supremacy. During slavery and after, Black and White women were thought of as being essentially different from one another and therefore treated as opposites according to the norms of southern paternalism, which turned Black women into inhuman sexual objects and White women into sacred symbols of sexual and racial purity. White women were "treated by southern gentlemen as if they were helpless damsels in distress," and consequently "derived power by being attached to a man of substance."[8] White women took full advantage of the twinned forces of White supremacy and White femininity in their dealings with Black women. Black women were thus victims of both southern paternalism and southern maternalism, powers which sought to police every aspect of their beings from their reproductive lives to their locations in space and place.

Southern White women saw the employment of Black domestics as a marker of their social success: "Gender roles in southern society . . . were distinctly marked. The class of women who were required to keep up a pretense of leisure required a staff of servants to do the heavy household chores and to provide care for the small children. . . . Southern women further down the social ladder could emulate their social betters by having a maid, as pay levels were relatively, indeed shamelessly, low."[9] Though Van Wormer, Jackson, and

6. Katherine Van Wormer, David W. Jackson III, and Charletta Suddeth, *The Maid Narratives: Black Domestics and White Families in the Jim Crow South* (Baton Rouge: Louisiana State University Press, 2012), 34.

7. Van Wormer, Jackson, and Suddeth, *The Maid Narratives,* 34.

8. Van Wormer, Jackson, and Suddeth, *The Maid Narratives,* 39.

9. Van Wormer, Jackson, and Suddeth, *The Maid Narratives,* 40.

Suddeth acknowledge that White women relied on Black domestics to bolster their status as ladies, their conclusion that White women suffered from a surfeit of requirements under southern paternalism is not correct. White women benefited greatly from doing their part to bolster southern paternalism, which provided them the financial means necessary to evade many of rigors of household labor and child-rearing. Southern paternalists provided the necessary conditions for southern maternalism; White women were able to direct the affairs of their households through the in/visible labor of Black women who served them.

I argue that out of the convergence of southern paternalists' and maternalists' need to reconcile the presence of Black women who supported them came the invention of the mammy, "the ultimate maternal figure," for whom Wormer, Jackson, and Suddeth argue White southerners had "feelings of trust and affection."[10] Those feelings of affection, however, were always coupled with violent affectual responses to Black women's bodies and beings, including rage, hatred, and envy. White southerners depended upon Black domestics to manage most aspects of their lives, including processes attending birth and death; Black domestics were often expected to be present at births, serving as midwives, and at bedsides as nurses during times of illness. As dependent as they were on Black women's expertise, White southerners paradoxically infantilized them, regarding them as overgrown children who could not be trusted to manage their own affairs. Van Wormer, Jackson, and Suddeth make the case that for Black domestics, "society treated her as someone who had to be mothered, although not always in the nurturing sense of the word."[11] I argue that mothering is always already an act of radical nurturing. To that end I see no evidence that society wished to see their mammies mothered. Rather, White southerners wanted and needed to strictly control Black women not only because their inexpensive labor was vital to maintaining their socioeconomic statuses, but also because of the importance of Black women's labor to the survival of White supremacist norms. Incorporating Black domestic laborers into the White family unit by mammifying them thus nullified any financial obligation White employers had to their Black servants by turning financial transactions into filial ones. Consequently, White southerners created conditions under which Black domestics were required to perform competence, deference, and the appearance of familial bonds, or face unemployment—or worse.

10. Van Wormer, Jackson, and Suddeth, *The Maid Narratives,* 36.

11. Van Wormer, Jackson, and Suddeth, *The Maid Narratives,* 36.

Kimberly Wallace-Sanders argues in *Mammy: A Century of Race, Gender, and Southern Memory*, that the "mammy-mother" was a creation and amalgamation of memories, material objects, and popular images that have taken the place of the history of the real Black women who lived and worked with White southerners.[12] To that end, the mammy-mother is simulacrum. Given the complex of ideas that surrounded Black domestic workers and their instantiation as mammies, Wallace-Sanders explains that "the mammy's body is the site where fiction, history, autobiography, memoir, and popular culture meet in battle over the dominant representation of African American womanhood, and African American motherhood more specifically."[13] Our inattention to the influence of the mammy on the US national psyche matters precisely because the mammy remains "the most widely recognized symbol of African American motherhood."[14] For centuries, Black slaves and domestics performed powerful feats of mothering, encompassing the physical, psychic, and spiritual needs of Black and White people. The overwhelming lack of critical attention to Black domestic workers as women and mothers in their own right is the result of the continued interrelation of southern paternalism, southern maternalism, and White supremacy, the production of a powerful White southern cultural imaginarium of Black slaves and servants in film, literature, and art, and the historical gaps and archival silences regarding the lives of Black women slaves and domestics.

If the mammy is the most recognized image of Black motherhood, then perhaps I turned down the offer to attend *The Help* because I did not want to conflate the symbol of the mammy with the real experiences of Black mothers. To put it another way: I didn't want to participate in my own mammification. My refusal to be conflated with or to conflate for myself the image of the mammy-mother maid was a rejection of that vision of Black motherhood in the minds of the White women who invited me, but also of the characterization of Aibileen Clark and Minny Jackson as represented by Kathryn Stockett. Tucker maintains that "in literature and in the popular imagination . . . the black domestic is cast as both mother to her own children, and mother surrogate to white children. More important, she is often seen as a strong mother to both races of children."[15] Black women, however, were far more

12. Kimberly Wallace-Sanders, *Mammy: A Century of Race, Gender, and Southern Memory* (Ann Arbor: University of Michigan Press, 2011), 2.

13. Wallace-Sanders, *Mammy,* 3.

14. Wallace-Sanders, *Mammy,* 7.

15. Tucker, *Telling Memories Among Southern Women,* 5.

than mother surrogates. Annie Victoria Johnson, a former domestic worker from Mississippi, remembers that her mother often served as wet nurse for her White charges:

> My mother would be there when the white woman's babies were born! She helped make baby clothes for them and feed them. They breast-fed their babies, but as soon as they got to be six months old, whatever you ate, the baby ate. The white women breast-fed and the black folks, too. . . . The black women would breastfeed the white babies. The black woman's milk would be there for the white baby. . . . The black woman would have a baby too. They both nursed their babies.[16]

As Johnson makes plain, Black women nursed their own children *in addition to* the children of White women, rather than *instead of* nursing their own biological children. Though there are stories of live-in domestic workers who saw their children only on the weekends, in oral histories far more women remember that their mothers took them to work, raising them alongside White children. Johnson recalls that she "started working for white people as soon as I was old enough to walk. . . . Wherever she [her mother] went, she took us with her. She would help take care of white babies and black babies. She would help bathe them and feed them. We just did all of that. As I grew older, that taught me."[17] Johnson's memory of her mother's radical mothering is striking and important—by taking her children with her to work and insisting upon nursing her own children, Johnson's mother demanded acknowledgment of her *own* maternity. Her children were not less important than her White employer's children. In fact, they were more so.

As Wallace-Sanders explains, one of the most destructive myths about the mammy is that she neglected her own children in order to care for White children: "Her own children are usually dirty and ill mannered, yet they serve as suitable playmates for her white charges. She is typically depicted as impatient or brusque (sometimes even violent or abusive) with her own children, in contrast to her lavish, affectionate patience for her white charges."[18] Though they were believed to be loving and indulgent caretakers to White children, mammies were often represented as abusive and intolerant of their biological children. In every way, White constructions of a mammy-mother who

16. Van Wormer, Jackson, and Suddeth, *The Maid Narratives,* 92–93.

17. Van Wormer, Jackson, and Suddeth, *The Maid Narratives,* 89.

18. Wallace-Sanders, *Mammy,* 6.

preferred White children to her own biological Black children reinforced the myth of White supremacy. Though many of the Black domestics interviewed by Van Wormer, Jackson, Suddeth, and Tucker recall having been raised in rich intergenerational mothering environments, where their mothers, grandmothers, aunts, siblings, and cousins were called upon to care for one another in complex and beautiful ways, there stubbornly persists the misconception that Black women did not love their children or care for them well enough. Indeed, even Van Wormer, Jackson, and Suddeth perpetuate the myth that "when mothers took care of white children, their own families were often neglected," because of "the extent to which all the attention lavished on the white child takes away from attention that could be given to the servant's own family."[19] I reject arguments that maintain that Black mothers who worked outside of the home were neglectful of their children—certainly, they are no more neglectful than mothers who work full-time jobs and employ daycare workers or ask family or friends to mind their children.

Rethinking the concept of the mammy-mother in both academic and popular imaginaries requires reading Black women as resisting southern paternalism, southern maternalism, White supremacy, ableism, classism, and misogyny. By rejecting narratives of Black mothers as neglectful, simple-minded mammy-children, we can see Black domestics as among the earliest progenitors of revolutionary mothering in the United States. Cynthia Dewi Oka argues in "Mothering as Revolutionary Praxis" that "the revolutionary struggle against a colonial, racist, heteropatriarchal capitalism which has for centuries separated us; arranged us in structured oppositions to each other; reduced our bodies to raw resources for abuse, exploitation and manipulation; and . . . occupied our breathing, is today the struggle for a world—no, many worlds—where we might exist and thrive as each other's beloved."[20] If we understand that Black mothers have always been at the frontlines of the struggle for their own liberation and that of their children, rather than passive participants in or ardent supporters of systems which maligned them and devalued their lives, we can come to see that "mothering is a primary front in this struggle, not as a biological function, but as a *social practice*."[21] When we place Black domestics within a framework of

19. Van Wormer, Jackson, and Suddeth, *The Maid Narratives,* 176.

20. Cynthia Dewi Oka, "Mothering as Revolutionary Praxis," in *Revolutionary Mothering: Love on the Front Lines*, eds. Alexis Pauline Gumbs, China Martens, and Mai'a Williams (Oakland, CA: PM Press, 2016), 51.

21. Oka, "Mothering as Revolutionary Praxis," 51. Emphasis in original.

mothering as a social practice, Black mothering becomes a necessary intervention into public life; in this paradigm, Black mothering is, as Oka puts it, "literally *priceless*."[22] Indeed, in a world where "women of color have been violently punished and stigmatized for mothering," the reclamation of Black motherhood and acts of mothering as a radical revolutionary struggle is a necessary and timely intervention into our present moment.[23]

I follow Alexis Pauline Gumbs in advocating a queer approach to the reclamation of the history of Black mothering:

> The complexity of the term "mother" (next to "Black") requires a queer theory that deuniversalizes race and highlights the function of racism in reproducing the heteropatriarchal status quo. . . . We are people of color. The whole system wakes up every day trying to exterminate our bodies and our spirits. Our very survival is queer. We were never meant to survive, and if mothers are part of why we are here (and they are), then they are the queerest of us all. . . . If we remember what Black women have been up to in the United States, we can just go ahead and let go of the assumption that mothering is conservative or that conserving and nurturing the lives of Black children has ever had any validated place in the official American political spectrum.[24]

Given the ways southern paternalism, southern maternalism, and White supremacy conspire to construct Black domestics and Black mothers as mammies, queering the mammy requires reading the contributions of Black domestic laborers outside of "the heteropatriarchal status quo" that makes invisible their labor of both mother love and housework, forms of labor that are fundamentally devalued in a capitalist structure. According to Gumbs's model of revolutionary mothering, "the use of the word 'queer' to describe a politics of sexuality is not based on a specific sexual practice, but rather a critical relationship to existing sexual and social norms."[25] To that end, Black domestic laborers queer conceptions and practices of normative heteropatriarchal White motherhood at multiple important intersections.

22. Oka, "Mothering as Revolutionary Praxis," 51. Emphasis in original.

23. Oka, "Mothering as Revolutionary Praxis," 51.

24. Alexis Pauline Gumbs, "Forget Hallmark: Why Mother's Day Is a Queer Black Left Feminist Thing," in *Revolutionary Mothering: Love on the Front Lines*, eds. Alexis Pauline Gumbs, China Martens, and Mai'a Williams (Oakland, CA: PM Press, 2016), 120.

25. Gumbs, "m/other ourselves," 20.

Black domestics kept their White employers and their families alive, providing them with ethical and moral guidance, affective care during childbirth and illness, medical care, emotional and physical comfort, and physical nourishment through the use of their own bodies and hands, even as "the U.S. state enacted domestic and foreign policies that required, allowed, and endorsed violence against the bodies of Black women and early death for Black children."[26] This is not to say that all Black women survived, or that they did not struggle to survive. I want to be clear that their love-labor was not performed out of a feeling that White people were superior, but rather out of a desire to survive and to enable their own children and families to survive. Though under White supremacist heteropatriarchal capitalist frameworks Black women have been and continue to be mammified, the power of Black women's mother love has always been a radical response to conditions of profound indifference to Black lives. As Gumbs explains, "To answer death with utopian futurity, to rival the social reproduction of capital on a global scale with a forward-dreaming diasporic accountability is a queer thing to do. A strange thing to do. A thing that changes the family and the future forever."[27] Indeed, I argue that Black women's domestic labor in White homes was in the service of protecting their Black communities, and it is a misapprehension of Black women's work to suggest that their survival was oriented in service of their masters or employers. Rather, Black women's mother love—to raise children, to care for themselves, and for their Black communities—is both pragmatic and utopian, future-oriented and historical.

In her oral history, Tucker reminds us that foundationally Black domestics were in close connection with one another, working cooperatively to keep themselves grounded and whole in a world hostile and unsympathetic to their fundamental human needs: "As generation after generation of black women entered domestic work, a body of knowledge about how to deal with white employers was formed. Black domestics repeatedly spoke of advice given to them by their mothers, aunts, older sisters, and friends. I heard such advice repeated so often that I feel that stories about it should be considered a standard part of how domestics coped in the world in which they lived."[28] I do not, unfortunately, have space to explore in great depth the many ways Black domestics worked together to mother their children and themselves. But I

26. Gumbs, "m/other ourselves," 21.

27. Gumbs, "m/other ourselves," 21.

28. Tucker, *Telling Memories Among Southern Women,* 198.

would like to end this essay by turning to Zelda Greene, who at the time of her interview had been working as a domestic for many years, and who expresses clearly how Black domestics saw themselves as mothers and daughters in their own right:

> A lot of things black people had to put up with, they went on and smiled and put up with it. People had to take and swallow a lot because they thought that they would lose their job. . . . My mother used to always tell us, "Never marry yourself to a job." You go out there; you're hired on a job; you do your part what you're supposed to do. You know how a lot of people think they own the people's houses and stuff like that. No, when I come home, *that's* my home.[29]

Greene draws clear distinctions between the substance of her employer's lives and that of her own, between the home of her employers and her own, between her personal affect and that of her employers. Furthermore, her testimony highlights the ways Black women made fundamental distinctions between "a job" and "my home." Though White maternalism conjured up an image of a mammy in order to justify their brutalization of Black women and their exploitation of domestic labor, Greene reminds us that Black domestic's behavior did not often align with their affect. By paying attention to Greene's insistence on a strict delineation of her home space and that of her White employers, we find the roots of a Black radical mothering that insists on the creation of community, home, and family in spite of systemic attempts to eradicate or undermine the practice.

By sending her daughter to college with money she earned working as a domestic, Greene sees herself as actively resisting mammification and queering the norms of Black motherhood: "They [White people] would say, 'Well, if your mother used to work for me, you grow up, and then after she got too old, the children will work for me.' They would just keep it coming down from generation to generation. I say, it's going to stop right there! My daughter she won't need to think she need to do that days work for a living."[30] This act of sacrifice, child-rearing, and mother love is, as Gumbs structures it, resistance: "It is an act of love to participate in the resistance work of child-raising. It is an act of love to envision and actualize an intergenerationally participatory movement. We honor and acknowledge the work of raising and caring for children as life force toward the world we

29. Tucker, *Telling Memories Among Southern Women,* 203.

30. Tucker, *Telling Memories Among Southern Women,* 204.

can only transform together."[31] I remember, once more, the afternoon of the film screening; I sat in a rocking chair, holding my small infant son to my breast, feeding him, motherful and mothering. I am the result of the revolutionary life force begotten by transformative radical mothering work done by generations of Black women. As a mother who is also a worker, I am myself continuing their legacy. By queering the mammy and actively resisting efforts to mammify Black mothering in our work and thinking about Black women, I argue that we can begin to understand the essential importance of the future-oriented work that Black mothering does and has done, work which is of survival and of moving beyond survival into spaces where Black mothers and Black mothering are regarded as a model for futurity, as a model of persistence, and as evidence of our continued existence in the presence of death.

Bibliography

Gumbs, Alexis Pauline. "m/other ourselves: a Black queer feminist genealogy for radical mothering." In *Revolutionary Mothering: Love on the Front Lines*, edited by Alexis Pauline Gumbs, China Martens, and Mai'a Williams, 18–31. Oakland, CA: PM Press, 2016.

———. "Forget Hallmark: Why Mother's Day Is a Queer Black Left Feminist Thing." In *Revolutionary Mothering: Love on the Front Lines*, edited by Alexis Pauline Gumbs, China Martens, and Mai'a Williams, 117–22. Oakland, CA: PM Press, 2016.

Harris, Trudier. *From Mammies to Militants: Domestics in American Literature*. Philadelphia: Temple University Press, 1982.

Oka, Cynthia Dewi. "Mothering as Revolutionary Praxis." In *Revolutionary Mothering: Love on the Front Lines*, edited by Alexis Pauline Gumbs, China Martens, and Mai'a Williams, 51–58. PM Press, 2016.

Tucker, Susan. *Telling Memories Among Southern Women: Domestic Workers and Their Employers in the Segregated South*. Baton Rouge: Louisiana State University Press, 1988.

Van Wormer, Katherine, David W. Jackson III, and Charletta Suddeth. *The Maid Narratives: Black Domestics and White Families in the Jim Crow South*. Baton Rouge: Louisiana State University Press, 2012.

31. Gumbs, "m/other ourselves," 26.

Wallace-Sanders, Kimberly. *Mammy: A Century of Race, Gender, and Southern Memory*. Ann Arbor: University of Michigan Press, 2011.

Joanna Davis-McElligatt is an assistant professor of Black Literary Studies at the University of North Texas. She teaches courses in Africana studies; critical race and ethnic studies; literary theory; women's, gender, and sexuality studies; comics studies; Southern studies; and twentieth and twenty-first century US literary studies. Davis-McElligatt is currently at work on her first monograph entitled *Black and Immigrant: The New Black Diaspora in American Literature and Culture*, a critical exploration of representations of immigrants of African descent to the U.S. from Afropolitans to Wakandan Americans. She is also co-editor of *Narratives of Marginalized Identities in Higher Education: Inside and Outside the Academy* (Routledge 2018), *Narrating History, Home, and Nation: Critical Essays on Edwidge Danticat* (under contract), and *BOOM! #*@&! Splat: Comics and Violence* (under contract). Her scholarly work on the numerous aspects of Blackness and comics appears in many publications and journals. She has also published a comic about living in Opelousas, Louisiana, in *Little Village Magazine*.

Part II

The Influence of Slavery and the Civil War on the Matriarch

Mary Chesnut's Civil War and the Evolution of the Southern Woman

Michelle-Taylor Sherwin

The elite socioeconomic class of the South in the nineteenth century housed the shining beacon of American femininity: the southern woman. She seemingly begins as a southern belle in her youth and upon marriage, then transforms into a plantation mistress, a woman given countless responsibilities, often in a strange new home. Following the American Civil War (1861–1865), the image of this particular southern woman is reminiscent of the over-idealization of the antebellum era. Today, she is remembered as the belle, memorialized forever in Hollywood's *Gone with the Wind* through images of corsets and hoops set against a bright green Georgia landscape. However, history shows the actual narrative works in reverse. Instead, the image of the southern woman moves from a plantation mistress, an established historical social class, to the southern belle, a stereotypical representation of White femininity developed after the Civil War. Complex gender dynamics evolve within and around the figure of this southern matriarch alongside ramifications of slavery as an economic practice. Beginning with the gendered and racialized ideals established in the Cult of True Womanhood, the creation of the trope of the overall "good southern woman" coincided with the southern belle/plantation mistress stereotype.[1]

Mary Chesnut's Civil War (1981) simultaneously deconstructs and reconstructs the idealized notion of the "good southern woman" both outside the domestic domain and immersed within a more complex moral space. For

1. The Cult of True Womanhood, also known as the cult of domesticity, was a value system that dominated the moral underbelly of the United States during the early part of the nineteenth century. Post-Revolutionary women were subordinated in the political and economic hierarchy and instead reallocated to the domestic domain wherein their autonomy was limited to moral, spiritual, and reproductive care of the family.

Chesnut, the southern matriarch is the paragon of the private *and* public sphere, and it is her sense of morality that not only comforts the home but also the nation at large. Given Mary Chesnut's position as a wealthy White woman in the South, an undeniable member of the elite planter class before the Civil War, her supposed "diary" is therefore a foundational White feminist text that explores the development of this new and improved (White) southern matriarch and, by extension, how such gendered antebellum archetypes evolved as a result of the Civil War and Reconstruction periods.[2] Rather than simply this idea of "nostalgia," wherein the psyche of the White South longs to return to the time before the Civil War, Chesnut's diary redirects her focus and reflects a certain desire to both retain the economic nostalgia of slavery as a constant practice, and her position in the house in addition to the freedom and mobility the White woman experienced during and after the war. Chesnut's rhetorical practice and ideology in the early entries of the "diary" clearly establish the early-nineteenth-century trope of privileged White women comparing their "plight" as wife/mother to that of enslaved persons. Such a conflation, of course, desensitizes slavery as a horrific, traumatic economic process and refocuses the attention on White women instead.

To return then, to the significance of the (White) southern matriarch, Mary Chesnut's work ultimately demonstrates a southern matriarch's complex development, one that cannot be stereotyped or reduced to a simple label of "good." Instead, her journey is a contradiction, filled with growth and regression, that ultimately ends in utter disillusionment and an irrevocable shift in morality that is not necessarily accounted for by current critics. Chesnut exposes the ramifications of such a shift by mirroring the national rift following the end of the Civil War, in which the White (and gendered) South moves toward a restoration of imagined nostalgia as opposed to truly reconstructing the fractured nation with persisting and unrelenting ramifications that not only further the racial and gender divide but expose the inauthenticity of White southern matriarchs.

As a historical framework, the concept of the southern woman functions in different stages with morality as the common linking thread. Although the

2. I use the term "diary" here loosely. While Chesnut did base this text on diary entries written during the war, as editor C. Vann Woodward elucidates in his paratextual essay, "Diary in Fact—Diary in Form," her "extensive diary" that she kept "intermittently during the years of the Confederacy" was "never intended for publication" (xvii). Instead, this book acts as an epic of her experiences based on those diary entries that were edited for more than twenty years, a point I argue and expand upon at a later juncture in my work.

southern belle first appears after the Civil War as a symbol of the White southern patriarchy's nostalgia, beginning the framework with this figure highlights the current understanding of the southern woman's progression from belle to mistress. Nestled in the heart of the antebellum era, the southern belle sits daintily under the magnolia tree surrounded by adoring suitors.[3] Catherine Clinton's appropriately, and cleverly, named scholarship, *Tara Revisited*, defines this archetype in all her glory. Clinton's use of what she calls "planter daughters," on the epitomical southern plantation provides another name for the loaded phrase itself. She states, "Planter daughters marry at a young age . . . [o]ne day a young white woman might be the pampered daughter of a planter family, free of responsibility, a carefree schoolgirl pursuing fashion and romance. But marriage would change all that."[4] The southern belle is a young White woman—this youthful factor is key. Despite *Gone with the Wind's* casual portrayal of the belle surrounded by men, the stereotype is more prudish than the film suggests. The nature of the planter daughter reveres a sense of innocence in the young woman: she is confined to an innocent space, apart and separate from men. She is a belle, a young girl before she is a wife, a mother, and an official slave mistress.

With youth, there is the potential for the young woman to eventually provide spiritual, economical, and sensual comfort to a plantation owner. Such potentiality allows room for hope—she fits any mold society demands. Initially, the world sits at the feet of a belle and the expectations of married life are unclear; as Clinton writes, "she could be torn from the bosom of her family and anchored on an isolated plantation, saddled with her own household and charged with the care and feeding of her husband's slaves."[5] Such an abrupt transition into a new reality robs the belle of her previous "innocence" and instead catapults her into a new role, one that is more dependent upon survival. The transition from southern belle to plantation mistress is not often showcased in its entirety as it disrupts the hypermediated portrayal of an innocent young woman gliding down the staircase in a beautiful white dress with green trim and a delicate hat. The Scarlett O'Hara image on the grand Tara plantation is just that, a remediated image of the "reconstructed South" that takes an already romanticized notion and twists it to suit a more dramatic purpose for a hungry Hollywood audience.

3. *Gone with the Wind*, directed by Victor Fleming (1939; Atlanta: Selznick International Pictures/Metro-Goldwyn-Mayer, 1985), Film.

4. Catherine Clinton, *Tara Revisited: Women, War, and the Plantation Legend* (New York: Abbeville Press, 1995), 42–43.

5. Clinton, *Tara Revisited*, 43.

The true stereotype of the southern belle follows the end of the Civil War where young women of the South are lost to "considerable mists of sentiment" and what Clinton calls a "complex interweaving of myth and memories" that is not found in Rhett Butler's embrace.[6] Instead, the belle's strength (and eventually, the plantation mistress's strength) manifests in her manner of survival in the destroyed South following the war. This notion of southern femininity and strength of morality rests with the Old South, which is a key factor considering the historical period after the war and how this is defined within scholarship today. In terms of morality, the belle is the paragon of goodness and the epitome of privilege, a symbol of when times were "simpler," and the demarcation of the social, economic, and political hierarchy that was blissfully uninterrupted. After the war in which the South is (meant to be) reconstructed, this image is pervasive and constant because of the film: there is no escape from the Scarlett O'Hara image. As long as the belle herself is considered moral and all that is "good," the nostalgia lives.

The transition from the southern belle to the plantation mistress is a form of upward mobility within the hierarchy of the planter class: the maturation of the young woman is commodified and exploited by the plantation owner. The antebellum era allotted very few roles for upper-class women outside of the marriage bed; as Clinton states, "Choice of church, marital partner, and perhaps family limitation were the only decisions left to women."[7] The role of the plantation mistress stretches to that of "preserving the health and well-being of slaves on the plantation."[8] With this mentality, there is logic in the sense of paternal guidance that plantation mistresses often felt. The key to understanding elite White women's morality lies in the study of the plantation mistress. Through Catherine Clinton's historical findings and analysis of Elizabeth Craven's survey of nineteenth-century slave narratives on the "reported physical punishments" against slaves by the plantation mistress, she concludes that "mistresses were accountable for only a small portion [10 percent] of the punishment inflicted upon plantation slaves."[9] Most likely, this

6. Clinton, *Tara Revisited,* 15.

7. Catherine Clinton, *The Other Civil War: American Women in the Nineteenth Century* (New York: Hill and Wang, 1984), 43.

8. Catherine Clinton, *The Plantation Mistress* (New York: Pantheon Books, 1982), 187.

9. Elizabeth Craven, unpublished survey of twentieth-century Works Progress Administration interviews of ex-slaves, quoted in Clinton, *The Plantation Mistress,* 187.

number does not include the punishment for any female slaves' alleged sexual encounter with a plantation owner. With such a "small" number of mistress-related punishments in comparison to the "over 80 percent" of reports naming men as the aggressors, this leaves the plantation mistress as the lessor of the two evils in an innately corrupt and inhumane system. She appears distant from the horrible atrocity of slavery, despite the numerical fact that she is undeniably complicit: she is still responsible for at least 10 percent of violence against slaves. Clinton and Craven's work demonstrates a false sense of morality on behalf of the southern matriarch, a concept held firmly in place both during and after the Civil War.[10]

Prior to the Civil War, this sense of morality emerged as a common theme amongst White women in the South, undeniably creating a mythos of its own. This belief, or "morality complex," was constructed by elite White women of the South in order to fit their needs. As Clinton states, "The plantation mistress saw herself as the conscience of the slave South" because of her sympathy for the enslaved.[11] While there is no doubt that this view was adopted for the White women to rationalize and therefore minimize their complicity in slavery as a system, I extend this conscience to include the comparison of the White women themselves to that of the enslaved. In other words, since the elite White women consider their troubles on a parallel line with that of enslaved persons, and yet, they also have the capacity to feel sympathy for those who are enslaved, the White women are therefore morally superior. Regardless of this so-called role as the "conscience," by no means does this morality indicate a belief in racial equality on behalf of elite planter women. It is this sense of situational morality that became the model for and of elite southern femininity. In order to fully understand the depth of such a particular ideology and how it manifests within the plantation system, I now turn to Clinton's examination in *The Other Civil War* of the feminine moral conscience in the North that specifically highlights the difference of the positionality for the women in the South.

During the early years of the Republic, women's fervor and spiritual enthusiasm were the mainstay of American religion. Missionary zeal led many women into moral opposition to slavery. In the North, this energy was directed into evangelical channels. In the South, elite males tried to prevent women from participating in reform campaigns. They expected women to

10. Clinton, *The Plantation Mistress,* 187.

11. Clinton, *The Plantation Mistress,* 189.

devote themselves to caring for slaves on the *plantations* rather than to the cause of antislavery.[12]

With such a binary established between the already-divided North and South, the southern moral conscience takes a different route—to and on the plantation, as I have emphasized based on Clinton's analysis. It is the plantation where the elite White women of the South were encouraged to feel "sympathy" for the enslaved, so long as the enslaved continued to work. In the North, we have a clearer picture, given the advent of "reform campaigns," that is more traditional when contemporary scholars consider what we would retroactively call "White feminism." Regardless of the stark difference between antislavery in the North and supposed compassion in the South, the (elite) White women of both regions held fast to their perceptions of morality.

Slavery as a system became the focal point for women's battles during the nineteenth century; and yet, with its different manifestations and progression, this furthered the divide between northern and southern women. It is significant to note that to this effect, scholar Drew Gilpin Faust states, "Women's associations and organizations had not blossomed in the antebellum South as they had in northern states."[13] Instead, the associations and organizations were of a social nature as opposed to a political or economic meeting of furthering women's rights. Southern women's morality seemingly fostered where it could: at the top of the plantation hierarchy as White women. Within this hierarchy, abolitionism became a jumping off point for other issues. Both northern and southern women used slavery to further their own rights. For the North, there was more of a political movement, evident in the 1848 Seneca Falls convention, featuring feminists such as Elizabeth Cady Stanton and Lucretia Mott who fought for the rights of women—or more so, White women, even while calling for the freedom of the enslaved. In the South, there was a social movement around slavery, seen in the detailed writings and activities of Mary Chesnut and Lucy Holcombe Pickens. By constructing slavery as, perhaps, a social issue rather than a political issue, this allowed the elite White women of the South to instead politicize their positions on the plantation itself, therefore solidifying the plantation mistress into the hierarchy of the plantation system. Socially and politically, this created, and in terms of a narrative, creates and repurposes the southern matriarch as just that—a White matriarch.

12. Clinton, *The Other Civil War*, 67. Emphasis added.

13. Drew Gilpin Faust, *Mothers of Invention: Women of the Slaveholding South in the American Civil War* (Chapel Hill: University of North Carolina Press, 1996), 23.

Mary Chesnut's writing explores what the role of matriarch, and therefore, moral matriarch, means for the southern White woman in her text, *Mary Chesnut's Civil War* diary, which took place before, during, and after the Civil War. The text alternates between stories of the domestic home front and battles, providing the reader with over eight hundred pages of heavily revised material that took nearly twenty years to write until her death. The revision process alone robs the text of its ability to be called a "diary."[14] Instead, I argue that the text is a White feminist epic on the Civil War masquerading as a diary, in which Mary Chesnut the author has created "Mary Chesnut" the character—a woman who is, at first, the epitome of proper southern domesticity and morality. She is a devoted wife who keeps the slaves, a devoted southerner who champions the South during the war, and finally, a survivor at the end of the war whose entire way of life is ripped apart. Contemporary critics have called her book "the best-known woman's war commentary."[15] Her first "entry" is dated February 18, 1861, merely a few months before the start of the Civil War. Mary (both author and character) is thirty-eight years old and has been married for twenty-one years, well past the age to be labeled a southern belle herself. At this point, she is undoubtedly a plantation mistress, and more specifically, a sympathetic plantation mistress.

A mere fifteen pages into the epic, Chesnut provides her unique perspective on slavery and what it means for her: an opportunity for empathy on the part of White women and sympathy for enslaved peoples. Chesnut describes a scene in which "a negro woman [is] sold—up on the block—at auction."[16] By the end of the entry, Chesnut switches the focus from the plight of slavery to the women's burden of marriage: "You know how women sell themselves and are sold in marriage, from queens downward, eh?"[17] Here is the moral

14. The editor of this text, C. Vann Woodward, writes in the editorial preface that there "is no evidence that Mary Chesnut ever used or authorized this title" (xxviii) of the first edition, *A Diary from Dixie, as Written by Mary Boykin Chesnut, Wife of James Chesnut, Jr., United States Senator from South Carolina, 1859-1861, and Afterward an Aide to Jefferson Davis and a Brigadier-General in the Confederate Army*, published in 1905 (eds. Isabella D. Martin and Myrta Lockett Avary). Within the context of my argument, I reference the contemporary use of the word in the title *Mary Chesnut's Civil War* and challenge the current notion of referring to this text as a "diary."

15. Elizabeth Young, *Disarming the Nation: Women's Writing and the American Civil War* (Chicago, University of Chicago Press, 1999), 4.

16. Mary Chesnut, *Mary Chesnut's Civil War*, ed. C. Vann Woodward (New Haven: Yale University Press, 1981), 15.

17. Chesnut, *Mary Chesnut's Civil War*, 15.

conscience, or the southern morality complex, at work. Chesnut is at first displaying a sense of sympathy for the slave woman, but she wastes no time in then stating that (White) women also experience a sort of bondage through marriage. Evidently, slavery is not the primary focus for Chesnut, both in this passage in particular and the whole book. This is further evident within the same passage when Chesnut compares the woman on the auction block to her own personal slave: "The creature looked so like my good little Nancy. She was a bright mulatto with a pleasant face."[18] Referencing her slave allows the reader to question if Mary only experiences sympathy for the enslaved woman because she reminds Mary of her personal slave—one who appears Whiter than the others. Such ambiguity tosses this entire passage into a strange, inconceivable space of moral negotiation because the true focus is how White women are affected by marriage, not the "monstrous system" of slavery.

Slavery is continually entrenched in ambiguity after Chesnut's description of the auction scene, exposing the crack in the moral hierarchy of the morality complex. A mere few pages past her first mention of slavery, Chesnut writes, "I wonder if it be a sin to think slavery a curse to any land."[19] By posing such a question, this indicates the South's heavy economic reliance on slavery. However, a few lines down the same page, she complicates this question by writing, "Who thinks any worse of a negro or mulatto woman for being a thing we can't name? God forgive us, but ours is a *monstrous* system and wrong and iniquity. Perhaps the rest of the world is as bad—this *only* I see."[20] Chesnut places herself (or character) into the position of power here, quite unnecessarily, as she is already in the position of power at the top of the planter class. The language in the text that calls slavery a "monstrous system," which is then not followed by a declaration to stop the practice, shows that Mary Chesnut considers slavery a necessary evil. Mary's world, and that of other elite plantation mistresses like Lucy Holcombe Pickens, was utterly reliant on the system of human bondage.

Arguably, with the language in the text used to describe slavery and the immediate parallels made to White women, the focal point of Mary Chesnut's epic is not slavery. To read this text as a microcosm for the political, economic, and social aspects rampant in the South during the Civil War is more than likely the authorial intent at play here. However, to read this text as a metaphor for the evolution of the White southern matriarch not only includes this

18. Chesnut, *Mary Chesnut's Civil War*, 15.

19. Chesnut, *Mary Chesnut's Civil War*, 29.

20. Chesnut, *Mary Chesnut's Civil War*, 29.

microcosm but also places the book into a different historical consideration in terms of morality. In a genre in which, as Young states, "white women not only populated but dominated the literary marketplace for Civil War fiction," Chesnut's blending of the public and private sphere during the war casts morality into an even murkier space.[21]

For instance, Mary Chesnut the character and woman interacts often with Lucy Holcombe Pickens, affectionately nicknamed the "Queen of the Confederacy" by contemporary scholar Elizabeth Wittenmyer Lewis. Lucy and Mary knew each other well; both plantation mistresses, both married to upstanding southern gentlemen, and both good friends of Varina Davis, Jefferson Davis's wife. In an entry dated days before the official start of the Civil War, Chesnut writes, "Met the lovely Lucy Holcombe, now Mrs. Governor Pickens, last night at the Isaac Haynes. I see Miles now begging in dumb show for three violets she had in her breastpin. She is a consummate actress and he well up in the part of the male flirt. So it was well done."[22] The idea of performing social graces is evident in Chesnut's description of meeting Lucy for the first time. Chesnut's use of the word "consummate" shows distinction in Lucy's skills of performance, befitting for a woman of Lucy's status, as the wife of the governor of South Carolina. Eventually, these social meetings throughout the antebellum would become more of place in which upper-class women would volunteer in groups, and, as Faust writes, "[adjust] their efforts to the changing needs of the Confederacy," therefore creating their own hierarchical system within the overarching southern order.[23] It is within this system dominated by women of the planter class that Mary Chesnut and Lucy Pickens clashed as social rivals. While Mary's direct language does not identify any argument or falling out between the two women, I read Mary's often sour and bitter descriptions of Lucy as indicative of a social rivalry, a competitive streak wherein both women yearned to be the most popular woman in the Confederacy, most likely beneath that of Varina Davis.

It is significant to note that this perceived rivalry is not simply in the social realm, but within the political and economic spheres as well. With the war in full swing by 1862, Chesnut's entry on the ninth of that year reads: "Called on Mrs. Pickens. We flattered each other as far as that sort of thing can be done. She is young, lovely, clever—and old Pick's third wife. She cannot fail to hate

21. Young, *Disarming the Nation,* 4.

22. Chesnut, *Mary Chesnut's Civil War*, 240.

23. Faust, *Mothers of Invention,* 24.

us. Mr. C. put as [a] sort of watch and ward over her husband."[24] Evident in Chesnut's note of Lucy as "old Pick's third wife," there is a sense of superiority there on Mary's behalf, which I read as indicative of a sense of competition between the two women, and by extension, their two husbands, since historically, both men were close to Jefferson Davis throughout the duration of the war. Chesnut's use of the word "us," references that of her husband, creating a binary between the Pickenses and the Chesnuts, that was played out in the drawing room and the battlefield, or at least as Mary's drama would lead her readers to believe. In terms of this possible connection to the evolution of the southern woman, the preceding section to this paragraph where Mary introduces Lucy states that the latter is "young, lovely, and clever," marking the second time within thirty pages that Mary refers to Lucy's looks, and she continues to do so a number of times throughout her epic. Although Mary does not use the word "belle" here specifically, the reference to youth is clear: Lucy acts like a belle, a reversal of the place Mary herself occupies in the story. Her behavior does not seemingly reflect a responsible woman but instead, an immature girl. By not acknowledging Lucy's status within the Confederacy as a respected woman, in terms of postwar imagination, Mary not only creates her system of morality in the domestic sphere, but in the public sphere as well. She writes herself into said sphere as a woman who runs both the plantation house and acts as a political asset to her husband when she demands that "Mr. Chesnut [not] be the colonel of a regiment" but rather the "same political role" as Colonel Laurence M. Keitt.[25] Since Mary so aptly extends the role of helping her husband to outside the home, her chastisement of Mrs. Lucy Pickens is presented in two ways: by insulting her youth and her inability to portray a noticeable, political presence.

A mere ten pages later, Chesnut describes an interaction with Governor Pickens's secretary that speaks to this insult: "He hung over the lovely Lucy, standing or bending over her from the back of her chair. It suggested the devil whispering in Eve's ear in the primeval days."[26] Since Mary was, as Lewis writes, "never considered a beauty," the constant iteration on Lucy's looks is possibly emblematic of a deeper resentment.[27] This language and biblical allusion lends itself to an scathing intertextual critique. As Chestnut

24. Chesnut, *Mary Chesnut's Civil War*, 275.

25. Chesnut, *Mary Chesnut's Civil War*, 274.

26. Chesnut, *Mary Chesnut's Civil War*, 285.

27. Elizabeth Wittenmyer Lewis, *Queen of the Confederacy: The Innocent Deceits of Lucy Holcombe Pickens* (Denton: University of North Texas Press, 2002), 149.

writes, "Flirtation is the business of society. That is, playing at lovemaking."[28] According to Mary, there is still a sense of decorum that must be acknowledged. There is only meant to be a "playing at lovemaking," not the promise of physical lovemaking. By referring to Lucy as "Eve," Mary shows that Lucy moves beyond southern social graces of mere flirtation and now has the potential to fall into decadence and corruption, as Mary's tone indicates with utter disgust. Mary's use of sentimental language robs Lucy of any moral traits, condemning her to the role of a constant temptress, a perpetual belle.

Mary's disapproving tone, particularly as it pertains to Lucy Pickens, is not surprising; instead, the sentimental rhetoric is indicative of a specific type of southern matriarchal identity, one that was under construction before Mary's very eyes. Chesnut's description reflects the label of a certain kind of woman in the South, one who is *not* a belle, but instead, a plantation matriarch. This obvious shift in the southern matriarchal phenotype moves distinctly away from lauding the association of youth with the belle and instead, promotes the image of the dependable, capable plantation matriarch. To this end, it is significant to note the *way* in which the word "belle" is used throughout her epic.[29] In one instance, she writes about an acquaintance named Mrs. Walker:

> —a Montgomery beauty (find her pretty, silly and, I really believe, half-crazy). Such magnificent dressing. She was also an heiress. So dissatisfied with Richmond. Seems to be accustomed to be a belle, but under different conditions. As she is as handsome and well dressed as ever, must be the men who are all wrong.[30]

28. Chesnut, *Mary Chesnut's Civil War*, 690.

29. The word "belle" is used a different number of times throughout the different editions of *Mary Chesnut's Civil War*. The version used in this paper, edited by C. Vann Woodward, uses "belle" a total of three times. *A Diary from Dixie* uses the word "belle" a total of seven times. While that observation in and of itself can be explored individually and extensively, for the purposes of this paper, it is pertinent to my current argument to note that the word was used at all and in a degrading manner.

30. Chesnut, *Mary Chesnut's Civil War*, 164. While there is no way to tell if this word was written during the 1860s or the 1880s due to Chesnut's extensive revision, according to C. Vann Woodward's editorial symbols chart in the beginning of the text, the word "belle" does not at any point have the "< >" symbols round it, which indicates "effaced or erased passages restored by the editor" (lviii).

By calling Mrs. Walker a "belle" hereafter labeling her "half-crazy" in the 1860s journal edition, according to editor C. Vann Woodward, this is not a term of endearment.[31] Instead, this is Mary's displeasure at a woman who is "silly," or not doing the work that Mary the character believes Mrs. Walker should be doing. This action places the concept of the southern "belle" into a different context than currently understood by a contemporary audience: this is not a romanticized word for Mary, but rather, her usage shows a more pertinent meaning during the war for the economic/political status of women. The "belle" itself is not the desire, but is instead, the hindrance. What is valued in Chesnut's text is maturity and experience; rather, "belle" is a label of immaturity, of youth, in which the labeled woman is not a political or social force in society. For Mary, Mrs. Walker is clearly not an asset for the Confederacy when relegated to such a space. On the other hand, while Mary does not call Lucy Pickens a "belle" directly, the sentimental language of dissatisfaction mirrors Walker's description and is clearly iterating a sense of moral superiority.

Despite Mary Chesnut's fluctuating disapproval of her "frenemy," Lucy's supposed decadence and intrigue led her onto the one-hundred-dollar bill of the Confederacy, forever cementing her southern belle image in history. While women, like Chesnut, did not approve of Lucy's demeanor and felt that she often "overplayed her part" as a southern belle, Lewis's text entitled *Queen of the Confederacy* describes how Lucy and Mary shared a common goal in attempting to further the Confederate cause. In the moments where their social rivalry was put aside, Mary Chesnut and Lucy Pickens became, as Faust writes, "a combination [of] hostess[es]/chaperone[s] for a bevy of eligible South Carolina belles whose romantic adventures absorbed much of Chesnut's attention," and consequently, much of her diary.[32] These former belles (considering the contemporary understanding of the stereotype) became mentors to other belles, perpetuating the same sense of morality and idealization of the South they were exposed to. For the upper class specifically, the moral path led to the support of the South, which relied fundamentally on slavery. The social scene merges then with the political and economic scene, placing Mary and Lucy on the same side.

Toward the end of the war and with the realization that the Confederacy would in fact lose, this morality manifested in a sense of bitterness and rage, evident in Mary's language at the end of her epic. Mary acutely blames the war for

31. C. Vann Woodward, introduction to *Mary Chesnut's Civil War*, ed. C. Vann Woodward (New Haven: Yale University Press, 1981), lviii.

32. Faust, *Mothers of Invention,* 147.

bringing "bad passions to the surface," thus highlighting her resentment at the South's positionality.[33] Such blunt rhetoric reinforces Clinton's historical context: "White women in the South felt especially oppressed by postwar hardships."[34] By the end of the war, Mary "spent [time] as a refugee without any negotiable currency, in makeshift quarters first at Lincolnton, North Carolina, then at Chester, South Carolina."[35] By the end of Mary's epic, the focus of morality has evolved: the South is indeed the victim. At least for the immediate period after the war, the loss of the South's social scene and economic system is palpable. There are many accounts in which upper-class women were "compelled to buy back a dress [they] had given one of [their] slaves several years before."[36] The alternative for these plantation mistresses and young belles was to use homespun fabric. These "bad passions" that Chesnut reveals within southern women provide more of an opportunity to preach and to rely on their morality to overcompensate for the economic and social loss of slavery at the hands of the North.

The Civil War disrupted an entire nation and even more so, the elite hierarchy that bound the South. The actual southern belle, lost somewhere between the battle of Gettysburg and the creation of Jim Crow South, is revitalized through Hollywood and White southern memory. The plantation mistress lives on in case studies and neo-slave narratives. Along similar lines in Mary Chesnut's epic, roles and rules for southern women are evident in twentieth-century writer Lillian Smith's text, *Killers of the Dream,* where Smith reiterates the moral codes of such a young woman in the South: "We were taught in this way to love God, to love our white skin, and to believe in the sanctity of both."[37] The daughter of parents who were born during the Civil War, Lillian Smith shows that Mary Chesnut's morality was and still is evident: Whiteness, and therefore White experience above all else. Chestnut equates Whiteness with a higher national power. This hierarchy is still utilized during the beginning of the twentieth century, even as the space for nineteenth-century southern women has been relocated to memory. Placing Mary Chesnut in the folds of White feminist writing as well as historical writing on the Civil War allows for a more pervasive look at the role and effect of these elite White women, exposing the lasting ramifications of such matriarchs as "moral" crusaders, with an unequivocal foothold in southern history, literature, and gender studies.

33. Chesnut, *Mary Chesnut's Civil War*, 827.

34. Clinton, *The Other Civil War*, 89

35. Woodward, *Mary Chesnut's Civil War*, xli.

36. Faust, *Mothers of Invention,* 222.

37. Lillian Smith, *Killers of the Dream* (New York: W. W. Norton, 1949), 83.

Bibliography

Chesnut, Mary. *A Diary from Dixie, as Written by Mary Boykin Chesnut, Wife of James Chesnut, Jr., United States Senator from South Carolina, 1859-1861, and Afterward an Aide to Jefferson Davis and a Brigadier-General in the Confederate Army*, edited by Isabella D. Martin and Myrta Lockett Avary. New York: Appleton and Company, 1905.

———. *Mary Chesnut's Civil War*, edited by C. Vann Woodward. New Haven: Yale University Press, 1981.

Clinton, Catherine. *The Other Civil War: American Women in the Nineteenth Century*. New York: Hill and Wang, 1984.

———. *The Plantation Mistress.* New York: Pantheon Books, 1982.

———. *Tara Revisited: Women, War, and the Plantation Legend.* New York: Abbeville Press, 1995.

Faust, Drew Gilpin. *Mothers of Invention: Women of the Slaveholding South in the American Civil War.* Chapel Hill: University of North Carolina Press, 1996.

Fleming, Victor, dir. *Gone with the Wind.* 1939; Atlanta: Selznick International Pictures/Metro-Goldwyn-Mayer, 1985. Film.

Lewis, Elizabeth Wittenmyer. *Queen of the Confederacy: The Innocent Deceits of Lucy Holcombe Pickens.* Denton: University of North Texas Press, 2002.

Smith, Lillian. *Killers of the Dream.* New York: W. W. Norton, 1949.

Young, Elizabeth. *Disarming the Nation: Women's Writing and the American Civil War.* Chicago: University of Chicago Press, 1999.

MICHELLE-TAYLOR SHERWIN is a doctoral student in English and instructor of First-Year Composition at the University of Georgia. Her primary research focuses on mentorship, motherhood, and women's writing in nineteenth- and twentieth-century American literature. In the *South Atlantic Review,* she has published "The Evolution of Foucault's Utopic Panopticon: Technology and the Creation of a Dystopia in Big Brother." She won the Graduate Student Essay Award at the South Atlantic Modern Language Association conference for this work.

The Death-Bound Matriarch in J. California Cooper's *Family*

Sidney Jones

The anguish of loss was a defining characteristic of enslaved Black motherhood. Scholars like Heather Andrea Williams have taken on the arduous task of going through diaries, slave logbooks, and public records to present the devastating extent to which Black families were torn apart.[1] Their work demonstrates that the rupture of Black families, especially after the closing of the American trans-Atlantic trade in 1808, was as normative and fundamental to the everyday operation of the plantation as the ceaseless labor was.[2] By dividing families, slave masters not only earned a profit but continued the strategic project of transforming the enslaved population from human beings with a traceable family lineage into objects of capital. For enslaved Black women, the experience of constant trauma and instability meant that mothering was a source of pain rather than fulfillment. The possibility of separation constantly reminded Black women that their control over their lives and their ability to protect their children didn't truly exist.

In bondage, Black mothers lacked both control of their families and their own bodies. They not only were expected to help build the plantation economy but through sexual assault and sequential child-bearing, they were expected to perpetuate the labor force as well. Their children were sequentially

1. Heather Andrea Williams, *Help Me to Find My People: The African American Search for Family Lost in Slavery* (Chapel Hill: The University of North Carolina Press, 2012).

2. According to Williams in *Help Me to Find My People*, thousands of African American enslaved families were forcefully separated. And in Barrett Holmes Pitner's "We've Had Family Separation Before—It Was Called Slavery and Jim Crow," approximately "one-third of enslaved children in the upper South experienced separation either by being sold themselves or from losing a mother, a father, or siblings."

property of the master, invalidating Black women's ownership of their children. Ultimately, as captive Black mothers were denied subjecthood, they became completely exteriorized and commodified as organic capital, fleshy machinery. Ironically, both their survival, and their continued subjugation, depended on them sustaining their body.

J. California Cooper's *Family* (1991) reimagines the embodied experience of the enslaved mother through the protagonist, Clora. Set in the South during the Civil War era, *Family* follows Clora as she tries to keep her family together. Clora's lineage is the direct result of sexual assault.[3] As Clora comes of age, she finds herself in a similar situation to that of her grandmother and her mother, as her master repeatedly rapes her, leading to several unwanted pregnancies. Rather than face the prospect of seeing her children sold to different plantations, Clora attempts to take her children's lives, as well as her own, by feeding them poisoned weeds. In a dramatic twist, Clora's children survive, leaving her to exist in the afterlife alone watching them grow up in slavery without her guidance.

As much as *Family* is a text about the everyday anguish of slavery for Black women, it is also a text about bad mothers and the stigma behind infanticide. Nikki Taylor points out the rarity of infanticide in chattel slavery, and asserts that when enslaved women did commit violent acts, "they typically killed their owners, and not their loved ones—especially not their own living, breathing children."[4] Despite the small number of cases of infanticide, it is a popular theme in contemporary re-imaginings of slavery like *Family* and Toni Morrison's *Beloved* (1987).[5] The thematic predominance of enslaved infanticide seems to stem from its rejection of naturalized assumptions about motherhood. If mothers are expected to nurture their children, how can infanticide be construed as a parallel act of compassion? If legal ownership legitimizes a mother's authority over her children, are Black women's claims to motherhood invalid as their children are the legal property of the slave master?

3. The pattern of rape that Cooper draws out in Clora's lineage connects to the institutionalized rape of Black women in US chattel slavery as a method of perpetuating the institution of slavery, and as Angela Davis has pointed out in *Women, Race, and Class*, a crucial method of social control.

4. Nikki M. Taylor, *Driven toward Madness: The Fugitive Slave Margaret Garner and Tragedy on the Ohio* (Athens: Ohio University Press, 2016), 1.

5. *Beloved* takes place right after the Civil War, and follows Sethe (a woman who escaped from slavery) as she tries to make a home for her and her daughter, Denver. Sethe's central problem is that the ghost of the child she killed (with the hopes of sparing her the agony of capture and bondage) occupies the home.

Infanticide illuminates the provocative reality that idyllic motherhood is not a naturalized gender role, but instead derives from the larger structure of White privilege.

Although infanticide can thematically draw out the complexities of enslaved kinship, critical conversations have largely focused on the power structure. Laura Dawkins, for instance argues, that authors like Angelina Grimké and Georgia Douglas Johnson revisit infanticide to "suggest that Christian mythology, in valorizing submission and renunciation, conspires with an oppressive social order to defuse maternal power. Portraying mothers who reject religious and cultural codes that demand the deliverance of their children into a brutal society."[6] In anticipation of the binary race politics of the Black Arts Movement (1960–1979), Harlem Renaissance writers present infanticide as a symbolic denunciation of White religion and its historic aim to keep Black matriarchal leaders passive and satiated with the racial status quo.[7] In Dawkins's summation, these Black maternal characters are strong, politically-astute figures, consciously sacrificing their intimate bonds with their children to make a social statement. It's certainly imperative to consider the complexities of Black female positionality within systems of oppression, and the ways that Black female characters go against the odds stacked against them. However, Dawkins's emphasis on positivistic resistance potentially reduces Black maternal figures to the restrictive archetype of the strong Black woman, overlooking the nuances of characters like Clora who don't fit within this mold.

In framing this essay around Abdul JanMohamed's death-bound-subject, notably his examination of the African American captive as a "bare life," my goal is to shift direction away from the moralistic conversations about defiance. I instead want to examine how slavery in *Family* transforms the life-giving space of motherhood into a space of death. While Clora's self-destruction virtually leaves her powerless in the afterlife, it also can't be denied that her decision to take her life ruptures the lineage of dispossession that her and her foremothers inherited. This disruption is rather brief, as Clora's death causes

6. Laura Dawkins, "From Madonna to Medea: Maternal Infanticide in African American Women's Literature of the Harlem Renaissance," *Literature Interpretation Theory* 15, no. 3 (2004): 223.

7. The Black Arts Movement (BAM) was a prolific period of artistic, cultural, and activist work amongst African Americans that occurred from the 1960s to the 1970s. As BAM was grounded in the Black Power movement, the focus was on nationhood and racial pride, in which White organizations and value systems were perceived as the primary enemy to Black consciousness.

her oldest child, Always, to become the family's matriarch. Always not only lives out Clora's fate on earth as an enslaved mother, but when considering the significance of her name, she embodies Clora's attempt to possess her children as her own. Clora names her daughter *Always* because it was "something didn't nobody have but me and my baby . . . was that name. Til I realized one day, people use that word all the time. But, still, I knew what I meant, and they didn't have that!"[8] The name *Always* symbolizes the permanence of Clora's bond with her daughter. The fact that the intimacy and individuation implied in Always's name is disrupted by the common grammatical use of the term, shows the ways that language can fail to transform the most dire of circumstances like that of Clora. It additionally suggests the impossibility of an intimate bond between mother and daughter in slavery. Although they present different kinds of embodiment, Always and Clora are bound by a singular pursuit out of the spiritual death of slavery. This essay draws parallels between death-bound-subjecthood and Black embodiment to argue that one of the primary antagonists to enslaved motherhood in *Family* isn't only White systems of oppression, as scholars have outlined in the past, but the troubled relationship between Blackness and corporeality.

In this essay, I will discuss the historic use of embodiment in African American literature, specifically slave narratives. Then I will explore how Clora's and Always's embodied experiences as death-bound-subjects shape their consciousness differently. After that, I will examine the sexualized and racialized nature of marginalization for Clora and Always, as enslaved women, and the ways that their embodied knowledge is unable to save them from the everyday violence of slavery. I will finally close with a consideration of how infanticide is presented in *Family* as a possible way out of the death-bound-subjugation for the two.

I center Clora and Always's experiences within the framework of embodiment, which I ground in phenomenology.[9] Just as phenomenology underscores the "lived experience"—knowledge acquired through a person's subjective consciousness—I define embodiment as coming to consciousness or coming to know what you know through the subjective experiences (tangible,

8. J. California Cooper, *Family* (New York: Anchor Books, 1991), 19.

9. Originally coined by Edmund Husserl (1905), phenomenology is the idea that reality and knowledge are entirely based on the subjective human consciousness and the individual's perception of phenomena (objects and events). Phenomenology differs from the Western notion of knowledge as objective, immaterial, and independent of human consciousness.

mental, emotional) of the body. To take a cue from Nirmala Erevelles, my use of phenomenology highlights the potential of embodiment as a tool for sociopolitical analysis.[10] In focusing on embodiment, my work acknowledges that the sensory experiences, perceptions, and differential treatment of bodies exist in raced, gendered, and classed contexts. The enslaved Black matriarch is a fundamental example of this phenomenological embodiment as she becomes through the definition of her as laboring flesh, completely void of individuating subjecthood.

Little critical attention has been given to *Family*, despite the fact that this novel significantly contributes to discourse around literal and figurative dis/embodiment in African American literature.[11] Antebellum slave narratives and contemporary texts on slavery have consistently battled with the politics of representing embodiment. Sherryl Vint notes that on the one hand, "the suffering body authorized and authenticated autobiographical accounts of slavery's horrors," but on the other hand "others invoked embodiment to deny full personhood to non-Whites and women."[12] Presenting abused Black bodies powerfully appeals to readers' emotions, providing unquestionable proof of the cruelty of chattel slavery. However, writers run the risk of perpetuating stereotypes about Black people as nothing more than bodies with no access to intellectual abstractions like language. Ultimately, authors and critics have wrestled with the razor-thin line between the strategic use of embodiment to promote a racially progressive agenda, and the possible exploitation of Black suffering.

Harriet Jacobs's *Incidents in the Life of a Slave Girl* (1861) notably illustrates this ambiguity as she illustrates eroticized Black embodiment to bolster the argument for abolition. Jacobs faces the task of persuading a White female readership of the urgency of abolition and addressing the obstacle to this objective—the widely-held stereotype of enslaved Black women as possessing an animalistic eroticism, diametrically opposed to propriety. To persuade readers, Jacobs presents slavery as the breeding ground for moral depravity.

10. Nirmala Erevelles, "Unspeakable Offenses: Untangling Race and Disability in Discourses of Intersectionality," *Journal of Literary and Cultural Disability Studies* 4, no. 2 (2010): 127–45.

11. A possible reason for the critical silence around *Family* could be the popularity of neo-slave narratives in the 1990s in the wake of *Beloved*, which is the poster child of the genre.

12. Sherryl Vint, "Only by Experience: Embodiment and The Limitations of Realism in Neo-Slave Narratives," *Science Fiction Studies* 34, no. 2 (2007): 242.

She alleges that "no matter whether the slave girl be as black as ebony or as fair as her mistress. In either case, there is no shadow of law to protect her from insult, from violence, or even from death; all these are inflicted by fiends who bear the shape of men."[13] Ultimately, Jacobs presents herself as a young Black woman, mired in sin—a trope readers come to expect. However, the institution of slavery holds the brunt of the blame, not an innate sexual desire exclusive to Black people. Jacobs implicitly argues that the sexual impetus of slavery makes it nearly impossible for young Black women like herself to live up to the gendered standards of piety that the cult of true womanhood dictates.

Since *Family* is a contemporary reimagining of slavery, there is no impetus for abolition. However, Cooper seems to use embodiment to provide greater insight into the interior lives of enslaved people, and consequently challenge one of the most enduring characterizations of Black mothers—the Mammy. Many critics have written extensively about the Mammy as an embodiment of masculinized Black maternalism, beloved by the White family she serves and despised within the slave quarters for her domineering harshness.[14] Her Blackness dictates her stereotypical qualities, brash yet diligent worker, and these characteristics in turn validate the otherness of her race. Cooper's illustration of Always and Clora seems to complicate the stereotype of the Mammy. Although the former possesses a physical body and the latter exists as a spirit, they not only share a matriarchal lineage, but also a physical and emotional pain that wracks their beings, complicating this caricature of Black motherhood.

In *Family*, the pain that Clora endures at the hands of her master comes to define her sense of embodiment. Once Clora's master begins sexually assaulting her, she reflects on the impact this has on her mind. She recounts how she "just hated him. Not only for ownin my body, but for blockin my mind, letting my heart dry and shrivel up cause it didn't have nothin to do but hate him."[15] Clora's consciousness and embodied experience center on an overwhelming sense of dispossession. As the pleasures and labor of her body

13. Harriet Jacobs, *Incidents in the Life of a Slave Girl* (New York: Penguin Classics, 2000), 45.

14. Trudier Harris, *Saints, Sinners, and Saviors: Strong Black Women in African American Literature* (New York: Palgrave, 2001); Patricia Hill Collins, *Black Feminist Thought: Knowledge, Consciousness, and the Politics of Empowerment* (New York: Routledge, 2000).

15. Cooper, *Family*, 21–22.

aren't her own to enjoy, and as her mind is consumed by a hatred of her master, Clora's daily experience is that of an exploited object, completely at the will of her master's hands.

This dispossession parallels the dehumanizing experience of JanMohamed's death-bound-subject. The death-bound-subject is a "relation, perceived from within the subjectivity of that 'bare life,' that never feels authorized to be, to do, or to possess anything; it is a subjectivity that can never feel securely grounded in the myriad social, political, and cultural values, rules, and procedures that 'normal' society takes for granted: the bareness of bare life permeates its finest capillary structures."[16] What defines the death-bound-subject as such is their contrast with the "normal" or normative center.[17] The death-bound-subject is completely cut off from the social processes of subjecthood and citizenship (for example, the narrative of rugged individualism that is frequently romanticized and championed in the United States) that the center would perceive as rites of passage. Without any larger sense of purpose, the life of a death-bound-subject is "bare" in that it essentially consists of base survivalism. The only real social role carved out for the death-bound-subject is to go from being objectified "flesh," metaphorically dead with no subjecthood, to physically dying at the hands of the center and becoming "meat" as JanMohamed articulates.[18] As a captive with no ownership of self or legal acknowledgment of her humanity, Clora demonstrates JanMohamed's death-bound-subject as a commentary on the experience of racialization for African Americans.

Always, in parallel to Clora, suffers through the same experience of bare life. However, where she differs is in the significant role land plays in her sense of self. As mentioned earlier, soon after Clora's death, Always is sold off and her life on the plantation is much like that of her mother's. The master, Doak Butler, forcefully takes her as his concubine, and she produces multiple children, who all get sold off to other plantations. Amidst the constant anguish, the only source of control that Always enjoys is in working the land. Once she finds out how potentially lucrative the plantation is, Always vows to till the land and expand it, stating "I wants silver and gold money from what I

16. Abdul R. JanMohamed, *The Death-Bound-Subject: Richard Wright's Archaeology of Death* (Durham: Duke University Press, 2005), 10.

17. The way that the term "normal" stands in as the boundary that the death-bound-subject is defined against seems to suggest that the process of racializing and metaphorically killing Black subjecthood is tied up with notions of bodily and performative difference.

18. JanMohamed, *The Death-Bound-Subject,* 10.

grow."[19] For Always to take a task that was commonplace in the everyday subjugation of enslaved Black people and transform it into a profitable enterprise is radical. Farming becomes more than just a lucrative business—for Always, it becomes a part of her sense of embodiment. After the Civil War, when she is faced with the prospect of losing the land she worked, Always exclaims, "I know this dirt like my own blood runnin in my body . . . This land is part of my body. My roots is deep in this ground. I came, they bought me, I slaved here, This my land. Even freedom, sweet as it be, ain't gonna make me leave this land."[20] Andreá Williams argues that many African American writers in the wake of the Civil War and Reconstruction were reconsidering the existential significance of labor outside of the forced exploitation of slavery. They used their work to explore the "extent to which their labor can 'speak for them' in shaping their identities" beyond slavery.[21] While Williams's commentary focuses on literary pieces produced at the turn of the twentieth century, in the novel *Family*, Always clearly demonstrates this idea that your work is an extension of your voice and your sense of self.

Her reflections on the interconnectedness of her body and the land and possessing equally consciousness of her physical body and the farm undoubtedly summons archetypal images of Black women as earthy, originary guardians of humanity. The commonplace metaphor of Earth as a feminized, compassionate figure who watches over humanity as her children, despite their callous neglect comes to mind as well. Ultimately, Cooper seems to complicate this metaphor of a Black Mother Earth in that the naturalized bond between mother and child is erased. As each extension of the field is the direct result of a child Always conceives with Doak, the land symbolizes the physical absence of her children and redefines mothering as the process of laboring to preserve the past and the memory of lost children.

While the land comes to redefine motherhood for Always, on a broader level, it also becomes a physical measure of her sexualized abuse. When

19. Cooper, *Family,* 110.

20. Cooper, *Family,* 202. The irony of the farm is that even though it is technically Doak's in name, it is the product of Always's literal blood, sweat, and tears. Toward the end of the novel, Always shows a deep investment in Doak's land because she not only tilled it, but every purchase Doak made to extend the property is the direct result of the sale of a child he conceived with Always. More importantly, through the novel's duration, Always develops her own profitable business selling the many crops she grows to neighbors.

21. Williams, *Help Me to Find My People,* 49.

Always first arrives at Doak's plantation, he brutally assaults her, which Clora vividly describes as such:

> She felt the damp dirt stickin to her, the gravel digging into her skin as he drug her across it. She smelled the dirt, the clay, indeed, it was in her nose, her mouth, her eyes. Tied arms bled. Tied arms could not fight. She could not understand what and why he had to do this, this way. She had been goin to wait to see how it all turned out before she would hate him, but now . . . she hated him now.[22]

Concrete details like smell, taste, and sight place a greater emphasis on Always's embodied experience of the assault than on Doak and his actions, viscerally positioning the reader in the scene with her. This assault essentially leads Always to foster a hatred of Doak and his wife, similar to the hatred that consumes Clora. Furthermore, in this instance, Always's sensory experience of the assault (for example, the smell of the dirt in her nostrils or the feel of the rope cutting into her wrists) and the way that her senses so bluntly betray her prior expectations of Doak's civility, makes the moment all the more humiliating and objectifying. Always's sexual assault suggests that the connections she forges between her physical body and the land can be a source of dehumanization, and not only a means out of subjugation.

This complicated interplay of sexual vulnerability and race speaks to contemporary Black feminist sentiments of the same unique positionality Black women find themselves in. Venetria K. Patton's observations about idealized womanhood in the antebellum period shed light on the ways Black women became culturally stigmatized through mythic narratives of sexual depravity. Placing her commentary in conversation with texts like *Family*, according to Patton, "true womanhood was based on four cardinal virtues: piety, purity, submissiveness, and domesticity. Although all four of the virtues were important, purity appears to provide the foundation for all the rest. The loss of purity was associated with madness or death, since its absence was considered unnatural and unfeminine."[23] The determining factor of idyllic womanhood and the sequential rationale for policing women was sexual purity. Although Patton doesn't explicitly reference race in this instance, it is evident that White women greatly benefited from this construct, as they have historically been upheld as the standard of womanhood and beauty. In the nineteenth century,

22. Cooper, *Family,* 84–85.

23. Venetria K. Patton, *Women in Chains: The Legacy of Slavery in Black Women's Fiction* (Albany: State University of New York Press, 2000), 58–59.

the elevation of White women as the symbol of chastity was met with the degradation of Black women as the embodiment of vulgarity.

Ultimately, Always's and Clora's mental and bodily abuse places them in a double bind, in which they are perpetually vulnerable to abuse, yet perceived as invulnerable because of their Blackness. We see this paradox of Black female embodiment, when Clora's mistress barges into the slave quarters and attacks her and her baby, who she notices resembles the master. As Clora threatens to hit the mistress with a poker in self-defense, she has a brief moment of heightened awareness, noting that "from somewhere the idea came that this woman who was built like me . . . had eyes, nose . . . and blood just like me didn't know what she was doin in this here thing either. The Master of the Land was Master of us both. . . . She should have helped me . . . not struck me for bein a slave to him."[24] In a sophisticated manner, Always notices how sexism victimizes her and her mistress. Always's gender subjects her to sexual assault and unwanted pregnancies at the hands of her master, while the narratives about her Blackness as excessively lewd both justifies the sexual assault she experiences and forces her to labor to perpetuate the system of slavery. Although the mistress undoubtedly enjoys a life of leisure in contrast to Always, it can't be denied the sexism of White patriarchy lies at the root of the roles she's expected to play as the chaste "damsel" and accessory to the master. While both women experience sexism, the mistress uses her racial privilege to brutalize Clora, prioritizing the violence of White supremacy over any common ties to sisterhood.

I highlight this moment of conflict between Clora and the mistress because this event preempts her attempt to kill herself and her children. Even though Clora doesn't actually harm the mistress, her instinct is to commit suicide because her attempt at self-defense within slavery warrants death as a punishment. Clora laments that her children would sequentially "have no more mother, worthless even as she was to them, they needed me for whatever I could do for em."[25] The aftermath of Clora's confrontation reveals the tragic irony of slavery. Within this system, White people can commit crimes and are free of reproach. In contrast, any attempts on the part of the enslaved to protect themselves and their family from injustices become punishable offenses. Janell Hobson argues that this "moral and legal paradox" is a lasting legacy of US chattel slavery as

24. Cooper, *Family*, 32.

25. Cooper, *Family*, 34.

> black resistance to white oppression becomes a criminal offense—the "facts of blackness" constantly grate against the "fictions of whiteness." After all, the white body, by virtue of representing the law and moral authority, legitimates the immoral acts of physical and sexual violence. . . . The black body is presumed guilty in relation to the presumed innocence of the white body.[26]

Hobson's commentary, in juxtaposition with Clora's rationale for suicide, reveals the stakes of embodiment. According to Hobson, slavery set up a fatalistic binary between Whiteness and Blackness, where the former is the embodiment of innocence, and the latter is the physical manifestation of criminality. When you're always already culpable just through the act of attempting to live with dignity, the only reprieve from this is death.

The moral quandary of infanticide channels the divide between the depravity of slavery and the shame and stigma of its memory in the present day. Sheldon George highlights the predominance of infanticide, and the explicit references to Margaret Garner in *Beloved*, as a part of a larger tradition in African American literature of "repetition and revision" in which the "persistence of a traumatic past . . . haunts the present through a subjective, psychic experience of trauma that defies the limits of time and space."[27, 28] While George specifically discusses *Beloved*, the idea of the memory of slavery not only resurfacing, but haunting those in the present, as Sethe's deceased child Beloved haunts her and her family, is a temporal framework that applies to countless slave reimaginings. Morrison's decision to concentrate the violent memory of slavery into the body of a phantom child, suggests an antagonistic relationship between the survivors of slavery and the ancestors.

Where *Family* departs from *Beloved* is in making Clora, the mother figure, the central phantom of the text. In contrast to Beloved, who torments her family throughout the novel, Clora is determined to maintain a watchful gaze over her children. Immediately after Clora consumes the poison and discovers that she has died while her children survived, she mentions, "I could feel my heart still grievin. . . . Wasn't no angel sent down to tell me nothin bout what was happenin

26. Janell Hobson, *Body as Evidence: Mediating Race, Globalizing Gender* (Albany: State University of New York Press, 2012), 71.

27. Margaret Garner was an enslaved Black woman who escaped with her family from Kentucky to the free state of Ohio in 1856. Upon being discovered by slave catchers, Garner killed her daughter instead of allowing her child to be captured and returned to slavery.

28. Sheldon George, "Approaching the Thing of Slavery: A Lacanian Analysis of Toni Morrison's *Beloved*," *African American Review* 45, no.1–2 (2012): 115.

to me. . . . I was just left. Just out there in nothin, bein nothin. . . . I blive I was left out here so I could watch over my children, my blood, my Always."[29] Ultimately, Clora's death is ironically anti-climactic. Her death refuses to give the readers the dramatic, romanticized death scene that we come to expect of slave narratives. Instead of experiencing a gut-wrenching death, and sequentially occupying a mystical afterlife requite with demons and angels, the afterlife for Clora is stripped of all these cultural constructs, and she merely inhabits a vast space of nothingness. She exists in "nothin" and is technically a disembodied, immaterial spirit, yet she inhabits the physical world and recounts the stories of her loved ones throughout the text from an intimate, first-person narrative voice. Unlike popular depictions of death as peaceful and distinctive from the physical world, Clora is still very much tied to the world, her family, and the pain she endured while alive. The fact that she can watch her children grow up without the worry of being separated, suggests that the only way enslaved mothers can enjoy some sense of belonging and ownership to their children is tragically in death. However, even in the afterlife, Clora's influence over her children is limited, as she has no supernatural abilities to intervene in their lives and truly protect them. Essentially, death is another form of powerlessness for the enslaved Black mother that parallels that sense of helplessness in the world.

Clora's failed attempt at infanticide pushes against critical readings of infanticide as potentially empowering, by suggesting that these violent acts do little to effectively change the lasting effects of slavery. Regardless of the structural or social impact of infanticide or lack thereof, focusing on the potential power dynamics of infanticide overlooks the messages it suggests about Black mothers' positionality. In a 2013 interview with Junot Díaz, Morrison recounts how second-wave feminism asserted that abortion, and the right to *not* have children, was the ultimate freedom. By contrast, the enslaved Black woman having and legally possessing a child as one's own truly signified freedom. Since Black female captives could never exercise this right, for Morrison, "when Margaret Garner cut that girl's neck, she was saying, 'This child is mine.' And to claim her, even if it had to go and become bloody . . . nevertheless, that was the freedom, that was the ability, that was the mothering."[30] Because the enslaved could never legally own their children without them eventually being stripped from their arms, Morrison points out that

29. Cooper, *Family,* 36.

30. Josh Begley, "Toni Morrison and Junot Díaz," December 13, 2013, Youtube Video File, accessed February 15, 2019, 45:57, https://www.youtube.com/watch?v=J5kytPjYjSQ&t=2770s.

taking their life and refusing to allow them to be a part of this institution was the only alternative way of protecting the child. The fact that taking the life of a child rather than giving and sustaining that life is the only way for Garner and (to extend this rationale to *Beloved* and *Family*) Sethe and Clora to actualize themselves as Black matriarchs truly speaks to the deeply-ingrained violence of slavery. It also suggests that within slavery, the only way to feel fully realized is to perform acts that ultimately perpetuate stereotypical notions of Black matriarchy as brutal and domineering. Clora's character arc suggests that the only way to transcend this web of violence and performance is through disembodiment and the destruction of one's physical self.

Despite the ways that autonomy creates self-actualization, Trudier Harris highlights Clora's preoccupation with agency, and this particular scene as potentially problematic. She asserts that Clora's attempted infanticide "has embedded in it the . . . possibility of her considering the children her property, objects with which she, like the Master of the Land, can do as she likes. Intention here . . . is the only thing that separates the mother from the master."[31] For Harris, Clora's preoccupation with control is problematic because she ironically strips her children of agency over their lives in the same way that a slave master strips his captives of autonomy. Harris's point sheds light on the potential dangers of the matriarch as she suggests that perhaps the matriarch might wield too much control over her family.

In contrast, Vint's exploration of infanticide in neo-slave texts suggests that although this act is incredibly violent and teases out problematic elements of agency politics, it still spares Black children the trauma of slavery. She points out that infanticide actually frees Black children from "the violence of slavery" that destroys individual subjectivity.[32] Furthermore, infanticide that we see in novels like *Beloved* "can be a sign of mother love" as Black authors refute "negative stereotype of black mothers" and illustrates how "slavery itself produces the very behaviors it then condemns as pathological in black women."[33] Even though infanticide recreates the master-slave dynamic between the enslaved Black mother and her child, it pales in comparison to the racist dehumanization of slavery. Essentially, Vint reiterates the claim that death is more honorable than a life in slavery. This is the same idea that we see maternal figures articulate in many neo-slave texts. The emphasis here on the context of violence that infanticide arises out of, rather than isolating it

31. Harris, *Saints, Sinners, and Saviors,* 93.

32. Vint, "Only by Experience," 247.

33. Vint, "Only by Experience," 247.

as an individualized, cruel act of learned behavior, rightfully draws readers' attention to the true culprit in this situation—the institution of slavery and the masters who perpetuate it.

The violence of slavery not only circumscribes subjecthood, but when we consider the conclusion of *Family*, it makes Clora's dedicated guardianship inconsequential. As the novel flashes forward to illustrate an elderly Always on her deathbed, surrounded by the family that she has made for herself, Clora eagerly awaits reuniting with her, only to note that "when my beloved daughter Always closed her eyes and rested her soul, she didn't come to me. She passed me by. Oh Lord."[34] Just like Clora's death, this final scene in *Family* refuses to give readers a sentimental reunion and satisfying conclusion to the novel. Instead, we see the gulf of distance between a mother and daughter, and the way that time has turned them into strangers. If *Beloved* implies that an antagonism exists between the past and the present, between ancestors and the descendants of the enslaved, *Family* suggests that there is a tragic dissociation between past and present generations. In spite of the dedication of a loving, matriarchal ancestry, and their effort to perform the gendered role of guardianship, these efforts can't seem to overcome the chasms that slavery creates between family members.

Despite what many critics argue, *Family* seems to suggest that death isn't a way out of the larger structure of chattel slavery. Clora's attempted infanticide merely actualizes her expected role in slavery as a dead, disembodied subject. Clora, prior to suicide, greatly parallels that of the death-bound-subject, in that she has nothing of her own (not her children or even her own sense of self). More importantly, she merely exists to give her labor and her body to her master. Ultimately, JanMohamed's theory dictates that there is no inspiration, no agency, no autonomy for death-bound-subjects like Clora. Although a subjugated individual can't wield possession over their life or their family, as Clora desperately wants, they retain absolute control in their literal death. For JanMohamed, "the slave's ability to appropriate the death that is brought by the master and to embrace his death as a property of his own subjectivity radically transforms the political economy that the master had constituted around the threat of death."[35] When we connect JanMohamed's work to *Family* and US chattel slavery, essentially the only outlet for self-making allotted to the enslaved is the ability to take their own life. The act of suicide is so subversive because it usurps power

34. Cooper, *Family*, 228.

35. JanMohamed, *The Death-Bound-Subject*, 15.

from the White slave master and it shatters the stigma and around death. In the social structure of slavery, where a Black child is determined to be dead at birth, suicide transforms dying from something to fear into a way out of the injustices of this institution. Ultimately, it's possible that infanticide isn't necessarily an imitation of the master's cruelty, but is instead an overturning of his influence.

Bibliography

Begley, Josh. "Toni Morrison and Junot Díaz." December 13, 2013. Youtube Video File, 1:22:20. Accessed February 15, 2019. https://www.youtube.com/watch?v=J5kytPjYjSQ&t=2770s.

Collins, Patricia Hill. *Black Feminist Thought: Knowledge, Consciousness, and the Politics of Empowerment.* New York: Routledge, 2000.

Cooper, J. California. *Family*. New York: Anchor Books, 1991.

Davis, Angela. *Women, Race, and Class*. New York: Random House, 1983.

Dawkins, Laura. "From Madonna to Medea: Maternal Infanticide in African American Women's Literature of the Harlem Renaissance." *Literature Interpretation Theory* 15, no. 3 (2004): 223–40.

Erevelles, Nirmala. "Unspeakable Offenses: Untangling Race and Disability in Discourses of Intersectionality." *Journal of Literary and Cultural Disability Studies* 4, no. 2 (2010): 127–45.

George, Sheldon. "Approaching the *Thing* of Slavery: A Lacanian Analysis of Toni Morrison's *Beloved*." *African American Review* 45, no. 1–2 (2012): 115–30.

Harris, Trudier. *Saints, Sinners, Saviors: Strong Black Women in African American Literature*. New York: Palgrave, 2001.

Hobson, Janell. *Body as Evidence: Mediating Race, Globalizing Gender*. Albany: State University of New York Press, 2012.

Jacobs, Harriet. *Incident in Life of a Slave Girl.* New York: Penguin Classics, 2000.

JanMohamed, Abdul R. *The Death-Bound-Subject: Richard Wright's Archaeology of Death*. Durham: Duke University Press, 2005.

Patton, Venetria K. *Women in Chains: The Legacy of Slavery in Black Women's Fiction*. Albany: State University of New York Press, 2000.

Pitner, Barrett Holmes. "We've Had Family Separation Before—It Was Called Slavery and Jim Crow." *The Daily Beast*, June 29, 2018. https://www.thedailybeast.com/weve-had-family-separation-before-it-was-called-slavery-and-jim-crow.

Taylor, Nikki M. *Driven toward Madness: The Fugitive Slave Margaret Garner and Tragedy on the Ohio*. Athens: Ohio University Press, 2016.

Vint, Sherryl. "Only by Experience: Embodiment and The Limitations of Realism in Neo-Slave Narratives." *Science Fiction Studies* 34, no. 2 (2007): 241–61.

Williams, Andreá N. "Black Women's Labor and the Melodrama of Class Mobility in Sutton Griggs's *Overshadowed*." *African American Review* 45, no. 1–2 (2012): 49–64.

Williams, Heather A. *Help Me to Find My People: The African American Search for Family Lost in Slavery.* Chapel Hill: The University of North Carolina Press, 2012.

Sidney Jones is a PhD candidate at the Ohio State University. She specializes in African American literature, Black feminist theory, and disability studies. She is currently completing her dissertation, *Performing Brawn and Sass: Strength and Disability in Black Women's Writing*, which considers how contemporary Black American authors complicate the Strong Black Woman trope in order to arrive at a more complex sense of Black womanhood.

In the Shadows at Dawn and Dusk
Southern Matriarchy in the Antebellum Era

Jericho Williams

At first consideration, American writers William Wells Brown and Willa Cather are an unusual pairing, particularly because of the two authors' strong associations with different pockets of American culture. After escaping slavery at the age of twenty, William Wells Brown became an abolitionist and a pioneer of African American literature during the nineteenth century. His slave narrative, *Narrative of William W. Brown, A Fugitive Slave* (1847), and *Clotel, or the President's Daughter* (1853), the first African American novel, remain his most celebrated works among an oeuvre that includes autobiographical narratives, speeches, a novel, a travelogue, a play, historical writings, and biographies. Cather spent her adolescence and early adulthood in Nebraska, and although she composed short stories, poetry, and literary criticism, her most popular novels—*O Pioneers* (1913), *The Song of the Lark* (1915), and *My Antonia* (1918)—comprise a Prairie Trilogy that illustrates the plights of immigrants who first settled in the Great Plains. Altogether, differences of gender, sexuality, class, and, for a period of two decades, freedom also illustrate the divide between Brown and Cather.

Although Brown and Cather had very different life experiences, their work is similar in significant ways. Both authors prized artistic innovation and reinvention throughout their careers, regardless of what others thought. They also bore witness to slavery's harmful repercussions for American society. In this regard, Brown and Cather were also especially insightful about the impact of a male-dominated, slave-based society on the formation of the southern matriarchy. The southern matriarchy was a set of societal customs and expectations that positioned White women as the principal figures of authority within their homes. At different points in their careers, each author exposed the troubling actualities of southern matriarchy prior to the Civil War through innovative novelization. Brown's *Clotel, or the President's Daughter* details the terrifying reign of a budding southern matriarch while

Cather's *Sapphira and the Slave Girl* (1940) peers closely at a southern matriarch's vengeful decline. In drawing from their private experiences to map new narrative contours, Brown and Cather illustrate the ease with which a slave-based society could legitimize corruption and abuse to uphold southern matriarchy. *Clotel* and *Sapphira* focus on the formation and decline of southern matriarchy in the antebellum era, and in the process, expose how a social system governed by White men and grounded in violence fostered competition and social pressure among White women—which abetted, sanctioned, and concealed the abuse of African American women.

Clotel (1853) and the Construction of Southern Matriarchy

Clotel is a story about the fictionalized daughter of former American President Thomas Jefferson. Described by one modern reviewer as "an American fairy tale in which the royal-blooded Cinderella isn't claimed by her royal destiny," but is instead "'deposited' into a beggar's grave,"[1] the novel traces Clotel's tragic descent from Thomas Jefferson's household into the destitution of slavery, which leads to the loss of her daughter and, eventually, the loss of her life. *Clotel* offers an impassioned rebuke against slavery, clearly demonstrating the power of White men who carelessly harm enslaved women. Brown presents the story through a host of experimental narrative strategies, drawing heavily from all facets of his living, reading, and lecturing experiences. Consequently, rather than a traditional novel, *Clotel* resembles a literary pastiche, or bricolage, of nonfiction and fiction in an effort to bring readers closer to understanding the great tragedy of the situation. Instead of one distinct voice, which is expected in an autobiographical slave narrative, *Clotel* suggests Brown as a "cultural editor" who draws from his personal life, and his encounters with others, speaking engagements, and tropes of sentimental fiction to assemble a panoramic story that reveals a collective "national disunity" stemming from slavery.

Within *Clotel's* multifaceted cultural critique, one of its central themes is the great damage that upholding the southern matriarchy inflicts upon women throughout the South, especially African American mothers and their daughters. As the father of two teenage daughters, Brown felt this concern acutely as he composed the novel. Although his children safely attended boarding school overseas, Brown knew that he, and by extension, they, could

1. Joyce Carol Oates, "'Tragic Mulatta': *Clotel; or, The President's Daughter,* William Wells Brown with an introduction by Hilton Als," *Uncensored: Views and (Re)views* (New York: HarperCollins, 2005), 252.

be counted as a White man's lost property. He understood the great threats his daughters would face in a society that allowed White men and women to harm African American women. The fine line that separated his daughters from slavery's horrors energized Brown's concern for the great injustices African American women experienced within slavery.

Clotel begins with more than thirty pages devoted to a revised account of Brown's earlier work, *Narrative of William W. Brown, A Fugitive Slave*, which stresses the painful separation from his mother and helps to frame the novel around the severed relationships between African American mothers and their children. Literary historian Robert Stepto notes that Brown's use of a lengthy introduction to himself prior to the story "authenticat[es] his *access* to the incidents, characters, scenes, and tales which collectively make up *Clotel*."[2] In other words, this personalized preface prepares readers by framing Brown as speaker of truth as much as an entertainer. Presenting a testimony about what he witnessed during his journey toward freedom, Brown signals that the greater message of his novel concerns the grave injustices that mothers and daughters experienced as the property of slave owners. In lieu of a note from a White abolitionist that might serve as validation, Brown asserts his own credibility. He strives for greater formality by describing himself from the third-person perspective for the entirety of the preface. This choice calls attention to a pivotal instance when Brown abruptly switches to the first-person perspective, when he details the harsh separation from his mother and sister. Recounting the final moment with his mother, Brown writes, "William approached her, threw his arms around her neck, kissed her, fell upon his knees begging her forgiveness, for he thought he was to blame for her sad condition."[3] The great pain associated with this memory overwhelms Brown, who breaks from perspective to add, "I could hear no more—my heart struggled to free itself from the human form."[4] This jarring shift in point of view uproots readers from following William's story of slavery and directly immerses them in the simmering emotional turmoil Brown associates with the separation from his mother.

When Brown transitions from his autobiographical preface to the beginning of *Clotel*, he continues the thread of family dynamics in the opening

2. Robert Stepto, *From Behind the Veil: A Study of Afro-American Narrative* (Chicago: University of Illinois Press, 1991), 30.

3. William Wells Brown, *Clotel; or The President's Daughter* (New York: Penguin, 2004), 15.

4. Brown, *Clotel*, 16.

paragraph, highlighting the fractured relationships between White southerners and African Americans. In the opening sentence, Brown notes a growing number of mulatto children conceived among slave owners and slaves. He writes, "With the growing population of slaves in the Southern States of America, there is a fearful increase of half whites, most of whose fathers are [slave owners] and their mothers slaves."[5] Here, he draws from his own experience as a child of a White man and a slave to set the scene for Clotel. Like Clotel, the fictionalized descendant of Thomas Jefferson, Brown, too, was a descendant of a careless father with established roots in the United States; someone whose public and private behavior was rife with contradictions. Brown proclaimed that the fact these relationships existed served as "the best evidence of the degraded and immoral condition of the relation of master and slave in the United States of America."[6] Continuing in *Clotel*, he moves from a cultural observation to how a faux-family might visibly appear in the next sentence. Brown writes, "Society does not frown upon the man who sits with his mulatto child upon his knee, whilst its mother stands a slave behind his chair."[7] The image, with a White father at rest and a slave mother standing behind him, emphasizes much of what Brown found abhorrent and contradictory about slavery. By honing in on this image, he identifies the family inequities associated with slavery, which allowed slave owners to take advantage of slaves and separate mothers from their sons and daughters.

Absent from *Clotel*'s arresting opening image is the slave owner's wife, the nineteenth-century symbol of southern matriarchy. Brown implies that she is left out, presumably carrying on with other social activities elsewhere or possibly in staunch opposition to her husband's affairs. Slavery, he shows, fosters spheres of social difference—dividing White husbands and wives, empowering the former to take advantage of enslaved women and leaving the latter to fend for themselves and work to establish their own forms of authority. To this extent, slavery impacts and shapes the nineteenth-century foundation of southern matriarchy by positioning the White woman within the plantation house as responsible for maintaining household and family appearances. Beginning with Clotel and looking outward at the people who influence her life, Brown shows how the accepted behaviors of White men and the southern matriarchy intertwine to foster tragic situations. At sixteen, Clotel falls in love with Horatio Green, a twenty-two-year-old man from a wealthy family

5. Brown, *Clotel,* 43.
6. Brown, *Clotel,* 43.
7. Brown, *Clotel,* 43.

in Richmond who returns home from college, becomes infatuated with her, arranges her purchase, and then rents her a cottage. Horatio promises Clotel freedom in time and claims that he will find a way to reunite her with her mother and sister. Their union is illegal, so with marriage impossible, they conceal their relationship and, soon afterward, their daughter Mary.

The situation becomes dire when Horatio pursues his political aspirations and Gertrude, the representative of southern matriarchy in *Clotel*, appears. Prior to Horatio's desire to become a politician, Clotel implores him to relocate with their daughter to France or England. Brown writes that when she looked at their daughter Mary, she feared for her safety. Although Clotel feels confident in the "sheltered home in Horatio's heart, which the world might ridicule, but had no power to profane," she recoils at what Mary's beauty may mean for her daughter after thinking about "the unavoidable and dangerous position which the tyranny of society had awarded her."[8] Clotel also cannot know the coming change her social status disallows her to see—that in time, Horatio feels compelled to marry Gertrude, the only daughter of one of his wealthy supporters. With this revelation, Brown attacks the slavery for the way it preys upon all women. Gertrude is no two-dimensional villain, for example, but rather a woman whose identity collapses violently in the wake of her husband's hidden relationship with Clotel. Like Clotel, she cannot fully know the workings of White men who dominate politics and business affairs. Her marriage to Horatio quickly becomes a trap, an irony that Brown does not miss, since Horatio remains in love and emotionally entangled with Clotel. With her security and reputation at stake, Gertrude strives to protect the public perception of her as a young southern matriarch at all costs.

In a short compression of narrative space, Brown infuses instances of cruelty, sensationalism, and chance—what Ann duCille refers to as the "realm of the fantastic and coincidental"—to show the damage of unchecked power of the southern matriarchy in White, slave-owning households.[9] First, he depicts a final parting moment between Horatio and Clotel, where the former confesses his love for Clotel and acknowledges marrying Gertrude as a means of social improvement. Then, the next paragraph fast-forwards a few months later, when Horatio and Gertrude cross paths with Clotel and Mary while traveling. Gertrude notices Mary's beauty and soon deduces the truth after intuiting Horatio's emotional response to Clotel's appearance. Brown writes that Gertrude "wept, but not as poor Clotel had done; for she never

8. Brown, *Clotel,* 65.

9. Ann duCille, *The Coupling Convention: Sex, Text, and Tradition in Black Women's Fiction* (New York: Oxford University Press, 1993), 18.

had loved, and been beloved like her, and her nature was more proud."[10] Afterwards, Horatio feels "the wintry chill of her polite propriety," a sharp contrast from the "gushing love" of Clotel, "who was indeed his wife."[11] The undoing of her assumptions alters Gertrude, who hesitates to act outside of her marriage at first. However, Horatio's relationship with Clotel awakens her to an ugly truth: that her sense of matriarchal authority is predicated on a hierarchical racial system that not only enables her comfort, but also proffers her the power to try to protect her way of life.

Gertrude's vengeful reaction to the situation further reveals the darkest side of southern matriarchy prior to the Civil War. Motivated by an urgent sense of revenge, she insists that Clotel should be sold while demanding that ten-year-old Mary be kept as a servant. As is the case of some southern women in similar positions, Gertrude betrays the common conception of a southern matriarch as representative of "leisure, passivity, dependence, [and] submission."[12] In his portrayal of this horrendous incident, Brown undermines the southern matriarch's common association with politeness, respectfulness, subservience, and virtue. Striking directly at the heart of the problem, he asks, "What social virtues are possible in a society of which injustice is the primary characteristic?"[13] Once Clotel has been sold, Gertrude treats Mary terribly. Mary resembles her husband in appearance, so Gertrude terrorizes the child as a means of condemning his prior affair. In a chapter Brown entitles "Retaliation," she sends the fair-complexioned child into a garden behind the house without a bonnet or handkerchief for protection from the sun. As a result, Mary is "broiled to sleep"; when questioned, Gertrude insists that she is merely "lying in the sun, seasoning."[14] Later, when Clotel dies after trying to find her way back to her daughter, Mary still remains a pawn in an ugly household game. Brown shows how Gertrude's unconscionable behavior derives from the great need to assert and maintain her position as a young southern matriarch. When Horatio stops showing that he cares about Mary, his wife changes her disposition and becomes his daughter's friend. No longer threatened, Gertrude relents and changes her behavior, yet not without great consequence for Mary. That this situation occurs in tandem with Clotel's

10. Brown, *Clotel,* 90–91.

11. Brown, *Clotel,* 91.

12. Anne Goodwyn Jones, *Tomorrow is Another Day: The Woman Writer in the South, 1859–1936* (Baton Rouge: Louisiana Sate University Press, 1981), 28.

13. Brown, *Clotel,* 121.

14. Brown, *Clotel,* 129.

death is no accident. As the novel comes to an end, Brown illustrates that for Clotel and many other slaves, revenge associated with the maintenance of southern matriarchy could mean the separation of a child or even death.

Sapphira and the Slave Girl (1940) and the Southern Matriarch's Decline

Published nearly ninety years after Brown's pioneering work, Willa Cather's *Sapphira and the Slave Girl* also offers a novel perspective about southern matriarchy in the nineteenth century. Like *Clotel's* prefatory autobiographical narrative, Cather's *Sapphira and the Slave Girl* features an unconventional narrative choice in the form of an epilogue based on the author's memory of witnessing the reunion of a runaway slave and her long-abandoned mother. Cather's recollection of the event became the basis of the novel. The profound importance of this reunion is stressed by the deliberate switching from a third-person to first-person perspective and recounting the incident through the eyes of a child. This creative conclusion was a gamble given Cather's mainstream popularity, the great amount of prepublication anticipation for the novel, and the cultural context of the late 1930s. At that time, Cather was in her mid-sixties and at the height of her popularity when she began writing *Sapphira and the Slave Girl.* Her two prior novels, *Shadows on the Rock* (1931) and *Lucy Gayheart* (1935), had been commercially successful; she had also composed a collection of short stories, *Obscure Destinies* (1932), and a set of literary essays, *Not Under Forty* (1936). Anticipating a bestseller, her publisher planned to print a greater number of copies of *Sapphira* than for any of its prior publications, and the nationwide Book-of-the-Month Club had chosen the novel as an upcoming selection. Undoubtedly, the story's setting and focus on an aging southern matriarch during the decade prior to Civil War generated even greater anticipation because of the appeal of Margaret Mitchell's Pulitzer Prize-winning *Gone with the Wind* (1936) and its influential film adaptation, which debuted a year prior to *Sapphira and the Slave Girl.*

The great buzz could in no way prepare readers for the depths of background, purpose, and emotion Cather channeled into the story. While writing *Sapphira*, Cather experienced the surprising deaths of two of her close companions, her brother Douglass Cather and dear friend Isabelle Hambourg, only a few months apart. Coupled with the passing of her parents within the prior decade and thoughts of her own mortality, these losses caused Cather to think more about preserving memories of their time in Virginia that she, as the oldest child, would be the last in her family to remember.

Cather spent the first nine years of her life living in the Shenandoah Valley of Virginia before she relocated with her family to Nebraska in 1882. As a child, she soaked in impressions and stories during the tumultuous Reconstruction era. Synthesizing a memory from long before with the painful, present-day circumstances associated with aging, she created her "most politically confrontational"[15] book, a direct challenge to romanticized snapshots of southern matriarchy that exposes the tangled and perilous relationships among women during the antebellum period. In lieu of idealism or a sense of dignity in pursuing a vanishing way of life, *Sapphira* adopts a cold realism. It reveals the difficult realities of an elderly southern matriarch within a racist and deeply divided society, detailing how one woman's insistence on control and cruel choices amount to an overwhelming sense of domestic horror that severs mothers from their daughters.

Cather channeled her outpouring of conflicting emotions into the creation of Sapphira Colbert, who stubbornly insists on upholding the nineteenth-century semblance of southern matriarchy even though she and her husband are the only slaveholders in their mountain community. She directs a household comprised of her husband Henry and several slaves, including a woman named Till and her teenage daughter Nancy. The novel traces Sapphira's gnawing fear that Henry and Nancy are having an affair. It observes her quietly aggressive response, which involves encouraging her disreputable nephew Martin to pursue and harass Nancy and portrays the great terror Nancy undergoes until Sapphira's daughter Rachel returns to the community and helps to orchestrate her escape.

Sapphira and the Slave Girl begins by asserting the powerful strength of the nineteenth-century southern matriarch in its first chapter. For thirty years, Sapphira and Henry Colbert have lived in Back Creek, Virginia, where he serves as the local miller while she oversees their household. The story begins with a heated argument at the breakfast table. As Sapphira urges Henry to sell Nancy, Cather highlights the imposing "icy quality" of her voice.[16] Henry, who objects to slavery and longs to grant freedom to all of their slaves, attempts to counter his wife by claiming the immorality of separating Nancy from her mother. The discussion continues for a few minutes, but Cather leaves the dilemma unresolved when Henry walks out of the house. She then

15. Ann Romines, "Willa Cather's Civil War: A Very Long Engagement," *Cather Studies* 6 (2006), 18.

16. Willa Cather, *Sapphira and the Slave Girl* (New York: Library of America, 1990), 781.

switches from presenting the Colberts' major disagreement to characterizing Sapphira's uncompromising presence. As her husband disappears, Sapphira says to herself, "Then we must find some other way," in a manner that mocks her husband and foregrounds her power.[17] Throughout this opening scene, Cather presents Sapphira as a towering and convincing woman with an uncompromising vision about how her household should appear and function. With Sapphira, she equates southern matriarchy prior to the Civil War as domineering and insistent within the realm of the household. In the chapter's surprising final paragraph, Cather reveals that Sapphira has dropsy, a condition presently known as edema and characterized by swelling due to the accumulation of fluid in bodily tissues or cavities, and that she commands everyone while bound to a wheelchair. She shows with great force the strength of southern matriarchy, which grants Sapphira the power to direct the household despite her ongoing infirmity that renders her the weakest member of the household.

Cather further critiques southern matriarchy by contrasting Sapphira's decisive power with Nancy's great vulnerability. In reflecting upon her childhood, Cather ruminates about the complexity of social relationships within southern households. The lives of White and African American women she witnessed were "deliberately entangled" before and after the abolition of slavery.[18] However, as she asserts in *Sapphira*, the latter suffered disproportionately within social arrangements of disempowerment. She suggests this imbalance in the novel's title, which positions Sapphira as the foremost and central figure and presents Nancy as an unidentified slave girl. Unlike the way that Sapphira dominates the novel's first chapter, Nancy first appears in the story at an odd angle from Sapphira's daughter's point of view, in a scene that reveals the way southern matriarchy stifled unfavorable thoughts and feelings for the sake of maintaining expectations and appearances. As Nancy irons clothes, Rachel notices that despite her kind words, her "lids were still red from crying," and that she appears to conceal greater worries.[19] Rachel reciprocates friendliness instead of inquiry while projecting "a resolute cheerfulness which she did not always feel" when speaking to her mother's slaves.[20] Yet, inwardly, she knows something has happened to Nancy since

17. Cather, *Sapphira and the Slave Girl*, 782.

18. Jessica Adams, *Wounds of Returning: Race, Memory, and Property on the Postslavery Plantation* (Chapel Hill: University of North Carolina Press, 2007), 22.

19. Cather, *Sapphira and the Slave Girl*, 787.

20. Cather, *Sapphira and the Slave Girl*, 787.

the slave whom her mother had always "shown her marked favoritism" now bears signs of physical violence.[21] At this point in the story, Cather asserts that not enough has happened to motivate Rachel to challenge the inequities found within the matriarchal structure. Rachel's fallback, in the face of Nancy's troubling appearance, is to replace her concern with distraction—to seek images of beauty and wellness elsewhere. She tells Nancy that she must leave and then departs to check on the status of some flower beds near the slave quarters. Walking away temporarily absolves Rachel from asking further questions or taking action, and it effectively sidesteps the implications of emotional and physical violence for the pursuit of something more pleasant.

Rachel's initial failure to consider or confront Sapphira's aggression leads to a more dangerous situation when her mother becomes even more threatening toward Nancy. Perhaps the novel's most damning irony about southern matriarchy is the fact that neither Sapphira's deteriorating condition nor how she responds to it enables her to consider the "powerlessness" of the African American women nearest to her.[22] In a situation separate from her interactions with Nancy, Sapphira cruelly announces to another slave that the consequence of a poorly planned funeral gathering will be the sale of her daughter.[23] Later, the general cruelty toward her slaves peaks when her nephew Martin Colbert arrives to stay with the family. A gambler and the "worst rake in the country" with a noticeable tooth replacement as a result of mistreating another woman, Martin soon begins aggressively pursuing Nancy.[24] His actions—which Sapphira notices, pretends not to see, and then actively supports—range from harassing Nancy to grabbing and kissing her to stalking her at night. Soon, others begin to notice Nancy's fear and exhaustion and seek to address the problem. When her husband questions Sapphira about Martin's length of stay six weeks after his arrival, as a means to encourage her to ask him to leave, Sapphira maintains that allowing Martin to stay is merely a sign of southern hospitality. Inwardly, she still fears that Henry is having an affair with Nancy, so she considers exacting torment on Nancy through Martin, and then defending her nephew remains "almost as good as play."[25] In the

21. Cather, *Sapphira and the Slave Girl,* 788.

22. Angela M. Salas, "Willa Cather's *Sapphira and the Slave Girl:* Extending the Boundaries of the Body," *College Literature* 24, no. 2 (1997): 97.

23. Cather, *Sapphira and the Slave Girl,* 834.

24. Cather, *Sapphira and the Slave Girl,* 872.

25. Cather, *Sapphira and the Slave Girl,* 889.

great power that Sapphira retains, which she uses to abet Martin's aggression toward Nancy, Cather undermines any sense of nostalgia for a way of life where the fates of African American women lie in the decisions of the all-powerful southern matriarch.[26]

Southern matriarchy crumbles toward the end of novel when Sapphira's daughter and health conspire against her. With Rachel's help, Nancy flees Martin and Sapphira's reign of terror. This shocking event upends Sapphira, who feels humiliated after Nancy's escape and eventually passes. It also sets the stage for Nancy's return twenty-five years later in *Sapphira*'s aforementioned controversial epilogue. Without this final chapter, Cather wrote, "the whole book would be constructed, not lived, like a hundred other stories of the South and of slavery."[27] The epilogue begins with a girl sharing what she remembers of Nancy's return. She is five and can recall the meeting between Nancy and her mother Till. The girl notes, "There was something Scriptural in that meeting, like pictures in our old Bible. . . . [Later,] Nancy and Till sat where they were, hand in hand, and went on talking as if I were not there at all."[28] Even though she is young, she realizes that the moment is special. The scene represents an instance of healing that only a much older Cather could contemplate and seek to make sense of, but also never truly understand.

Relaying the situation from the child's point of view not only remains true to what Cather witnessed, but it also aligns with *Sapphira*'s contention that White women reared within southern matriarchy could never fully comprehend the abuse and mistreatment common in the lives of African American women in the South. If the novel neglects to offer Nancy's point of view, a move that has sparked subsequent criticism—most strongly conveyed by author Toni Morrison, who considers Nancy and other African Americans in the novel as either "silenced" or "acquiescent"—it may be all that Cather could confidently or comfortably share, knowing that what she saw and felt failed to approach what women like Till or Nancy felt.[29]

Clotel and *Sapphira and the Slave Girl* spotlight the dark corners in the grand ballroom of southern matriarchy. In abrupt and disconcerting ways,

26. Traci B. Abbott, "'A Good Girl Like Nancy': Willa Cather's *Sapphira and the Slave Girl*," *Southern Quarterly* 46, no. 1 (2008): 27.

27. Willa Cather, "To Roscoe Cather." 26 August 1940. *The Selected Letters of Willa Cather*. (New York: Alfred A. Knopf, 2013), 587.

28. Cather, *Sapphira and the Slave Girl*, 932–33.

29. Toni Morrison, *Playing in the Dark: Whiteness and the Literary Imagination* (Cambridge: Harvard University Press, 1992), 27.

these novels elucidate the hardships of African American women living in relationships with powerful southern women who sought to establish and retain their grasp of household affairs. Brown's and Cather's personal experiences shaped these haunting novels, which share how the curse of slavery blanketed southern matriarchs with competition, aggression, and fear. By peering into shadows that conceal harm and immense pain, Brown and Cather also expose the trickle-down effects of violence that White men enacted and justified during the antebellum era. They also question any form of southern matriarchy, pre- or post-Civil War, that depends on the abuse of African American women. Finally, their novels suggest that in order to come to terms with the evolution of southern matriarchy, readers must consider the function of slavery to comprehend the thin line between respectability and the appearance of social goodness versus what these appearances demand.

Bibliography

Abbott, Traci B. "'A Good Girl Like Nancy': Willa Cather's *Sapphira and the Slave Girl.*" *Southern Quarterly* 46, no. 1 (Fall 2008): 26–45.

Adams, Jessica. *Wounds of Returning: Race, Memory, and Property on the Postslavery Plantation.* Chapel Hill: University of North Carolina Press, 2007.

Brown, William Wells. *Clotel; or, The President's Daughter.* 1853. New York: Penguin, 2004.

Ernest, John. *Resistance and Reformation in Nineteenth-Century African-American Literature.* Jackson: University Press of Mississippi, 1995.

Cather, Willa. *Sapphira and the Slave Girl.* 1940. New York: Library of America, 1990.

———. "To Roscoe Cather." 26 August 1940. *The Selected Letters of Willa Cather.* ed. Andrew Jewell and Janis Stout. New York: Alfred A. Knopf, 2013: 587–88.

duCille, Ann. *The Coupling Convention: Sex, Text, and Tradition in Back Women's Fiction.* New York: Oxford University Press, 1993.

Greenspan, Ezra. *William Wells Brown: An African American Life.* New York: W. W. Norton & Company, 2014.

Jewell, Andrew. *The Selected Letters of Willa Cather.* New York: Alfred A. Knopf, 2013.

Jones, Anne Goodwyn. *Tomorrow is Another Day: The Woman Writer in the South, 1859–1936.* Baton Rouge: Louisiana State University Press, 1981.

Kerrison, Catherine. *Claiming the Pen: Women and Intellectual life in the Early American South*. Ithaca: Cornell University Press, 2006.

Levine, Robert S. "Introduction." *Clotel; or, The President's Daughter*, 3–27. 1853. New York: Bedford/St. Martin's, 2000.

Morrison, Toni. *Playing in the Dark: Whiteness and the Literary Imagination.* Cambridge, MA: Harvard University Press, 1992.

Oates, Joyce Carol. *Uncensored: Views and (Re)views.* New York: HarperCollins, 2005.

Romines, Ann. "Willa Cather's Civil War: A Very Long Engagement." *Cather Studies* 6 (2006): 1–27.

Salas, Angela M. "Willa Cather's *Sapphira and the Slave Girl*: Extending the Boundaries of the Body." *College Literature* 24, no. 2 (June 1997): 97–108.

Stepto, Robert. *From Behind the Veil: A Study of Afro-American Narrative.* Chicago: University of Illinois Press, 1991.

Jericho Williams is a professor of English at Spartanburg Methodist College who researches American, African American, and Southern literature. He is the editor of *Critical Insights: Frederick Douglass* (Salem Press) and has published essays about environmental education and injustice in American slave narratives in *Ecogothic in Nineteenth-Century American Literature* (Routledge), childhood in the fiction of Nella Larsen (*South Atlantic Review*), racial isolation in Zora Neale Hurston's fiction in *Representing Rural Women* (Lexington Books), and literary naturalism in relation to the writings of Claude McKay (*The New Centennial Review*). He is currently editing a collection of essays to celebrate the upcoming fortieth anniversary of Alice Walker's *The Color Purple* in 2022.

Othering the Mother
Navigating Southern Matriarchy in Morrison's *Beloved*

Gabriella Greco

Toni Morrison's novel *Beloved* presents an intricate display of trauma's impact within a family unit, especially the mother-daughter relationship. This trauma is compounded further by mother and former slave Sethe's willingness to commit infanticide to spare her unnamed daughter from the same traumas she just escaped. Sethe's trauma is further aggravated by the arrival of a childlike mystery woman who calls herself Beloved—the same name inscribed on the late infant's headstone. Beloved's presence is complex. She becomes a substitute daughter that Sethe attempts to mother in order to free herself from the guilt she feels having lost her biological daughter. Thus, she is not just the reason the memories come rushing back, but rather the antagonist pulling the memories from Sethe—often against her will—forcing her to remember and relive the pain of her original traumas. Beloved's antagonistic presence serves as a new source of trauma while also bringing a second wave of trauma through Sethe's memories.

As a text based heavily on tropes from both American Gothic literature and the slave narrative genre, Morrison's novel serves as a complex and delicate commentary on African American trauma and the psychologically haunting effects of that trauma on motherhood. Through various key characters, Morrison gives the reader several lenses through which to view the value placed on the mother-daughter relationship, or in many cases how the absence of motherly love is a trauma with long-lasting effects on the successful formation of identity. Morrison's female characters share a collective maternal identity, unique to their traumatic experiences as slaves. Their painful memories, both of being owned as slaves through adolescence and of their later struggle to adapt to motherhood, blur the conventional lines of what it means to nurture and protect, the stereotypical qualities of a strong matriarch. Aside from the most blatant and gruesome trauma of the novel—the infanticide that Sethe commits as an act of mercy for her unnamed child—many of the recurring traumatic memories evoke the challenges of motherhood during slavery. The cause of Sethe's eventual decline into madness is the complex traumatic role of the mother-daughter dynamic in her life. For these women, the act of storytelling, the sharing of their traumatic childhood memories, becomes an attempt to claim selective ownership over their own pasts—their "rememories" as Morrison writes—with the hope of navigating their own traumatic identities as mothers.

Despite Sethe's newly found freedom, the freedom to choose whether to remember or repress certain memories is taken from her upon Beloved's mysterious arrival in Ohio. Beloved becomes a haunting reminder of the baby Sethe tragically lost, as well as the catalyst that causes Sethe to remember and retell other traumatic, formerly repressed memories from her own childhood. Beloved, the haunt, becomes a stand-in for the baby Sethe killed as she tries to make amends and justify her actions to free her from her own guilt. The traumatic effects that both Beloved's haunting presence alone and the remembering of such damaging memories have on Sethe are witnessed as the reader watches the two women's gradual descent into the codependent madness of their convoluted mother-daughter bond.

As slaves, these women were denied the familial bonds necessary for the formation of an identity and have thus learned to perpetuate this denial of self and family as a means to defend themselves against loss; if something does not belong to you it cannot, logically speaking, be lost or taken from you. This extends to the women's inability to claim their own children and further complicates the role of mother. The terrorism of slavery lies in the original actions that dehumanized the women as children, but is made more complex by the secondary and tertiary traumas that come when, later in life, the women are unable to understand or adapt to the traditional expectations of motherhood; they were not nurtured and thus they cannot nurture. In his article, "Art and the Ambiguity of Terrorism," Gorman Beauchamp opens a discussion surrounding race, terror, and the ambiguous relationship between the two. He is particularly concerned with the gray area that many African American literary genres rely on as a source of ambiguity along the ethical spectrum of victim and criminal. The characters he references were once maligned as the savage, evil representation of their race, but are now seen by many modern readers as martyrs capitalizing on some small window of opportunity to regain the precious freedom—by any means necessary—that had been stolen from them by the *truly* savage White man. Beauchamp perpetuates the presence of this gray area falling between the two extremes of acceptance and denial by referencing

Auden's "September 1, 1939": "Those to whom evil is done/ Do evil in return."[1] Whether the evil done justifies the consequently evil acts is precisely where the ethical ambiguity thrives. It is not, however, the responsibility of the reader to take on this impossible task of condemning or forgiving Sethe for her tragic act of infanticide, but rather to navigate these ambiguous spaces that Morrison artfully creates in an attempt to gain further understanding of the complexity faced by southern matriarchs.

Gorman Beauchamp has an intriguing treatment of what he terms "terrorism," which focuses on the ability of a single act to be "condemnable by one set of values, laudable by another."[2] Having grown up an orphaned, abused slave, Sethe's set of values are very different from those of the motherless Schoolteacher and his White nephews, despite their own lack of a mother figure throughout the novel. This contradictory dichotomy of judging terror can be seen from the condemning attitude of Schoolteacher's nephew upon witnessing Sethe's acts in the shed. The same nephew who had no trouble perpetrating such horrific trauma on another (Sethe) by robbing her of her maternal milk, "cannot understand why Sethe would bring harm to her children."[3] The nephew's psyche, or "set of values," to quote Beauchamp, leaves room to justify the committing of his own horrible acts and yet allows him to stand in judgment of the acts of another. Despite the nephew's openly judgmental and arguably hypocritical opinions of Sethe, few of the other characters are as hypercritical as she is in recounting her own motivations for the infanticide.

In her description of the act, recounted to Paul D, Sethe explains that her reason for the infanticide was something unexperienced by and incomprehensible to many of her female peers: love. Sethe *attempts*, though not without struggle, to claim herself and her children as truly free from Schoolteacher and his boys, and from the radically traumatic slave life she left behind in Kentucky. This openness to love was a blessing and a curse for Sethe. It motivated her to be strong enough to survive for her children, while simultaneously ostracizing her from the other women in the community who were not willing to open their hearts and leave themselves quite as vulnerable.

1. Gorman Beauchamp, "Art and the Ambiguity of Terrorism: 'Benito Cereno' to the Death of Klinghoffer," *Southwest Review* 100, no. 3 (2015): 347, ProQuest.

2. Beauchamp, "Art and the Ambiguity," 378.

3. Jeanna Fuston-White, "'From the Seen to the Told': The Construction of Subjectivity in Toni Morrison's *Beloved*," *African American Review* 36, no. 3 (Autumn 2002): 464, JSTOR.

Often, Morrison artfully and intentionally leaves these controversial instances of claiming oneself hanging in the realm of ethical ambiguity. To reiterate, it is not the purpose of Morrison, or the reader, to decide if Sethe is to be forgiven or damned, but rather to understand how these complex traumatic motherly actions blur the lines on what qualifies as "good mothering." Molly Abel Travis, expounding on the ethical dilemma proposed by James Phelan states: "The design of Morrison's narrative calls for identification with Sethe, while also ultimately making that identification impossible. We feel sympathy for Sethe, but the 'inability to fix a position on the central action complicates our relation to Sethe as the central actor.'"[4] The reader's sympathetic feelings parallel those of Sethe's female community in the novel, but interestingly, while there is sympathy for Sethe she still remains an "othered" character both among the novel's other women and Morrison's readers. Travis focuses largely on the empathetic burden placed on the reader to align themselves with Sethe's point of view—one who commits infanticide to establish herself as "an agent of resistance against slavery."[5] However, while Travis highlights the authorial ambiguity that Morrison has mastered in *Beloved*, it is vital for the reader to push past the superficial judgment of Sethe's actions to understand the effects of othering that are a result of Sethe's struggling attempts to love her children. Instead, the focus should be placed on Sethe's psychological grounding for her actions: her troubled understanding of what and how the task of mothering is to be undertaken.

Just as Sethe is hypercritical of her actions, Toni Morrison is hypercritical of her own role as author. While several of her critical comments focus on the role of the "Africanist other"[6] in canonical texts, Morrison's *Playing in the Dark: Whiteness and the Literary Imagination* takes the analysis one step further. Othering is the action of separating yourself or being ostracized from a person/people based on how well you adhere to their expected characteristics. Typically, those that are othered are considered outliers—be it of their race, religion, gender, sexuality, or any combination thereof. In Morrison's critical explanation, the "Africanist

4. Molly Abel Travis, "Beyond Empathy: Narrative Distancing and Ethics in Toni Morrison's *Beloved* and J. M. Coetzee's *Disgrace*," *Journal of Narrative Theory* 40, no. 2 (2010): 236; The text Travis is referencing is James Phelan, "Sethe's Choice: Beloved and the Ethics of Reading," *Style* 32, no. 2 (1998): 329.

5. Travis, "Beyond Empathy," 233.

6. Toni Morrison, *Playing in the Dark: Whiteness and the Literary Imagination* (New York: Vintage, 1993), 47.

other . . . permitted opportunities for the exploration of ethics and morality."[7] Through Sethe's controversial character, set amongst a backdrop of racially equalized characters, Morrison is able to take the previously stereotypical portrayal of "Africanist others" in the White Anglo-Saxon Protestant literary canon and turn it on its head playing on the assumptions of the modern reader. Morrison explains, "That assumption is . . . that slave women are not mothers; they are 'natally dead,' with no obligations to their offspring or their own parents."[8] She goes on to explain, "The absence of mother love . . . is connected to the assumption of a slave's natal isolation."[9] Sethe seems open to the potential for love *despite* her trauma, but she is alone in her thinking and is misunderstood and ostracized in her "free" community. She moved from being racially othered as a female slave, to being socially othered because of her openness to love and motherhood. Morrison takes the canonical trope of the African other as "natally dead" and dives headfirst into Sethe's ambiguous relationship as both a daughter who lost her mother, and, later, a mother who lost a daughter. Exploring this duality within Sethe gives Morrison's reader the opportunity to view othering from a social and psychological context rather than the more traditional racial context. Although the memories of childless mothers and motherless children become the recurring source of trauma for the women in Morrison's works, the character Sethe is one of the few to actively attempt to work through these traumas.

Memory and, more importantly, the *rememory* of failed acts of mothering become important themes chasing Sethe and the other Ohio women throughout the novel. These memories of motherhood become the lens through which Sethe must cope with her past traumas. Sethe's inexperience with a mother figure during her terrifying childhood has affected her own ability to mother her children. Sethe acted out of what she identifies as love, but clearly her inexperience with more stereotypical, nurturing, motherly love has given her no foundation for how to express her emotions or offer protection to her own offspring in a way that is deemed socially appropriate. This viciously cyclic dynamic between mother and child is what makes condemnation or forgiveness of Sethe difficult for the reader and for the community's women, many of whom experienced similar traumas related to motherly bonds. Navigating the ambiguity of motherhood is the journey that Morrison takes the reader

7. Morrison, *Playing in the Dark*, 48.

8. Morrison, *Playing in the Dark*, 21.

9. Morrison, *Playing in the Dark*, 23.

on through Sethe's own character arc. Of her intentionally authored ambiguities, Morrison states:

> These spaces, which I am filling in, and can fill in because they were planned, can conceivably be filled in with other significances. That is planned as well. The point is that into these spaces should fall the ruminations of the reader and his or her invented or recollected or misunderstood knowingness. The reader as narrator asks the questions the community asks, and both reader and "voice" stand among the crowd, within it, with privileged intimacy and contact, but without any more privileged information than the crowd has.[10]

The questions present in *Beloved*'s ambiguities are not solely about race, despite its inherent presence in a novel about an escaped female slave, but rather about the vulnerability of motherhood and these women's subsequent inability to express mother love. This inability is perpetuated until the climax of the novel when the female collective arrives—in many ways assuming the motherly role they previously struggled to embody—to protect one of their own damaged women, Sethe, from the further damage experienced in her destructive relationship with Beloved. Only together can these women achieve the nurturing they previously struggled to find for their own children.

While the exact psychologically damaging effects of growing up motherless and enslaved nineteenth-century Kentucky are outside the realm of experience for modern readers, Morrison was able to highlight this moral ambiguity as a powerful commentary on the long-term effects of childhood trauma. Despite the arguable authorial motive, the effect is the same: Sethe's explanation for her infanticide should not be read as a testimony to her innocence, but an explanation of the trauma she endured throughout her life and how she coped with those memories. Her retelling becomes a necessary means of working through the issues. Sethe's recognition of her own memories of the barely-there relationship with her mother is emphasized with the introduction of Beloved's character. For Sethe, Beloved is the haunting reminder of her failed attempts at mothering, having turned to the mercy killing of her baby to spare her from the same fate Sethe had just escaped. To clarify, Sethe's regret would be that she is not with her daughter either in life or death; if she had succeeded with her homicidal/suicidal intentions, there would be nothing to regret because she would have kept the family unit safely intact—her

10. Toni Morrison, "Unspeakable Things Unspoken: The Afro-American Presence in American Literature," *Toni Morrison: Modern Critical Views*, ed. Harold Bloom (New York: Chelsea House publishers, 1990), 157.

idea of protection. Instead, Sethe is left with the all-too-familiar feelings of abandonment from not knowing her own mother. Not only does Beloved directly symbolize a second chance for Sethe to succeed at motherhood, but also serves as the catalyst for Sethe's rememories of her own psychologically damning adolescent experiences with her mother. Through the glimpses back into Sethe's psyche, Beloved grants the reader access to Sethe's first terrifying experiences within a flawed mother-daughter relationship.

In one of her first examples of claiming ownership over something, an instance retold as a memory, Sethe recalls her arrival in Ohio. Sethe "was big," she explains to Paul D, "and deep and wide and when I stretched out my arms all my children could get in between. . . . Look like I loved em more after I got here. Or maybe I couldn't love em proper in Kentucky because they wasn't mine to love."[11] She presents her fleeing to Ohio as an attempt to truly reclaim her own role as a mother, and a fulfillment of her longing to "get to a place where you could love anything you chose—not to need permission for desire."[12] Unfortunately, while Sethe understands that this claiming ownership is the first step in deepening her motherly connection, the next steps are unfamiliar territory for her. In the bleak world of Sethe's childhood, she was raised, sold, purchased, and consistently treated as property. For Sethe, finally having the freedom she desired for herself and her own most prized possessions, her children, was motive enough for her to ensure that freedom remained—by whatever means necessary. It is vital to note that Sethe's understanding of motherhood can be better explained as an understanding of ownership.

Her adolescence was lived not through a mother-daughter relationship, but through the damaging lens of the slave-master relationship. Sethe is more familiar with how one demonstrates ownership than how one shows love. When highlighting this childhood dynamic, there is an interesting comparison that can be made between slave ownership and the "ownership" experienced in a parental role. Both slave owner and mother may feel a sense of entitlement or responsibility to protect what is theirs. As can be seen with Sethe the means of protection, namely the act of infanticide, are not without their psychological repercussions. The reasoning behind the acts, however, is where the important difference can be noted; slave owners protect their property to protect their *own* investments, whereas in motherhood, as far as Sethe can understand it, one may sacrifice her own self and mental well-being

11. Toni Morrison, *Beloved* (New York: Vintage, 2004), 190.

12. Morrison, *Beloved,* 191.

to ensure a better life for her children—even if that better life can only be preserved through death. There is a *selflessness*—a *giving* of one's body—present in motherhood that stands in direct contrast to the *selfishness* of slave ownership—the *taking* of another's body. These contrasts can be more clearly understood in analyzing the sacrificial portrayal of breastfeeding in order "to draw a link between slavery and motherhood, which not only exposes how slavery in fact horrifically disrupted motherhood, but also traces how these issues of ownership and mastery, of possession and possessiveness, are always present as anxieties in the early mothering relationship."[13] Sethe's motivation to cross the river is not solely to gain freedom for herself, but more importantly to bring milk to her waiting baby.

Milk becomes an important symbol of life and an indicator of motherhood as it is "the essence of mother love."[14] The first instance is in Sethe's emotional recounting of Schoolteacher's boys taking her milk, an act of "appropriation and commodification of slave women's mother love."[15] Sethe remembers, "All I knew was I had to get my milk to my baby girl. Nobody was going to nurse her like me. . . . I told them to put sugar water in cloth to suck from so when I got here in a few days she wouldn't have forgot me. The milk would be there and I would be there with it."[16] For Sethe, who was not nursed by her own mother, providing nourishment for her children becomes one of the driving forces behind her escape. It is an obligation she must fulfill for her daughter in order to prove herself as a mother, as well as maintain the fragile connection between mother and child. Sethe is validated as a mother by her children's dependence on her. Again, milk's importance is witnessed as Sethe nurses Denver immediately following the incident in the shed. Sethe is covered in the blood of the infant, but regardless, "Denver took her mother's milk right along with the blood of her sister."[17] In this instance, there is a complex juxtaposition of life and death. The milk provides Denver with nourishment and life, while the blood of her slaughtered sister is a clear indicator of death. This duality can also be attributed to Sethe, who has the

13. Rebecca Stone, "Can the Breast Feed the Mother Too? Tracing Maternal Subjectivity in Toni Morrison's *Beloved*," *British Journal of Psychotherapy* 31, no. 3 (2015): 303.

14. Andrea O'Reilly, *Toni Morrison and Motherhood: A Politics of the Heart* (Albany: State University of New York Press, 2004), 129.

15. O'Reilly, *Toni Morrison*, 129.

16. Morrison, *Beloved*, 19.

17. Morrison, *Beloved*, 179.

strength and ability to both create and nourish life or to quickly end it, becoming the epitome of the complex Devouring Mother archetype. Sethe's desire to provide milk to nourish her child can be juxtaposed with the violent taking of her milk by Schoolteacher's nephews. There is a reciprocation in the mother-child relationship be it one of affection or protection that is just not present in the slave-master relationship. Note also that Sethe's intention in the shed was not to turn her beloved daughter into a martyr as a solitary sacrifice, but rather to sacrifice her whole family, as well as herself, to protect their newfound freedom. Death became a more appealing option for her than returning her children to the circumstances she worked so hard to free them—and herself—from in Kentucky, where she would never truly have been able to love her children the way she deemed fit.

The overwhelming source of terror for Sethe throughout the novel is her inability to understand her relationship with motherhood. She is justifiably fearful of furthering the vicious cycle of failed mother-child relationships, and thus she struggles to understand or appropriately express her motherly instinct, as opposed to her instinct for survival, which as a slave has been a primary instinct her entire life. The act of infanticide is not the sole source of trauma in Morrison's novel; there also lies the trauma of motherly abandonment and desertion. Thus, "the infanticide is one more desertion. If Sethe is the mother who killed her daughter to protect her from being re-enslaved, she is also *the* mother separated from *the* child in Middle Passage."[18] It is the loss of connection between mother and daughter—the lack of mother love—that haunts Sethe's psyche. She was deserted by her mother, who was hanged during Sethe's childhood, and she goes on to desert her own two-year-old by succeeding in her infanticide while failing to complete her intended suicide. She knows both the trauma of being deserted and the guilt of being the deserter.

Sethe's whole life has been a perpetual onslaught of traumas, beginning with her own memory as a nursing infant being removed from the breast of her mother to be nursed instead by someone whose *job* it was to provide nourishment. Keeping this motherless childhood in mind, one could easily argue that the rememories that the various characters work so diligently to keep at bay, including the "baby ghost" herself, can all be characterized as "intrusive phenomena" for Sethe.[19] Sethe is "repeat[ing] the traumatic aspects of

18. Naomi Morgenstern, "Mother's Milk and Sister's Blood: Trauma and the Neoslave Narrative," *Differences: A Journal of Feminist Cultural Studies* 8, no. 2 (1996): 114, MLA International Bibliography.

19. Cathy Caruth, "Unclaimed Experience: Trauma and the Possibility of History," *Yale French Studies* 79 (1991): 181.

[her] past life in relation to a current and tragic situation."[20] She is essentially a product of her traumatic environment, and thus her perception of trauma is heightened. She was deprived of love and treated poorly and thus the lines between the two have been blurred, causing Sethe to love "too hard" once she is free from the primary trauma.

The most complex trauma of the novel, despite the various ambiguities mentioned, is the *shared memory* of the originally traumatic events. Each character has their own perspective on the events, including the infanticide, that are shaped by their previous life experiences as orphaned children and later as abused mothers. The trauma can be considered subjective as each woman's experience with losing or giving up a child is unique; however, the emotions those losses bring are shared by many in a type of "collective trauma."[21] The newly freed women in Ohio "are collectively *possessed* by the long-term insidious effects of racism: they are psychically 'owned' to a greater or lesser degree by events beyond their control."[22] While they may have fought for and achieved their physical freedom, their shared memories of abuse and trauma still serve as a collective limiting factor to their psychological freedom.

For as much blame as critics place on Beloved as a parasite or devourer of memories, blame could also be assigned to Sethe, who becomes symbolic of the "Devouring Mother archetype" which highlights "the dangers attendant on the woman who needs to wean herself from mothering as her children grow up so that she can develop other parts of her identity."[23] All of Sethe's children—but especially her daughters—serve as stand-in, substitute fragments of her identity. If Beloved is an externalized fragment of Sethe's identity, "Sethe is both mother and daughter: she occupies that "double position" of mother-daughter . . . Sethe's maternal identity is inseparable from her identity as daughter."[24] Her own identity is hard enough to claim, but if she can claim or understand her daughters as reflections of herself perhaps there is a chance that their collective life will turn away from chaos.

20. Maria-Sabina Draga Alexandru, "Love as Reclamation in Toni Morrison's African American Rhetoric," *European Journal of American Culture* 27, no. 3 (2008): 196.

21. Victoria Burrows, *Whiteness and Trauma: The Mother-Daughter Knot in the Fiction of Jean Rhys, Jamaica Kincaid, and Toni Morrison* (Basingstoke: Palgrave Macmillan, 2004), 130.

22. Burrows, *Whiteness and Trauma*, 130.

23. Stephanie A. Demetrakopoulos, "Maternal Bonds as Devourers of Women's Individuation in Toni Morrison's *Beloved*," *African American Review* 26, no. 1 (1992).

24. O'Reilly, *Toni Morrison*, 87.

Unfortunately, Sethe lost an opportunity to mother after killing her daughter in the shed, and thus instead of weaning herself away from the role of motherhood, she adopts the role full force and becomes the mother that the mysterious Beloved desperately desires. Sethe's projection of her own fragmented identity onto her daughters becomes even more complex when juxtaposing her previous actions in the shed with her later actions inside their house at 124 Bluestone Road. Rather than grow apart from Denver and her newest "daughter" Beloved, Sethe locks them in the house to try and make reparations for her previous inability to keep them all together. She is trying to forcefully regroup the shattered pieces of herself because "to kill her daughter is to kill her own best self, to kill her best and self-gendered fantasy of the future. The act is like killing time itself, especially its redemptive gifts, which the daughter, as a potential mother, symbolizes."[25] This potential for motherhood parallels Beloved's own pregnancy at the novel's end. Owning and protecting oneself is a struggle exacerbated by the lack of motherly love and protection, and thus the act of storytelling becomes the first line of psychological defense in defining one's identity. Remembering and retelling are ways for the characters to navigate and cope with their timelines of traumatic experiences. By employing these methods, the characters can attempt to claim psychological ownership of their personal history. Storytelling becomes a source for the African cultural phenomenon of *nommo*,[26] defined as "the magic power of the word to call things into being, to give life to things through the unity of word, water, seed, and blood."[27] To call something into existence is to name it and give it a story, to tell or retell its history. The same is true for Sethe's and the other female characters' own identities. Their names are given to them, they are branded, their children and their own bodies are commoditized; it is no wonder that identifying oneself or claiming motherhood over one's children is such a struggle. Prior to her decline into disjointed madness, we see an instance of Sethe's more coherent storytelling. To clarify, it is not the infanticide that signifies or even necessarily causes her madness, but rather the devotion to Beloved once the three women lock themselves inside the house. She forces them into reclusivity in an attempt to protect her children from the outside threats and judgment of those who cannot understand their

25. Demetrakopoulos, "Maternal Bonds."

26. Morrison, "Unspeakable Things," 162.

27. William R. Handley, "The House a Ghost Built: *Nommo*, Allegory, and the Ethics of Reading in Toni Morrison's *Beloved*," *Contemporary Literature* 4 (1995): 677, Literature Resource Center.

mother-daughter dynamic—the same dynamic Sethe struggles to understand herself. Before this declining spiral into madness, however, Sethe remembers for Denver and Beloved a memory of a mark that her mother had on her ribs, a brand given to her by her owner to designate her as property; this was her only distinguishable identity. Beloved has implored Sethe to tell a story about her own mother, and in doing so has brought another traumatic memory into the foreground of Sethe's psyche. Sethe remembers most prominently not her biological mother, but the woman called Nan who was responsible for raising her. Sethe recalls for her daughters a memory of Nan, retold to Sethe as her mother is hanged:

> She threw them all away but you. The one from the crew she threw away on the island. The others from more whites she also threw away. Without names, she threw them. You she gave the name of the black man, she put her arms around him. The others she did not put her arms around. Never. Never.[28]

The physicality of this memory is important when remembering Sethe's own identifying scar and her later description of wanting to have arms wide enough to hold and protect all her children at once. Both her mother's branding scar, Sethe's own "chokecherry tree" scar[29] and the scar from the saw on Beloved's neck become permanent signifiers of their identities, as well as signifiers of the trauma they experienced. These scars become symbolic of the identities constructed *for* them rather than by them, and because of their permanent nature, must be dealt with and given meaning in order to reclaim their identity and move forward. Sethe must learn to own her scars in order to redefine and reclaim her identity as a free woman, and more importantly as a free mother. Unfortunately, in order to own the scars, the traumatic memories of their infliction must be remembered, relived, and retold.

Sethe's powerful childhood memories serve as a psychological grounding for her own struggle toward motherhood. Sethe is not familiar with how to form an adequate or healthy motherly bond because she was denied that luxury. Her only understanding of a relationship similar to motherhood is one of slave ownership and chosen property. The issue of claiming a child is similar to an issue of choice: to claim a child is to actively choose to be a mother. From this arises the motif of the chosen child; Sethe was the only child her

28. Morrison, *Beloved*, 74.
29. Morrison, *Beloved*, 93.

mother wanted, having been born out of love, the rest she abandoned or killed in her own acts of infanticide. If the inherent issue of race were not present in the plot, the dilemma the reader is faced with is an ethical animal all its own. Sethe is not condemned because she is a Black slave woman who chose merciful death for her child, but rather she is condemned and ostracized by her African American community because she chose to try to love *all* of her children. During a time that a child was not a blessing but a cursed innocent born into a system of exploitation and suffering, to desire such deep emotional attachment(s) was to leave yourself vulnerable to inevitable pain and future trauma.

Motherhood then, the act of providing, sustaining, and protecting the lives of one's children, is a struggle for many of the women in *Beloved* because it requires the naming and claiming, nurturing and protecting of another external thing by women who grew up unable to define or protect identities of their own. Dealing with the recurring traumatic memories and trying to keep *oneself* sanely intact is enough of a burden for Morrison's freed women; the thought of investing emotion in something external was an unwelcome danger in their nineteenth-century slave lives. There is a fine line between the "too thick"[30] love that Sethe feels for her children, and the lack of connection between Ella and her child, or Sethe's mother and her other children, for example. Because Sethe is willing to externally invest her love in the lives of her children, she is othered among her community of women who survived their childhoods as unloved orphans, and who struggle with their inability to take on the role of motherhood. Sethe is faulted for her differing opinions on "maternal nurturance" which is "situated as a political act that seeks to defy two different, although intersecting ideologies: the first deems black children as nonsubjects and the second defines slave mothers as breeders and so not mothers."[31] Despite her limited maternal experience, Sethe chooses to reject these ideologies and navigate motherhood on her own terms. Sethe has had four children, born out of love, that she hopes to nurture, raise, and protect. Her peers cannot comprehend these hopes for not just the survival, but the happiness of her children, thus Sethe is othered for her "too thick" attempts at mother love. Not until Sethe herself descends into madness do the community of women realize their long-standing motherhood potential and come to nurture and protect her—despite their own traumatic bouts with motherhood.

30. Morrison, *Beloved*, 193.

31. O'Reilly, *Toni Morrison*, 127.

Bibliography

Alexandru, Maria-Sabina Draga. "Love as Reclamation in Toni Morrison's African American Rhetoric." *European Journal of American Culture* 27, no. 3 (2008): 191–205.

Beauchamp, Gorman. "Art and the Ambiguity of Terrorism: 'Benito Cereno' to the Death of Klinghoffer." *Southwest Review* 100, no. 3 (2015): 371–403. ProQuest.

Burrows, Victoria. *Whiteness and Trauma: The Mother-Daughter Knot in the Fiction of Jean Rhys, Jamaica Kincaid, and Toni Morrison*. Basingstoke: Palgrave Macmillan, 2004.

Caruth, Cathy. "Unclaimed Experience: Trauma and the Possibility of History." *Yale French Studies* 79 (1991): 181–92.

Cutter, Martha J. "The Story Must Go On and On: The Fantastic, Narration, and Intertextuality in Toni Morrison's *Beloved* and *Jazz*." *African American Review* 1 (2000): 61–75.

Demetrakopoulos, Stephanie A. "Maternal Bonds as Devourers of Women's Individuation in Toni Morrison's *Beloved*." *African American Review* 26, no. 1 (1992): 51–59.

Durkin, Anita. "Object Written, Written Object: Slavery, Scarring, and Complications of Authorship in *Beloved*." *African American Review* 3 (2007): 541–56.

Fuston-White, Jeanna. "'From the Seen to the Told': The Construction of Subjectivity in Toni Morrison's *Beloved*." *African American Review* 36, no. 3 (Autumn 2002): 461–73. JSTOR.

Handley, William R. "The House a Ghost Built: *Nommo*, Allegory, and the Ethics of Reading in Toni Morrison's *Beloved*." *Contemporary Literature* 4 (1995): 676–701. Literature Resource Center.

Morgenstern, Naomi. "Mother's Milk and Sister's Blood: Trauma and the Neoslave Narrative." *Differences: A Journal of Feminist Cultural Studies* 8, no. 2 (1996): 101–26. MLA International Bibliography.

Morrison, Toni. *Beloved*. New York: Vintage, 2004.

———. *Playing in the Dark: Whiteness and the Literary Imagination*. New York: Vintage, 1993.

———. "Unspeakable Things Unspoken: The Afro-American Presence in American Literature." *Toni Morrison: Modern Critical Views*, edited by Harold Bloom, 201–30. New York: Chelsea House Publishers, 1990.

O'Reilly, Andrea. *Toni Morrison and Motherhood: A Politics of the Heart.* Albany: State University of New York Press, 2004.

Stone, Rebecca. "Can the Breast Feed the Mother Too? Tracing Maternal Subjectivity in Toni Morrison's *Beloved.*" *British Journal of Psychotherapy* 31, no. 3 (2015): 298–310.

Travis, Molly Abel. "Beyond Empathy: Narrative Distancing and Ethics in Toni Morrison's *Beloved* and J. M. Coetzee's *Disgrace.*" *Journal of Narrative Theory* 40, no. 2 (2010): 231–50.

Gabriella Greco received her MA from Stony Brook University in 2016 and is currently a PhD candidate of English at St. John's University in Queens, New York, and an adjunct professor at St. Joseph's College in Long Island. This project was adapted from her Master's thesis, which focused more broadly on themes of ownership and motherhood across Morrison's *Beloved.*

Part III

Subverting the Matriarch Archetype

FROM MAMMIES TO SOUTHERN BELLES
Redefining Southern Matriarchy in Sherley Anne Williams's *Dessa Rose*

Ashley Burge

Harriet Jacobs begins her harrowing sentimental slave narrative *Incidents in the Life of a Slave Girl* with a vivid description of the intricacies apparent in interracial relationships between White children and Black wet nurses on southern plantations. As she traces her familial upbringings from happy, though naive, delusion to stark detriment, she recalls her grandmother and mother's role within the White household: "My mother's mistress was the daughter of my grandmother's mistress."[1] She continues, "They were both nourished at my grandmother's breast. In fact, my mother had been weaned at three months old, that the babe of the mistress might obtain sufficient food." Though Jacobs never utters the word "mammy" in her narrative, in this concise description she both introduces the pervasiveness of this role on antebellum plantations while simultaneously contesting the veracity of its portrayal. It was commonplace for the Black children of enslaved wet nurses to go without so the slaveholder's White children could flourish both physically and emotionally through the bonds of Black female surrogacy. What Jacobs contests more than the reality of this role on antebellum plantations is the southern mythology that the mammy reveled in this forced devotion to her White charges at the expense of her own children, who withered in lack. Popular media representations of the mammy figure have cemented these ideologies in the American psyche to the detriment of Black womanhood and Black motherhood. Films such as *Gone with the Wind* (1936) portray Black women, like the nameless character only designated as "Mammy," as fiercely devoted to White superiority, subservient, sassy, self-sacrificing, and one-dimensional. The film's romanticized Black female servant parallels the female character birthed out of the imagination

1. Harriet Jacobs, *Incidents in the Life of a Slave Girl* (New York: Dover Publications, 2001), 10.

of Margaret Mitchell's novel of the same name. These media representations, however, only gave mass appeal to the detrimental stereotypes that were already existent in the mythology of the Old South. As Kimberly Wallace-Andrews argues, "The success of their portrayals was predicated upon its [the mammy figure] being deeply embedded within the popular imagination long before *Gone with the Wind* opened in Atlanta in 1936."[2]

Despite the pervasiveness of the mammy caricature in American media and literary discourse, African American slave narrative and neo-slave narrative authors have consistently, and effectively, countered these White supremacist patriarchal narratives by crafting revisionist histories that give enslaved Blacks voice and agency within the confines of the tyrannical system of slavery. Elizabeth Ann Beaulieu posits that "neo-slave narratives depend on the historical reclamation efforts of slave narrative scholars and contribute to attempts to revise history to include the perspective of enslaved Americans."[3] Like Jacobs before her, Sherley Anne Williams engages in this mode of reclamation in her neo-slave narrative *Dessa Rose* (1987). By deconstructing the mammy figure through the interactions of the titular character, Dessa Rose, and her would-be mistress, Ruth Elizabeth, Williams reconfigures Black motherhood and subverts ideologies that have consistently silenced the voices of Black women. Throughout the narrative, Williams attacks two major tropes used to reify race, class, and gender stereotypes in southern mythology: the mammy figure and the southern belle. While the mammy figure caricature has historically been used to define the parameters of race, class, and gender in the White household, the southern belle trope has been used to further define these parameters while simultaneously elevating the racial and maternal superiority of the White mistress. In *Dessa Rose*, Williams discredits both caricatures by reconfiguring the racial and gender norms that customarily reinforce the role of the mammy on the antebellum plantation. One of Williams's primary aims in *Dessa Rose* is to rebuff and reclaim the fragmented mammy character in ways that engender Black female subjectivity. Further, she uses the deconstructed role of the mammy figure as a transitional figure that engenders a unique family structure in *Dessa Rose*, which transcends the racial and class barriers between the fugitive Black runaways and the White mistress that inhabit the rural Alabama plantation of Sutton Glenn.

2. Kimberly Wallace-Sanders, *Mammy: A Century of Race and Gender, and Southern Memory* (Ann Arbor: University of Michigan Press, 2008), 2.

3. Elizabeth Ann Beaulieu, *Black Women Writers and the American Neo-Slave Narrative: Femininity Unfettered* (Connecticut: Greenwood Press, 1999), xiv.

The mammy figure has been prevalent in the mythology of the antebellum South with its peak visualization coinciding with anti-abolition sentiments during the pre-Civil War and postbellum eras. Many early depictions of the Black mammy portray her as the caregiver, wet nurse, and nanny to the White children of slaveholders. In literary and autobiographical discourses of the times, White authors lamented the disintegration of White child/Black mammy dichotomies as an inevitable and detrimental consequence of the abolition of slavery. Many proponents of slavery used these interracial surrogacy relationships as proof that slavery was advantageous to both the slaveholder's offspring, who received comfort and care at the bosom of the Black mammy, and the Black mammy, whose natural predilection was to care for and nurture her superior White charges with complete devotion and self-sacrifice. According to Wallace-Sanders, proslavery authors use the images of the mammy figure to reflect, "a symbol of racial harmony within the slave system."[4] And these images were often demeaning and dehumanizing to Black women while they simultaneously validated White supremacy. Many visual and literary depictions of the mammy characterized her by the physical dimensions of her body, the color of her skin, and the subservient behavior she exhibited toward her master and mistress. Trudier Harris argues that descriptions of the mammy as a large Black woman affirms the "institutionalization of white power" when she states, "comforting images of black women were favored over others . . . images range from the large black women who keep black men in line for white Americans, to the very large black women who are eternally happy to be in the kitchen making pancakes for their white charges."[5] In further writings, Harris also critiques characteristics that many literary effigies have deemed as the epitome of the mammy figure. In her definitions of the varied embodiments of southern and northern maids, she argues, "The true southern maid is the mammy whose ineffective compromise in the home of the white mistress cause her to identify completely with the status quo; she believes within her heart in the rightness of the established order of which she is a part. She has lost her black cultural identity (if she ever had one) and all sense of spiritual identification with black people."[6] Indeed, these types of "ideal" mammy figures are scattered throughout various works

4. Wallace-Sanders, *Mammy,* 13.

5. Trudier Harris, *Saints, Sinners, Saviors: Strong Black Women in African American Literature* (New York: Palgrave, 2001), 2.

6. Trudier Harris, *From Mammies to Militants: Domestics in Black American Literature* (Philadelphia: Temple University Press, 1982), 24.

of African American and American literature from Toni Morrison's character Pauline Breedlove in *The Bluest Eye* to Harriet Beecher Stowe's Chloe in *Uncle Tom's Cabin*. These images have been manufactured infinitely in various forms of American literary and cultural expressions and have, consequently, pigeonholed Black women into what Patricia Hill Collins calls "controlling images." According to Collins, images such as those of "stereotypical mammies," "matriarchs," and "hot mamas" only further perpetuate and justify the oppression of Black women in America because they allow racism and sexism to appear natural.[7] Though these Black caricatures persistently reify the oppressed status of Black women, exaggerated White caricatures such as the southern belle also aid in solidifying their existence in the American imagination.

The southern belle archetype has also been firmly situated in the essentialism of the Old South. Alexis Girardin Brown defines the ideal southern belle as "an endearing image, encompassing visions of delicacy, gentility, and hospitality within the domestic sphere of the household."[8] This archetype was both advantageous and detrimental to White women because it enabled them a certain amount of agency in southern society, but only in the realm where their superiority was bolstered by the inferiority of Black women. In American patriarchal society, sexist ideologies have historically oppressed White women and limited their access to the same privileges and rights that their White counterparts freely possess. In order to sustain some semblance of agency, images such as that of the southern belle were used to elevate the superiority of White womanhood, especially in the domestic sphere. bell hooks illuminates these race dynamics as she critiques the paradoxical status of White women and Black men in the American patriarchal system: "White women and black men have it both ways. They can act as oppressor or be oppressed. . . . White women may be victimized by sexism, but racism enable them to act as exploiters and oppressors of black people."[9] hooks's theory is especially apt when considering the rigid race, class, and gender dynamics of the antebellum period. The romanticized South dictated a caste system that oppressed some while validating others, and those that defined these roles enforced them with laws and codes that elevated the superiority of Whiteness. According to Brown, these gender and racial stratifications

7. Patricia Hill Collins, *Black Feminist Thought: Knowledge, Consciousness, and the Politics of Empowerment* (New York: Routledge, 1990), 69.

8. Alexis Girardin Brown, "The Women Left Behind: Transformation of the Southern Belle, 1840–1880," *The Historian* 62, no. 4 (2000): 759.

9. bell hooks, *Feminist Theory: From Margin to Center* (Boston: South End Press, 1984), 15.

"served to socialize both men and women into their appropriate spheres. The private sphere of women embraced femininity, beauty, simplicity, and submissiveness; the highest roles to which a southern woman could aspire were those of nurturing mother, dutiful wife, and social moral pillars."[10] Caricatures of the ideal White mistress and matriarch paralleled those of the southern belle at the expense of the Black mammy. Though Black women were forced into the domestic realm as dutiful surrogate mothers and nannies to White children, they were denied the validation associated with the noble femininity of the southern belle and matriarch. This was true even in cases where Black women were caretakers and nurturers of their own children. Further, because the Black mammy was denied access to the maternal realm, her very existence as the demeaned Black mammy solidified the veracity of the southern belle. This is analogous to Toni Morrison's argument that Whiteness is constructed as a consequence of the construction of Blackness in that "blackness and enslavement could be found not only in the not-free but also, with the dramatic polarity created by skin color, the projection of the not-me."[11] In the context of this argument, the southern belle archetype is often bolstered in opposition to the dehumanized portrayal of the Black mammy. Though Williams acknowledges and portrays both caricatures in *Dessa Rose*, she progressively deconstructs and reconfigures them through her portrayal of the formerly enslaved Dessa Rose and Ruth Elizabeth, known as Rufel, a White woman who is portrayed as an "antibelle," which is the antithesis of the romanticized southern belle trope, a construct that I will expand as I deconstruct the caricature. Using the mammy figure as a transitional figure, Williams transcends the roles of race, gender, and class in the antebellum south in order to forge a new type of family unit that defies the injustices of slavery.

Dessa Rose tells the story of the titular character, Odessa Rose, from three different perspectives and modes of narration. Williams captures Dessa's complex persona by tracing her journey from enslavement to freedom in three different sections of the work: "The Darky," "The Wench," and "The Negress." In each section, Dessa's character evolves as she encounters various people that either aid or hinder her as she attempts to emancipate herself from slavery. The first section begins shortly after Dessa attacks her master, who brutally killed the love of her life and husband, Kaine. Dessa, who is pregnant during the tragic scenario, is promptly sold and confined to a coffle

10. Brown, "The Women Left Behind," 759.

11. Toni Morrison, *Playing in the Dark: Whiteness and the Literary Imagination* (New York: Vintage, 119), 38.

with several other fugitive slaves. Though she is far along in her pregnancy, Dessa leads a revolt with her fellow coffle-mates and kills several White men. Dessa and her accomplices are captured, with the offending males hanged. Dessa is spared, however, because her value is intertwined with that of her unborn child, who will be sold once she delivers. After the delivery, her death is imminent. While she awaits her fate, Dessa is confined to a cellar where an opportunist, Adam Nehemiah, attempts to appropriate her story for wealth and fame in the aristocratic southern circles. In the second section, Dessa is rescued by two of her former coffle-mates, Nathan and Harker. As they flee, Dessa delivers her baby and Nathan and Harker transport Dessa and the newborn to Sutton Glen plantation where the matriarch, known by her pet name, Rufel, has been harboring runaway slaves in order to survive in the absence of her wayward husband. The second section and the final section portray the symbiotic relationship forged by Dessa, Rufel, Nathan, and Harker as they attempt to overcome the limitations of their respective race, class, and gender status in rural Alabama. In both sections, Williams portrays the burgeoning relationship between Dessa and Rufel as a transcendent bond that subverts race and class social norms of the antebellum era. The success of their relationship, however, is largely predicated upon undermining oppressive images that plague individual subjectivity, like that of the southern belle.

Williams meticulously crafts Rufel's persona as that of a southern aristocrat living lavishly in a rural Alabama town only to progressively expose its inconsistencies with the southern belle archetype. Initially, Rufel experiences the privileges of southern nobility as a debutante in Charleston, South Carolina. Born into a prosperous, well-respected family in the cotton industry, Rufel is given access to all the graces of southern gentility. Though she is not a "brilliant match," with her sister being the more attractive of the two, she is expected to do well, marry up, and carry on the tradition and heritage of the Old South. Once Rufel arrives in rural Alabama, she expects her affluent background to guarantee her unmitigated access to the aristocratic social circles, especially since she looks and acts the part. Rufel's physical attributes are reminiscent of a stock southern belle character, created to highlight the delicate femininity, purity, and beauty of the caricature. Williams depicts her in ways that simultaneously highlight and mock the one-dimensional portrayals of southern White women. When Dessa awakens from a coma-like sleep and finds herself in Rufel's bed, she makes note of Rufel's face, which "was very white and seemed to radiate a milky glow."[12] However, to counter

12. Sherley Anne Williams, *Dessa Rose* (New York: William Morrow, 2018), 86.

this superficial trope, Williams later contests, "Sometimes it seemed to Dessa that she was drowning in that milky skin."[13]

Rufel's interactions with the formerly enslaved tenants of Sutton Glenn plantation also suggest that she has been indoctrinated by standard racial and social norms of the antebellum south. She is aware of the privileges associated with her Whiteness and she expects the former enslaved people to adhere to spoken and unspoken racial codes. This is glaringly apparent with her interactions with Annabelle, the mentally disabled daughter of another enslaved person living with Rufel. As Rufel prattles on about balls, fashion, and hairstyles, the girl furtively retreats into the hallway to escape her frivolous conversation. Rufel's response reflects the entitled superiority that she wields in the midst of enslaved Blacks: "Why—I'm telling you more joy and, and happiness, yes! and excitement, too, than you can ever imagine in that paltry black hide. Nigger."[14] As the girl moves closer and closer into the hallway, Rufel snaps, "You know you don't just walk away from a white person without a by-your-leave." In these early interactions between Rufel and the formerly enslaved people on her plantation, she embodies the stereotypical southern belle caricature that relies on race and class codes, like the "by-your-leave" rule, to order the social and cultural interactions around her. In order to solidify her status as southern belle and matriarch in the plantation home, she must demand that Blacks are confined to a dehumanized lower class status in which they blindly adhere to these unspoken codes, thus validating the social order of the South. Further, by contrasting her life of "joy," "happiness," and "excitement" to the unimaginable life that Annabelle must endure, she designates the appropriate spheres that were customary for genteel southern women. Balls that symbolized "coming out" events where the beauty and femininity of White women were celebrated would be incongruous to the lifestyle of an enslaved Black woman, who would toil in the kitchen and the field in servitude to White families. In this instance, the role of the southern belle is validated and elevated in the midst of an oppositional Black enslaved person.

Though Williams acknowledges the tenacious presence of the southern belle caricature, she methodically undermines it by uncovering the gender and class limitations that define Rufel's existence in her small rural town. The facade begins to slowly fade as Rufel relinquishes her domestic sphere to Dessa and her Black tenants who have found a haven at Sutton Glenn. Dessa quickly learns that the runaways call her "Miz Ruint" to reflect the plethora of misfortunes

13. Williams, *Dessa Rose,* 117.

14. Williams, *Dessa Rose,* 99.

that she endures at her modest plantations. Through the characterization of Miz Ruint, Williams undermines the southern belle trope by creating the antibelle. Once again, she acknowledges the parameters of this one-dimensional caricature only to mock and subvert it. Williams does this convincingly by eroding three major constructs of southern nobility: the plantation home, the aristocratic society, and the devoted slave. The plantation home has historically been a staple in the romanticized Old South because it reflects the wealth and nobility of White families. This is especially pertinent for the southern matriarch because the domestic sphere was designated as her dominion. However, Rufel's time at Sutton Glenn is only marked by heartbreak and disappointment. Her husband, Bertie, whisks her away from Charleston with promises of a gallant South that he cannot produce because of his restless spirit and gambling problem. Bertie promptly buys land to cultivate and builds a Georgian plantation only to leave both behind with his estranged wife. Rufel's position is greatly diminished because her housemates know she is a fraud who is barely surviving. Ada, a formerly enslaved fugitive, poignantly relays this to Dessa as she explains the arrangements on the plantation: "We runned away. . . . She let us stay here; she need the he'p. Man gone; slaves runned off."[15] She continues, "Tell you honey, these some poor white peoples. Oh this room and the parlor fine enough, but you know what's outside that door? A great big stairway lead straight up to nothing cause they never did finish the second floor."

Rufel's antibelle status is even more apparent in her interactions with the formerly enslaved people who live with her. Though she initially demands that they treat her with the blind reverence of other southern Whites, her vulnerable status dictates the reality of their relationship. Ada reminds Rufel of this after she has an intense exchange with her daughter, Annabelle: "Shaken and angered by the incident, Rufel had complained to Ada. And Ada, while allowing that the girl was slow and oftentimes silly, had defended her, reminding Rufel in that abrupt way she had that neither belonged to her, that in fact they did her a favor by working for her at all!"[16] Without the devotion of Black slaves, or a grand plantation home, or a husband to solidify her status in the southern sphere, Rufel's character contradicts the clichéd archetype of the southern belle. Williams subverts this caricature in order to uncover the foundations of its prevalence: a culture fortified by the demeaning institution of American slavery. Every facet of antebellum southern culture correlates with the exploitation of African American slave labor—the plantation

15. Williams, *Dessa Rose,* 116.

16. Williams, *Dessa Rose,* 100.

homes, the wealth of southern aristocrats, and the rigid social norms that reinforce White supremacy all fueled the romanticization of the Old South. By challenging the validity of the southern belle, Williams challenges the very foundation of southern culture and its exploitation and dehumanization of enslaved Blacks. Further, by challenging the parameters of the stereotypical southern belle archetype, Williams reveals other fragmentations that connect to gender, race, and class confines. Rufel cannot trust in her Whiteness to survive in the rural South because her vulnerability lies in her diminished status as a poor White woman in a society ruled by prosperous White men. Once Williams deconstructs the archetype, she is able to forge a reconfigured southern matriarch that transcends race and class in the antebellum south. She does this through her manipulation of the mammy figure.

Initially, the mammy figure is manifested through Rufel's distorted image of Black female servitude. In standard paternalistic fashion, Rufel constructs her mammy's persona only in ways that elevate her White superiority and validation in southern society. Though Rufel is an antibelle, she fabricates a memory of southern gentility through the one-dimensional caricature of her Black mammy. Rufel even appropriates her mammy's history to align with the narrative of the southern mammy trope. Though her mammy was initially a servant for a family in France, Rufel disregards this information and deceivingly tells people that she has been in her family for some time and was given to Rufel as a wedding gift. When Dessa arrives at Sutton Glenn plantation, Rufel's mammy has just died, and with her the last visage of Rufel's imagined southern aristocracy. Rufel frequently reverts to memories of her mammy to cope with the inconsistencies and ambiguities of her life as a single, impoverished woman in an unfinished southern plantation. She placates her tragedy by ruminating on the comforting images of her mammy. This is especially true when Rufel attempts to mollify herself in the presence of Dessa, who she is initially intimidated and intrigued by. In her first encounters with Dessa, she contemplates the veracity of the nickname that the other former enslaved Blacks have given her, "the devil woman." Williams writes,

> What could there be to fear in this one little sickly, colored gal? Oh, she was wild enough to have some kind of devil in her, Rufel would think, smiling, remembering the way the girl's eyes had bucked the first time she awakened in the bedroom, just the way Mammy's used to when something frightened her. Mammy, Mammy's hands in her hair—Sudden longing pierced Rufel. Mammy's voice: "Aw, Miz 'Fel"; that was special, extra loving, extra.[17]

17. Williams, *Dessa Rose,* 93.

Here Williams reveals how Rufel uses the mammy stereotype to make sense of her interactions with other Black women. Rufel has created a monolithic caricature that she projects onto all Black women, which evokes Collins's "controlling images" that continually prevent female Black subjectivity. This is even more apparent in her internal constructions of mammy's persona. In her purview, mammy is not a separate entity. Her validity as an individual is predicated upon how Rufel defines her in her psyche. As she revels in her stupor of deception, she sees mammy as "almost an extension of herself."[18] In this instance, mammy's distinct characterization is irrelevant as her figure is only used to bolster Rufel's manufactured persona.

Williams simultaneously discredits the manufactured Black mammy while reconfiguring its construction to promote Black female subjectivity. In this instance, Williams uses the redefined mammy as a transitional figure that leads to a type of reconciliation between southern matriarchy and Black subjectivity. Williams uses the initially contentious relationship between Dessa and Rufel as a platform to renegotiate the construct of the Black mammy. She orchestrates this exchange as Dessa is forced into intimate interactions with Rufel. The women sleep together in the same bed in Rufel's room because Dessa is sickly after she has given birth. Their sleeping arrangements are also necessitated by the needs of Dessa's newborn. Dessa is unable to breastfeed her baby, Desmond, and, to her chagrin, she must depend on Rufel to breastfeed her baby along with Rufel's own daughter. Dessa is both shocked and unnerved by this arrangement and her frustrations reach their limit in a pivotal scene between Dessa and Rufel. As Rufel has customarily done throughout the narrative, she reverts to Charleston society, gowns, fashion, and the comforting images of the mammy figure to entertain herself and bolster her superiority before her Black tenants. Dessa, weak and indifferent, suddenly becomes enraged and confused as Rufel begins to describe her relationship with Mammy. Her construction of this maternal figure is incongruous to everything Dessa's own mammy, who is her biological mother, represents. As Rufel continues her fabrications, Dessa thinks, "No white woman like this had ever figured in mammy's conversations. . . . And this would have been something to talk about: dinner and gowns—not just plain dresses."[19] Dessa balks at the fact that Rufel would confine Mammy to such a superficial role. Before she continues with her tales of ball gowns and fashion, Dessa snaps, "Mammy

18. Williams, *Dessa Rose,* 146.

19. Williams, *Dessa Rose,* 117.

ain't made you nothing!"[20] Though Rufel aggressively protests, Dessa retorts, "Mammy ain't nobody name, not they real one."[21] Dessa vehemently rejects that the forced relationship between the entitled White women and her enslaved nanny was anything but the exploitation of Black female servitude. She further undermines the Black mammy caricature by acknowledging and validating Mammy's role as a caregiver and nurturer to her own children, a role that was often denied in constructions of Black maternity. Rufel continues to prove the veracity of the White child/Black mammy dichotomy by arguing, "She just had me! I was like her child." Williams counters this statement by illuminating a more accurate image of Black maternity through Dessa's construction of Mammy's history. Williams writes,

> Mammy gave birth to ten chi'ren that come in the world living. . . . The first one Rose after herself; the second one died before the white folks named it. Mammy called her Minta after a cousin she met once. Seth was the first child lived to go into the fields. Little Rose died while mammy was carrying Amos—carried off by the diphtheria. Thank God, He spared Seth.[22]

In this instance, Williams creates a revisionist history that denounces the master narrative and subverts the White child/Black mammy dichotomy. Here Dessa elevates and validates Black maternity through the reconfiguration of her mammy's narrative. Dessa's revelation also creates a form of self-definition and subjectivity that was denied to Mammy when she was exploited in Rufel's White household. Even Rufel does not dismiss these new revelations of Black subjectivity. They, consequently, prompt her to question the nature of her own relationship with her mammy. "Had mammy had children?" she asks herself. Had she "suckled a child at her breast?" she wonders. And further had they been taken away?[23] In turmoil, she fearfully asks herself the question that fractures her fabricated relationship with Mammy: "How could you love someone who used you so?"[24] In this existential moment, Rufel realizes that the image she has created of Mammy is self-serving and false, only created to uphold the demeaning social constructs that have also hindered Rufel's subjectivity.

20. Williams, *Dessa Rose,* 118.
21. Williams, *Dessa Rose,* 119.
22. Williams, *Dessa Rose,* 119.
23. Williams, *Dessa Rose,* 128.
24. Williams, *Dessa Rose,* 143.

Williams portrays this reconfigured mammy character as a transitional figure that engenders a redefined southern matriarch that transcends race and class barriers and creates a family unit that can withstand the detriments of the antebellum south. Williams accomplishes this primarily through inversions and subversions of social and familial norms on Sutton Glenn plantation. This is most evidently reflected in Rufel's necessitated maternal instincts toward Dessa and her newborn son Desmond. Because Dessa is incapacitated for a significant amount of time when she first arrives at Sutton Glenn, Rufel must act as wet nurse to Desmond to ensure his viability. When Dessa's cofflemates transport her to Sutton Glenn, thrashing and volatile, Rufel is encumbered with sympathy for her and her crying child. Without thought, she takes the child and nurses him to comfort. Though nursing a Black child is initially arbitrary to Rufel, she progressively gleans the weight of the action once she bonds with the infant. As she reflects on the act in light of its cultural and social diversions, she is empowered by the fact that she acts of her own volition despite the racial norms of the times. She thinks,

> She shouldn't have done it; Rufel had been over that countless times, also. If anybody ever found out. If they had been followed. But nothing of that had entered her head as she picked her way carefully up the steep back steps, the baby hugged close to her body. The girl's desolate face, the baby's thin crying—as though it had given up all hope—had grated her; she was a little crazy, she supposed. But she could do something about this, about the baby who continued to cry. . . . She—Rufel—could do something.[25]

Williams uses Rufel's cross-racial breastfeeding as a pivotal moment that symbolizes Rufel's evolution in the narrative. In this inverse mammy interaction, Rufel taps into her humanity while simultaneously discrediting the dehumanization of Black people. Choosing to breastfeed a hungry child, despite society sanctioned race and class chasms, reflects her evolved status as not merely a one-dimensional southern belle caricature but an evolved southern matriarch with the capacity to empathize with the plight of the formerly enslaved Blacks on her plantation. Though she initially defines her Black tenants as "darkies" that are a necessary evil to uplift herself in southern society, after her transformative bond with Dessa and Desmond, Ada notes that "where white people look at black and see something ugly, something hateful, she [Rufel] saw color."[26] The redefined mammy construct is the transitional

25. Williams, *Dessa Rose,* 95.

26. Williams, *Dessa Rose,* 170.

figure that allows Rufel, Dessa, and the other fugitive enslaved people to bond and form distinct relationships that mirror the foundations of a family unit.

Though Dessa is initially heartbroken that she must depend on Rufel to nurse her child and equally unnerved that Rufel enters into a romantic relationship with Nathan, who she likens to a brother, she cannot disregard the survival opportunities that Rufel offers to her, her coffle-mates, and her baby at Sutton Glenn plantation. Similarly, Rufel is grateful to find support and value in a makeshift family that does not reify the constricting caste system of the antebellum South. Their symbiotic relationships are further reinforced as Rufel, Dessa, Harker, and Nathan devise a dangerous scheme to disguise themselves as White mistress, Black mammy, and Black studs to counterfeit the institution of slavery by selling themselves back into slavery only to escape and continue the con for financial profit. In this scenario, Williams continues to subvert the race and class conventions of the antebellum South by using the very devices of stratification that discredit the institution of slavery.

Williams uses reconfigurations of the southern belle and the mammy figure to redefine southern matriarchy as a tool to emancipate individuals from the limitations of race and class constructs. The emancipated Mammy figure is the key component to understanding the evolution of southern maternity in *Dessa Rose*. By using the reconceived mammy figure as a catalyst that engenders the transcendent family unit exhibited by Rufel, Dessa, and the other fugitive enslaved people, Williams authenticates Black motherhood and Black womanhood in the midst of an inequitable system of oppression.

Bibliography

Beaulieu, Elizabeth Ann. *Black Women Writers and the American Neo-Slave Narrative: Femininity Unfettered.* Connecticut: Greenwood Press, 1999.

Brown, Alexis Girardin. "The Women Left Behind: Transformation of the Southern Belle, 1840–1880." *The Historian* 62, no. 4 (2000): 759–778.

Collins, Patricia Hill. *Black Feminist Thought: Knowledge, Consciousness, and the Politics of Empowerment.* New York: Routledge, 1990.

Harris, Trudier. *From Mammies to Militants: Domestics in Black American Literature*. Philadelphia: Temple University Press, 1982.

———. *Saints, Sinners, and Saviors: Strong Black Women in African American Literature*. New York: Palgrave, 2002.

hooks, bell. *Feminist Theory from Margin to Center*. Boston: South End Press, 1984.

Jacobs, Harriet. *Incidents in the Life of a Slave Girl.* New York: Dover Publications, 2001.

Morrison, Toni. *Playing in the Dark: Whiteness and the Literary Imagination.* New York: Vintage Books, 1992.

Wallace-Sanders, Kimberly. *Mammy: A Century of Race and Gender, and Southern Memory.* Ann Arbor: University of Michigan Press, 2008.

Williams, Sherley Anne. *Dessa Rose.* New York: William Morrow, 2018.

Ashley Burge received her PhD from the University of Alabama in English literature with a concentration in African American literature. Her research focuses on race, gender, class, and sexuality, with prominent emphases on civil rights, social justice, Black feminism, and ecocriticism. She completed her dissertation on the works of Toni Morrison and several of her contemporaries, and she is currently transforming it into a book-length manuscript. The manuscript articulates a theoretical paradigm that uses Morrison's oeuvre as a pathway to convert trauma into healing, redemption, and liberation. She has published articles in the *North Carolina Literary Review* and the *Encyclopedia of African American Culture*. Her other current projects include an upcoming book chapter in *MLA Approaches to Teaching Harriet Jacobs.*

Rebels of Southern Womanhood
Faulkner's Depictions of Unconventional Matriarchs

Austin Svedjan

Considered by many to be *the* pillar of post-Reconstruction southern literature, William Faulkner's oeuvre presents women, as Kelly Reams notes in her book *Women and Race in Contemporary U.S. Writing*, "as the bearers of culture; they maintain its artifact and pass down its oral history."[1] While this duty of upholding one's culture and sustaining its history may at first seem—albeit superficially—noble, the burden placed upon southern women concurrently deprives them of their agency as fully realized subjects. The epitome of this restricted womanhood can be found in Faulkner's matriarchs, who find themselves tasked with preserving, and often personifying, southern identitarian structures, but remain unable to reap its benefits. In this regard, Faulkner's depictions of southern womanhood remain largely a reflection of the sociocultural conservatism of his time. However, there are numerous portrayals of matriarchs present in his works who all in some way subvert the societal norms of their, and Faulkner's, environment. In particular, the instances in which this subversion is made most apparent can be found when the women occupy spaces of societal otherness, either in facets of their race, class, or sexuality.

Dilsey of *The Sound and the Fury* (1929)

In his breakout novel, *The Sound and the Fury*, Faulkner introduces the reader to the Compson family, formally headed by the middle-aged blue blood Caroline. It does not require a close reading for one to quickly discern that Caroline is not, however, the matriarch of the Compsons. Rather, the African American servant, Dilsey, arguably holds the most influence over the

1. Kelly Lynch Reames, *Women and Race in Contemporary U.S. Writing* (New York: Palgrave Macmillan, 2007), 46.

Compson children, and even over Caroline herself. While it has been long argued that Faulkner's idolization of Caroline's daughter, Caddy Compson, manifests itself in the lack of narrative voice, the placement of Dilsey as morally superior to those around her eventually renders her the character Faulkner appears most fond of. Phillip Weinstein perhaps asserts this best, noting that the "women in *The Sound and the Fury* . . . [are] essentially on display, dramatized not through any bond with others but through [their] impact on them. The exception is of course Dilsey."[2] In lieu of severing the bonds Dilsey has with those around her, Faulkner instead emphasizes Dilsey's ethical superiority almost exclusively in her interactions with the Compson children. One example of this can be found in an early, infamously chaotic section of the novel, wherein Dilsey instructs Caroline to "give [Benjy] a flower to hold. . . . That's what he wanting."[3] In this instance, Dilsey is starkly juxtaposed against Caroline as the only one with any intuition on how to best placate the youngest—cognitively disabled—Compson brother, Benjy—an ability that would typically be reserved for his mother. Although Dilsey occupies the same imposed domesticity as other matriarchs in the South, she ultimately destabilizes her White counterpart Caroline's matriarchal claim to the Compson family. This subversion operates to present a stark—though not necessarily binarist—contrast between genuine and faux matriarchy. While southern society traditionally associates motherhood and familial matriarchy with biological maternity, it consequently neglects the representations of matriarchy exhibited by women like Dilsey, who becomes a matriarch in her own right to a family not biologically hers. Although Caroline is, as Sally Page notes, "the ghastly embodiment of the destructiveness that results from the perversion of the mother's role," Dilsey, "on the other hand . . . is a matriarch, the source of life . . . and [is] the active mother of the Compsons."[4] Neo-antebellum society may indeed assess Caroline as the matriarch of the Compsons as a result of her genealogical maternity, but this maternity should not be conflated with relational motherhood. Dilsey, on the contrary, acts as the sole unifier in a family that would otherwise find themselves perpetually

2. Philip Weinstein, "Meditations on the Other: Faulkner's Rendering of Women," in *Faulkner and Women: Faulkner and Yoknapatawpha, 1985*, ed. by Doreen Fowler and Ann J. Abadie (Oxford: University of Mississippi Press, 1985), 85.

3. William Faulkner. *The Sound and the Fury: The Corrected Text* (New York: Vintage, 1990), 10.

4. Sally R. Page, *Faulkner's Women: Characterization and Meaning* (De Land, FL: Everett-Edwards, 1973), 180–81.

divided, thereby becoming a matriarch whose motherhood extends beyond the superficial realm of genetic lineage.

However, in order to fully acknowledge the matriarchy embodied by Dilsey, one must additionally contemplate the contextual implications of Dilsey as a character of servitude. Critics such as Deborah Clarke have argued that Dilsey is "more [of] a mammy than a mother,"[5] alleging that, "[Dilsey] cannot function as a mother to these children, not because she didn't give birth to them but because she lacks selfhood and power in a white racist world."[6] Despite this lack of access to larger, racialized, systems of power—a lack of access that, as I will argue, is shared by all of Faulkner's unconventional matriarchs in varying contexts—Dilsey *does* appear to wield some power in the dynamic of the Compson family. Southern writer and social critic Lillian Smith elucidates this contradictory relation to power for "mammy" figures nicely:

> Her role in the family was involved and of tangled contradictions. She always knew her "place," but neither she nor her employers could have defined it. She was given a limited authority, but it was elastic enough to stretch into dictatorship over not only children but the white mother and sometimes even the male head of the family.[7]

Smith's illumination of this duality of power within the family and oppression within general society certainly aligns with Faulkner's own depiction of Dilsey, who—while demanding obedience from the children and even at times from Caroline—can do very little systematically to actually enforce this obedience. Although she is not necessarily interchangeable with the nameless Mammy from *Gone with the Wind*, Dilsey is still barred from outwardly expressing any frustration toward the Compson family.[8] The only instance in which she does so, and the only instance in which her vague authority over the family is consequently questioned, is to protect Quentin Compson from her uncle, Jason, who thus chastises the family: "That's the trouble with nigger servants, when they've been with you for a long time they get so full of self-importance that they're not worth a damn. They think they run the

5. Deborah Clarke, "Erasing and Inventing Motherhood," in *Robbing the Mother: Women in Faulkner* (Oxford: University of Mississippi Press, 1994), 22.

6. Clarke, "Erasing and Inventing Motherhood," 33.

7. Lillian Smith, *Killer of the Dream* (New York: Doubleday, 1962), 110–11.

8. Kimberly Wallace-Sanders, *A Century of Race, Gender, and Southern Memory* (Ann Arbor: University of Michigan Press, 2008), 123.

whole family."[9] The issue with this criticism, however, is that the "run[ning] of the whole family" is not a duty that Dilsey necessarily desires, but is rather inscribed upon her due to an absence of any other matriarchal authority in the family. Though the reader should acknowledge critiques like Clarke's, and thereby recognize Dilsey's characterization as an idyllic, White vision of Black womanhood—which prioritizes servility and a nurturing demeanor—it is difficult to refute that Dilsey, despite being so entangled by White supremacist systems of power, rebels against the status quo of her position on the societal hierarchy, displaces Caroline in figural maternity, and consequently emerges as the matriarch of Faulkner's novel. Although she transgresses the bioessentialist and racist barriers of matriarchy, that is not to say that she supersedes racism completely. Sixteen years after *The Sound and the Fury*'s first publication, Faulkner added an appendix to the novel, which cataloged the happenings of the Compson family in those sixteen years hence. While the majority of entries are extensive, Dilsey's, by contrast, is reduced to two words: "They endured."[10] Though she may endure, there exists no avenue for a Black woman to truly prosper in the twentieth-century South—and arguably even today. As Diane Roberts notes, Dilsey "endures, but she does not escape."[11]

Faulkner's depiction of Dilsey in *The Sound and the Fury* acts as a symbol for the southern matriarchy he idealized. Rather than establishing her matriarchy on a biological familial relation, she instead becomes a matriarch through the forming of affective relationships of care for the Compson children. Although she acts as a mother for the Compsons, Dilsey still ultimately exists as a figure born from a culture continually plagued by Black subjugation. Her physical decline as a matriarch and a mammy mirrors the deterioration of the Old South itself and illustrates the integral role matriarchs play in maintaining a collective southern identity. As the Compson estate and legacy eventually fall into disarray, Dilsey's matriarchy—and thereby Faulkner's ideal South—endures.

Miss Reba of *The Reivers* (1962)

Another example of subversion of the traditional boundaries of matriarchy presented by Faulkner can be observed in the Memphis brothel madam,

9. Faulkner, *The Sound and the Fury*, 207.

10. Faulkner, *The Sound and the Fury*, 343.

11. Diane Roberts, *Faulkner and Southern Womanhood* (Athens: University of Georgia Press, 1994), 68.

Miss Reba. When initially thinking of prostitution, one may conjure visions of dark alleys and dirtied street corners; Miss Reba's brothel, however, challenges presumptions of a home/whorehouse binary. The atmospheric domesticity and Reba's role as matriarch in the brothel are best surmised by one of her first descriptions in the novel, from one of the sex workers in her care, Miss Corrie: "By the time you've known Miss Reba a few hours longer, you'll find out you done learned something else about ladies too: that when she suggests you do something, it's a good idea to do it while you're still deciding whether you're going to or not."[12] This assessment by Corrie does not so much place Reba in the role of a madam, but rather as a matriarch wielding authoritative power over those in her household. Although she does hold control over her house, Miss Reba also deeply cares for the women who live with her, and even protects them from her landlord/lover Mr. Binfold. When Mr. Binfold calls the women in the house "whores," Miss Reba immediately acts to defend the girls, swinging a bottle at him and proclaiming, "I can throw you out too. Don't think I won't. What the hell kind of language is that!"[13] Though Mr. Binfold holds financial dominance over the home as its landlord—and is generally granted more authority as a White man in the South—Miss Reba continually opposes such aggression toward those who she considers akin to daughters. Not unlike Dilsey, Reba is perpetually shown to be acting in the best interest of those she looks after.

While the bulk of Reba's description as a matriarch in the brothel lies in only one of the novel's chapters—it is clear her subversion of traditional matriarchy has left a lasting impression upon the novel's protagonist, Lucius. After Corrie's nephew, Otis, refuses to answer Reba's questions because of her position as a woman, Reba continues to ask him, refusing to concede to the young man. Lucius notes that Reba refuses to forfeit because

> Miss Reba was still fighting. Because women are wonderful. They can bear anything because they are wise enough to know that all you have to do with grief and trouble is just go on through them and come out on the other side. I think they can do this because they not only decline to dignify physical pain by taking it seriously, they have no sense of shame at the idea of being knocked out. She didn't quit, even then.[14]

12. William Faulkner, *The Reivers: A Reminiscence* (New York: Random House, 1962), 103.

13. Faulkner, *The Reivers,* 108.

14. Faulkner, *The Reivers,* 111.

Similar to his characterization of Dilsey, Faulkner affixes Reba's position as a matriarch to her aptitude to endure. Although Dilsey's endurance is directly related to the implications of her race, Reba also must endure as an untraditional woman in a conservative, patriarchal society. Like Lucius, the reader is intended to become enamored with Reba and her continuation of resistive defiance. By presenting matriarchs who rebel against the social norms so deeply intertwined with the cultural definitions of matriarch itself, Faulkner's hope for the matriarchy is that, like Reba, it will "come out the other side," reformed and relieved of its limitations on southern women.

Ruby Lamar of *Sanctuary* (1931)

While most of Faulkner's unconventional matriarchs become matriarchs unconsciously through their actions, Ruby Lamar represents one who wishes to attain traditional southern womanhood at all costs. The common-law wife of bootlegger Lee Goodwin and the mother of his child, Ruby is a former sex worker from Memphis who only desires to be a wife and mother of southern tradition.

Much in the same way he treats Dilsey, Faulkner first introduces Ruby as embodying the ethical qualities of a matriarch but nonetheless removed from the traditional aesthetics of southern maternity: "A woman stood at the stove. She wore a faded calico dress. About her naked ankles a worn pair of man's brogans; unlaced, flapped when she moved."[15] Although she is performing a culturally intelligible action of a matriarch, cooking, her drab appearance is what ultimately prevails in both the sentence's focus as well as her overall struggle toward matriarchy. Signified by the "faded" color of the dress and her modest shoes, Ruby's class clashes with her ability to acquiesce to the normative ideals—here via their aesthetic productions—of the southern matriarch. Faulkner develops this struggle further by juxtaposing Ruby with an affluent counterpart, Narcissa Sartoris. Perhaps the earliest example of the contrast between Ruby and Narcissa is in the description of their homes, the antebellum symbols of southern womanhood and maternity. While Narcissa "liv[es] in a big house with her son and the great aunt of her husband,"[16] where she is frequently depicted as roaming the gardens, Ruby's home, "the Old Frenchman Place," is decrepit and unkempt:

> The house was a gutted ruin rising gaunt and stark out of a grove of unpruned cedar trees. It was a landmark, known as the Old Frenchman place, built

15. William Faulkner, *Sanctuary* (New York: Random House, 1931), 8.

16. Faulkner, *Sanctuary*, 23.

> before the Civil War; a plantation home set in the middle of a tract of land; of cotton fields and gardens and lawns long since gone back to the jungle, which the people of the neighborhood had been pulling down piecemeal for firewood for fifty years or digging with secret and sporadic optimism for the gold which the builder was reputed to have buried somewhere about the place when Grant came through the county on his Vicksburg campaign.[17]

Although such physical descriptions of Ruby's poverty are not as abundant throughout the novel as in the expository portions, the restriction of her acceptance by society is still explicitly reflected through Narcissa's criticism of her brother, Horace Benbow, who acts as lawyer for Lee and a generally supportive figure for Ruby. When Narcissa refuses to take in the homeless Ruby, Horace begs for his sister to provide her refuge, lest she be turned away to the streets. Narcissa, however, remains unmoved by her brother's plea, answering that it "shouldn't be a hardship. She ought to be used to that."[18] Narcissa's perceived apathy toward Ruby then quickly develops into animosity: "I don't care how many women you have nor who they are. But I cannot have my brother mixed up with a woman people are talking about. . . . I don't see that it makes any different who [murdered Tommy]. The question is, are you going to stay mixed up with it?"[19] Although Lee did not murder Tommy, Narcissa recognizes here that the scandal attached to Ruby by being in proximity to Lee would call her own obedience to the classist aspects of southern womanhood into question. Through Narcissa's condemnation of Ruby, Faulkner displays the willingness for southern society to preserve and propagate an image of matriarchy directly correlated to class and to guard it against those who do not fit its strict form.

It is made overwhelmingly evident that Faulkner sympathizes with Ruby and her plight, insinuating that her morality and adherence to traditional ideals of womanhood make her a more righteous figure than those who are more customary matriarchs. Certainly, the reader is made to sympathize with Ruby as well, and Faulkner's most prolific tool for creating that sympathy is found in Ruby's devotion to her husband Lee. Perhaps the most apparent example of this is when Ruby recounts the time Lee was last in prison, noting that with no money for a lawyer she turns to sex work to avoid abandoning him:

17. Faulkner, *Sanctuary*, 8.
18. Faulkner, *Sanctuary*, 182.
19. Faulkner, *Sanctuary*, 184.

> I got him out of jail once that way. Out of Leavenworth, too. When they knew he was guilty . . . I got a job as a waitress . . . so I could see Lee every other Sunday afternoon. We decided to get a lawyer. . . . I hadn't told Lee how I was getting the lawyer. He thought I had saved some money. . . . So when Lee got out, we had nothing. He said we'd get married, but we couldn't afford to. And when I told him about the lawyer, he beat me.[20]

Despite her awareness to Lee's "guilt" and her experiences of abuse, Ruby's loyalty to Lee seems to be prioritized over the pursuit of her own self-preservation. Some critics have agreed with this idolization of spousal loyalty as well, such as Sally Page, who asserts that "the evil of [Ruby's] past life of prostitution has been negated by her loyal devotion to her common-law husband"[21] and that, "[in *Sanctuary*,] the alternative to Popeye's evil is to be found in the qualities of responsible motherhood which Ruby Goodwin embodies."[22] This assessment, while not only vilifying female sexuality, reinforces one of the most rigid of traditional ideals of southern matriarchy—unwavering obedience to one's husband. Although Lee Goodwin is a criminal and beats Ruby, she is still expected to stay will him; her "negation" of her "evil," as it were, is translated to enduring such abuse, which would be of hardly any import to her competency as a mother. Though her class prevents Ruby from formally attaining matriarchal recognition by general southern society, she may still be regarded as a matriarch by the reader due to her adherence to the traditionalist ideals of southern womanhood and maternity. That adherence, as venerated by Faulkner, functions to indict how the rigid model of matriarchy subjugates southern women. Her matriarchy is not contingent upon affective relationship to her child, but rather her acceptance of abuse by her husband. Thus, while Faulkner's depiction of Ruby Goodwin as a matriarch is unique in that it subverts and criticizes the classist restrictions on matriarchy, the basis of this subversion ultimately aligns itself with an equally nefarious belief that women must suffer even abuse in order to be regarded as a devoted wife and mother.

Temple Drake of *Requiem for a Nun* (1951)

For those born in the American South, it does not require intensive research to comprehend how pervasive moral and social conservatism is in the

20. Faulkner, *Sanctuary*, 276–78.
21. Page, *Faulkner's Women*, 72.
22. Page, *Faulkner's Women*, 87.

region. In Faulkner's time, such adherence to social tradition was even more extensive—especially in the policing and ritualization of the female body. To be a woman in the early twentieth century was to live in duality, women's worth as belles directly connected to their sexual virtue, while simultaneously being viewed as objects of desire by their male counterparts. Faulkner observes this sexual dyad himself in *Sanctuary* through the character of Miss Myrtle, who notes that "men just can[']t seem to take us and leave us for what we are. They make us what we are, then they expect us to be different. Expect us not to never look at another man, while they come and go as they please."[23] In this regard, southern womanhood is a quality of carnal restraint that later matured into sexual domestication, in which it was a matriarch's responsibility to look after all domestic matters, fulfill the desires of a husband, and further perpetuate those customs of southern womanhood onto her children.

Unlike Faulkner's other matriarchs, Temple Drake—who appears as a sexually traumatized debutante in *Sanctuary* and later as a despondent wife and mother in *Requiem for a Nun*—is a wealthy, White woman of noble birth, and thus has no innate societal restrictions she must prevail over in order to attain traditional matriarchy. Instead, Temple would rather prevail over the concept of matriarchy itself. While *Sanctuary* primarily concentrates on the implications of Temple's rape by the criminal Popeye and subsequent time as a prostitute at Miss Reba's brothel, *Requiem for a Nun* resumes eight years later and finds Temple as a well-off housewife and mother. Despite that many of her contemporaries, such as Ruby, would consider this an ideal circumstance, Temple appears utterly disenchanted with the constraints on agency matriarchy necessitates.

Several critics have suggested that the events of *Sanctuary* are indicative of Temple's descent into moral corruption, though these tend to favor an ideal of chaste morality similar to those which Temple finds herself bound by, in which erotic innocence is conflated with ethical virtue. Her rape at the hands of Popeye has forcibly liberated Temple from virginity, and—while that is not to say that Popeye is by any means a righteous character to do so—as a result, Temple is no longer bound by the internal restrictions of sexuality linked with virginity that a culture idolizing chastity compels. No longer bound by her virginity, Temple is free to consensually pursue sexual intimacy outside the forum of courtship.

Later in *Requiem for a Nun*, when Temple finds herself returned to normative society as "Mrs. Gowan Stevens," her sexuality is once again restrained,

23. Faulkner, *Sanctuary*, 254.

now by matriarchy rather than virginity. Her husband, Gowan—whose incompetence and alcoholism in *Sanctuary* directly led to Temple's rape—marries Temple not only because he believes that by doing so, he will absolve himself of guilt, but that he is also doing Temple a favor in that he is making her once again agreeable to southern society. Temple's sexual encounters, both her rape and subsequent sex work, have rendered her unintelligible to the society she occupies. By marrying her, Gowan believes that he can remedy this by making Temple a wife rather than a former sex worker. Instead, however, it forces a new set of societal restraints, those of maternity, onto Temple. In this instance, one may view the expectations of Temple's matriarchy akin to Diane Roberts's observation of White southern womanhood as "represented as a vessel or as a garden or as a statue on a high, narrow pedestal; disruption is a fall—[an] expulsion from Eden."[24] Although Temple, whose name alone conjures visions of bleached stone and aesthetic purity, desires to be banished from this "Eden," she does not find herself in a position to adequately sustain herself outside of her marriage to Gowan. She attempts to make her condition more bearable by employing the former sex worker Nancy as a nanny to her children. While Temple is initially hopeful that Nancy will be a confidante whom she may openly discuss her sexuality with, Nancy eventually betrays that hope, murdering Temple and Gowan's newborn in order to prevent Temple from fleeing with her lover Pete. Nancy does not do this because she fears for Temple's happiness, but because she fears that the structure of southern family will somehow disintegrate should its biological matriarch escape her domestic confines.

While it may be easy to superficially pass off Temple's desire for sexual agency as a signal of corruption or, as Beverly Sheftall claims, a "complete and striking example of [a] rebel who lacks . . . honesty,"[25] if anything Temple's characterization is that of one who embraces "honest" self. What critics such as Sheftall perceive to be a lack of "honesty" is instead a refusal to adhere to normative sexual ethics. One is urged to further question if Temple's desire for sexual agency would be as scrutinized if she were a man. Faulkner provides his own answer throughout the novels Temple appears in, such as in *Sanctuary*, where Temple—fearing sexual assault—attempt to disguise her femininity under a coat and rain jacket:

24. Roberts, *Faulkner and Southern Womanhood,* 103.

25. Beverly G. Sheftall, "Faulkner's Treatment of Women in his Major Novels" (Master's thesis: Atlanta University, 1969), 74.

> She hurled the dress away, her hand reaching for the coat. She scrabbled it up and swept it about her, pawing at the sleeves. Then, the coat clutched to her breast. . . . She took the raincoat from the nail and put it on over her own coat and fastened it. . . . Temple lay, her hands crossed on her breast and her legs straight and close and decorous, like an effigy on an ancient tomb.[26]

It is not necessarily a desire for perceptually male genitalia that Temple yearns for, but rather the subsequent privileges a man in the South is granted. Although she is only a college student at the opening of *Sanctuary*, Temple is able to observe the freedoms offered to men but are conversely denied to women. By depicting Temple's desire to be removed from femininity so intently, Faulkner presents a complex view of female sexuality as a reflection of his own South. This sentiment is again echoed in *Requiem for a Nun*, where Temple, in a confession to Gowan—whom she believes at the time to be the governor—provides Faulkner's own understanding of the relation between southern womanhood and sexual agency: "You've got to be able to resist it . . . you must have already said no to it long before you even know what it is."[27] The novel closes with Temple still in her marriage to Gowan and "playing a part; that of the righteously bereaved mother."[28] This performance can also be interpreted as a wider "playing" of southern matriarchy. Akin to the restraints of agency race imposed upon Dilsey, Temple may be able to endure the onus of matriarchy's repudiation of sexual agency, but she by no means escapes it.

Thus, the burden of traditional southern matriarchy ultimately places barriers on southern women's social, economic, and sexual liberation. Although nostalgic idolizations of matriarchy and womanhood more broadly are deeply interwoven into the fabric of southern culture and identity, Faulkner indicts a distinctive form of matriarchy that isolates women from their own autonomy. Some of these matriarchs, however—as displayed by Dilsey, Miss Reba, Ruby, and Temple—attempt to resist against the restriction of agency this matriarchy insists. Depicting deeply complex and nonstandard matriarchs in his fiction, Faulkner offers his hope that southern women will reclaim their own personhood, rather than continuing to be regarded as purely ornamental objects. Encapsulated in a society which envisions them only as wife/widow

26. Faulkner, *Sanctuary*, 82–84.

27. William Faulkner, *Requiem for a Nun* (New York: First Vintage, 1951), 138.

28. Lonnie Dean Hefner, *The Concept of Love in the Novels of William Faulkner* (Austin: University of Texas, 1955), 122.

and maiden/mother, Faulkner's matriarchs embody a self-determinant womanhood unsubdued by their oppressors. They do not exist as rebels due to the monumental stature of their subversion per se, but rather because any resistance to such a rigid template of womanhood could be considered significant. Although the more formal aspects of this template have been eroded in the decades since Faulkner, much of its rigidity can still be observed in the oppression of southern woman today. By viewing the ways in which Faulkner's matriarchs rebel against the limitations enacted upon them, one is able to assess the greater implications of southern matriarchy throughout southern culture, both of past and present.

Bibliography

Clarke, Deborah. "Erasing and Inventing Motherhood." In *Robbing the Mother: Women in Faulkner*. Oxford: University of Mississippi Press, 1994.

Faulkner, William. *The Reivers: A Reminiscence*. New York: Random House, 1962.

———. *Requiem for a Nun*. New York: First Vintage, 1951.

———. *Sanctuary*. New York: Random House, 1931.

———. *The Sound and the Fury: The Corrected Text*. New York: Vintage, 1990.

Hefner, Lonnie Dean. *The Concept of Love in the Novels of William Faulkner*. Austin: University of Texas, 1955.

Page, Sally R. *Faulkner's Women: Characterization and Meaning*. De Land, FL: Everett-Edwards, 1973.

Reames, Kelly Lynch. *Women and Race in Contemporary U.S. Writing*. New York: Palgrave Macmillan, 2007.

Roberts, Diane. *Faulkner and Southern Womanhood*. Athens: University of Georgia Press, 1994.

Sheftall, Beverly G. "Faulkner's Treatment of Women in his Major Novels." Master's thesis, Atlanta University, 1969.

Smith, Lillian. *Killer of the Dream*. New York: Doubleday, 1962.

Wallace-Sanders, Kimberly. *A Century of Race, Gender, and Southern Memory*. Ann Arbor: University of Michigan Press, 2008.

Weinstein, Philip. "Meditations on the Other: Faulkner's Rendering of Women." In *Faulkner and Women: Faulkner and Yoknapatawpha, 1985*, edited by Doreen Fowler and Ann J. Abadie, 81–99. Oxford: University of Mississippi Press, 1985.

AUSTIN SVEDJAN is a doctoral student at Louisiana State University, where he studies queer negativity and French existentialism in twentieth-century literature. His essays appear or are forthcoming in *Glass Mountain* and *Remediating Region: New Media and the U.S. South.* He is currently at work on a book project concerning voyeurism, eroticism, and the inherency of fantasy in social relation.

Part IV

The Matriarch and the Male

On Southern Matriarchy Not Migrating to Harlem

Hannah Baker Saltmarsh

The southern matriarchs of twentieth-century African American fiction eternalize and ease the burdens of traumatic, transformational knowledge in the psyches of their daughters and sons. Hortense Spillers asserts that "the 'romance' of African American fiction is a tale of origins that brings together once again children lost, stolen, and strayed from their mothers."[1] However, such stories of identity are never easily resolved by a maternal presence, but rather suggest perennial embattlement and estrangement, foregrounding the child-protagonist's attempt to wrestle with ancestral oppression and resilience. As Trudier Harris, Patricia Hill Collins, Melissa Harris-Perry, and many others have argued, the archetype of the Black southern matriarch has done damage to African American families and to Black mothers themselves. The negative stereotype of the aggressive, domineering, loquacious, emasculating, self-sacrificing, pious, pedantic, suprahuman Black southern matriarch was forged in the context of enslavement. Slavery delineated in obvious, public ways that Black mothers were fecund beasts of burden—"insatiable breeder[s]"[2] and "carriers of malignancy"[3]—who perpetuated slavery through gestation. Today, the archetype of the praying, Black mother who privately accepts long-suffering and sacrifice yet publicly decries every injustice and error of judgment in her family, community, and social world

1. Hortense J. Spillers, "In the Time of the Daughters and the Fathers," in *Black, White, and in Color: Essays on American Literature and Culture* (Chicago: University of Chicago Press, 2003), 249.

2. Melissa Harris-Perry, *Sister Citizen: Shame, Stereotypes, and Black Women in America* (New Haven: Yale University Press, 2011), 71.

3. Harris-Perry, *Sister Citizen,* 114.

preserves the notion of weakness as strength.[4] Reviled and revered, the quintessential best and worst mother, devouring and nurturing, the Black matriarch is the infamously smothering "nurse shark."[5]

Great Migration literature, such as work by James Baldwin and Ralph Ellison, thematizes the struggles of sons and daughters to reckon with their southern past, which is embodied nowhere more explicitly than in their southern mothers. Adolescent migrant-protagonists react to matrilineal history in complex ways, such as rejecting shameful dependence on a maternal figure to navigate the northern experience; internalizing matrilineal knowledge; empathizing with aspects of maternal oppression; or entertaining acts of symbolic matricide through exile, excommunication, or rebirth. A question that clearly troubles migrant-protagonists is whether a southern matriarch represents a distant but hypothetical safe haven or necessitates a different safe haven from her. Protagonists of migration literature learn from, abandon, invoke, dream of, and reckon with their mothers with such consistency that a migrant-hero's journey cannot be imagined without such resolute women as irresolute touchstones of identity.

This analysis focuses on Ralph Ellison's *Invisible Man* (1952) and John Baldwin's *Go Tell It on the Mountain* (1953) because these novels worry and wonder what happens to Black southern matriarchy during the Great Migration. Ellison's and Baldwin's male protagonists cannot define themselves without reacting—in guilt, pity, shame, despair, empathy, love, or total disregard—to a southern Black matriarch in Harlem. I argue that the fight for reclaiming the narrative about one's own mother/mother figure becomes central in Ellison and Baldwin's migratory identity stories where home is a "mobile place,"[6] and son-protagonists consider how they want to "negoti-

4. Trudier Harris, *Black Women in the Fiction of James Baldwin* (Knoxville: University of Tennessee Press, 1985), 59. Harris says, "It could be posited, in the vein of the old argument used to discuss black women and their long-suffering, that their strength is in their very weakness. They continue; they thrive quietly within the limited space available to them, and they hope for better days for their children."

5. Toni Morrison, "The Kindness of Sharks," in *Playing in the Dark: Whiteness and the Literary Imagination* (New York: Vintage, 1993), 85. In this book chapter, Morrison analyzes the metaphor of the "nurse shark" used, disturbingly, to describe Black femininity in Ernest Hemingway's *To Have and Have Not.* Morrison writes, "The strong belief here is that of a black female as the furthest thing from human, so far away as to be not even mammal but fish. The figure evokes a predatory, devouring eroticism."

6. Edward Michael Pavlić, "Syndectic Redemption: Above-Underground Emergence in David Bradley's *The Chaneysville Incident*," *African American Review* 30, no. 2 (1996): 167.

ate" not just the "urban landscape,"[7] but the interior landscape of home. Rejection can be understood as part of a negotiation, and ultimately, while each protagonist rejects plenty, each carries within himself a vestige of an internalized southern matriarch. Ellison's Invisible Man and Baldwin's John Grimes reflect on what stays the same when the options seem to be a hybrid, changing identity or a buried one. For Blacks migrating north, particularly for young men in search of a new identity, the questions, "What's your name?" and "What's your story?" bring back the image of one's mother. Baldwin and Ellison suggest that traumatic upheaval, shame, and institutionalized racism and sexism have made it impossible to maintain a nostalgic mother-son bond, and so their Great Migration bildungsroman end in shaky epiphany or exile. The modernist alienation of Ellison's nameless narrator and Baldwin's John Grimes bespeak a young man who has buried the story of his mother's southern heritage, interring in his subconscious mind the stereotypes of the strong, Black woman and the formerly enslaved grandmother; the maternal warmth of comfort foods; and the vociferous folk wisdom of southern matriarchy effervescent in biblical language and the blues. As these characters develop throughout these books, the buried stories of their mother are often unearthed.

Preceding Baldwin and Ellison by almost two decades, Richard Wright's fictional migration story "Big Boy Leaves Home" (1936) speaks to the deep ambivalence the northern-bound protagonist "Big Boy" feels toward his southern mother. Wright's story opens with "the dozens" through a Yo' Mama joke in a bucolic, Edenic countryside,[8] shifts to a harrowing racial terror through the spectacle of lynching, and ends with Big Boy losing cornbread on a train to Chicago. The bittersweet moment of the falling crumb of cornbread suggests ambiguity over the sustainability of southern matriarchy. Wright visualized the migrating flow and jolting loss of the southern matriarchy in Big Boy's life by writing: "The truck sped over the asphalt miles, sped

7. I borrow Farah Jasmine Griffin's notion of the migration narrative, of which the third step is "the portrayal of the way migrants negotiate the urban landscape." Found in "*Who Set You Flowin'?": The African American Migration Narrative* (New York: Oxford University Press, 1996), 8.

8. Keneth Kinnamon writes, "Into the pastoral innocence of Big Boy's world intrudes violent white racism, driving him from the Southern garden toward the uncertain freedom of the North," and discusses the symbolic contrast between rural Mississippi and Chicago in the story. Found in Keneth Kinnamon, "The Pastoral Impulse in Richard Wright," *Midcontinent American Studies Journal* 10, no. 1 (Spring 1969): 43–45.

northward, jolting him, shaking out of his bosoms the crumbs of cornbread, making them dance with the splinters and sawdust in the golden blades of sunshine."[9] This traveling crumb of southern comfort food dances, nourishes, and yet fails to satisfy young male migrant-narrators in 1950s novels of the Great Migration so traumatized by Jim Crow era racial violence and the looming memory of enslavement felt in their own homes. Even so, some go looking for the tastes of home in their new environments while simultaneously avoiding the stigma of southern culture, as if their down-home culture was just a messy lap filled with fatty crumbs or, worse, a mockery of maternal protection to intercede in either southern or northern injustices. Big Boy calls to mind the emerging John Grimes and the Invisible Man in spiritual and sociological bildungsroman on tumultuous paths to manhood and iterates the dilemma of what from home a growing man will savor, hide, lose, or rediscover at the threshing floor.

Harlem, Part 1: On Elizabeth Grimes and John, Who Doesn't Know He's Nameless

James Baldwin's novel, *Go Tell It on the Mountain,* takes place over the day of John's fourteenth birthday, followed by the next dawn, as John receives salvation through his terror-filled, wondrous spiritual birth. As he comes of age, John experiences a deep, subversive split between himself and his father, whom he competes with at a game of spiritual megalomania. This text opens with one of the most telling lines in American literature: "Everyone had always said that John would be a preacher when he grew up, just like his father."[10] The irony is the man whom John presumes to be his father—the hypocritical, emotionally abusive Deacon Gabriel Grimes—is, in fact, his stepfather. During this same "awakening" he also experiences an estrangement between himself, as a new convert and aspiring preacher, and his long-suffering, silent mother, Elizabeth, who is fettered by patriarchy. Playing the role of deacon's wife and pregnant with her fifth child, Elizabeth still feels she must atone for having John out of wedlock in a previous relationship. Having migrated from Maryland to New York, Elizabeth is emblematic of what happens to Black mothers experiencing the internalized racism of the South and the institutionalized racism of the North: she has never been good enough in the eyes

9. Richard Wright, "Big Boy Leaves Home," in *Uncle Tom's Children* (New York: HarperCollins, 1991), 61.

10. James Baldwin, *Go Tell It on the Mountain,* 6th ed. (New York: Dell Books, 1981), 3.

of her racist, southern White relatives nor in the eyes of her husband, such that nearly every social institution casts blame upon her. All the while, she is attuned to the hatred and hypocrisy that fuels racism and sexism. Thus, the bastard-protagonist John carries with him empathy for his proud, abused mother even as he avoids her fate by claiming his male privilege as a pastor's "son" in the Black church.

The church stimulates fear of judgment in women overcome by sexual shame, internalized blame, or a general sense of fatedness in relationship to a vengeful, male God. Florence, Gabriel's virulent sister who is close to Elizabeth and John, struggles with whether to return to God as she is in the throes of colon cancer yet cannot quite accept the God of her hypocritical, urbane brother buffeted in prayer by their formerly enslaved mother who favored Gabriel. Each of the women, Florence and Elizabeth, who appear at the altar in prayer, come in dread for their lives, and in Elizabeth's case, in dread of her fatherless son's fate as well. Thus, the motif of the praying southern matriarch[11] becomes a space where Baldwin rewrites the archetype, peeling back the surface spirituality and submission of his female characters to reveal internal doubt, bitterness, effrontery, and revolution, which substantiates a quiet protest against patriarchal religion.

If "the story of Baldwin's treatment of black women is really the story of freeing them from the church,"[12] then John's "*new* name" and eternal, "ineffaceable"[13] salvation and prophesied pastoral call threatens Elizabeth further. Ironically, John's rebirth foreshadows a long, difficult spiritual journey due to John's closeted sexuality; his acceptance in a heteronormative church can only be seen as temporal. John knew himself to be assigned to "the back door, and the dark stairs, and the kitchen or the basement" in public space as a Black man, and would "break his neck trying"[14] to realize his ambition, but at the cost of Black womanhood. Baldwin suggests that in light of emasculation in the public sphere, men in the Black church create a safe space that thrives on casting women in supportive roles, with mothers cheering, clapping, crying,

11. Though Florence doesn't bear children, she takes John under her wing and plays a maternal role in his life. She rejects the matrilineal legacy of her formerly enslaved mother out of bitterness and shame, and, having had enough of her mother's apparent favoritism for Gabriel, Florence migrates to New York so she can finally leave Gabriel with the responsibility of caring for their mother.

12. Baldwin, *Go Tell It on the Mountain*, 59.

13. Baldwin, *Go Tell It on the Mountain*, 225.

14. Baldwin, *Go Tell It on the Mountain*, 31.

and praying on the periphery. Throughout this narrative, Baldwin intuits that Black churches posit more power in men than women, regardless of what "sins" they have committed. Even in creating a narrative of rejection that a closeted son and a mother with a past might seem to share, Baldwin intuits that Black women have less power than closeted men, as revealed in John's rise to power.

As the novel ends with John's spiritual rebirth, the figure of Elizabeth "in the doorway, in the long shadows of the hall"[15] symbolizes the lack of power, recognition, or love for Black women within church or family. Consequently, the novel ends with John's understated acknowledgment of his mother in contrast to Gabriel's flagrant abuse of her. Though domestic abuse is evident in one of the earliest scenes in the novel, where Gabriel slaps Elizabeth and then beats their son Roy with a belt,[16] the beaten, crying mother-and-son pair do not comprise the full story.[17] Baldwin closes the novel with Elizabeth and John looking into each other's eyes as a sign of triumph over Gabriel, the flawed family and spiritual leader. While mother and son smile, the father significantly does not. John has quite possibly caused his mother to feel pride in her illegitimate child who, in the words of a fellow congregant, is now "a holy son [who] is going to comfort [his mother's] gray hairs"; yet, his mother's "tears [fall] slowly, bitterly,"[18] as if to say that Elizabeth's heart is more than the battleground for a husband and stepson to confront each other. Thus, after his conversion, John senses that his mother's "smile remained unreadable" and that "he could not tell what it hid."[19] Elizabeth kisses John, and they seem to affirm each other in the doorway, but it's unclear if the threshold is a homecoming or not.

Rather than simply accuse Baldwin of writing a sexist cast of women characters, derivative of southern matriarchs and mammies who are resilient beasts of burden, I credit Baldwin for creating a space of recognition by which a fourteen-year-old protagonist sees aspects of his mother that no

15. Baldwin, *Go Tell It on the Mountain*, 226.

16. Baldwin, *Go Tell It on the Mountain*, 43–45.

17. In the novel, Baldwin describes Elizabeth and Roy crying in each other's arms: the mother "crying as John had never seen a woman, or anybody, cry before" and Roy "[holding] on to her as though he were drowning." Baldwin, *Go Tell It on the Mountain*, 44.

18. Baldwin, *Go Tell It on the Mountain*, 212.

19. Baldwin, *Go Tell It on the Mountain*, 225.

other character, not even the women in the church, understand.[20] Just as John realizes he can "not bow before the throne of grace without first kneeling to his father,"[21] he intuits the same process for the women in his family. Just as John hates his father for beating his mother, so does his paternal aunt: Florence despises a God who would anoint her brother, a former alcoholic, philanderer, and hypocrite, while blessing her with the bitter cup of cancer and widowhood.

John, as a very young man, wrestles with the kind of religion that "had bent his mother's back"[22] and wonders at the hidden sources of his mother's suffering, attune to the emotional hieroglyphics of her face. He acknowledges the existential crisis he and his mother share in being despised and disenfranchised: "His mother . . . was silent . . . and her silence made him feel that she was weeping. And why did she weep? And why did they come here . . . calling out to a God who cared nothing for them . . . if there was any God at all?"[23] John's main struggle in accepting salvation concerns his mother's pain: again, he asks, "Why did his mother weep? . . . If God's power was so great, why were their lives so troubled?"[24] The oppression of Black women is nowhere more evident than in Elizabeth's story: the stigma of carrying a nameless child in New York and the grief of losing a great love to racial injustice became a burden too heavy to carry. Soon after running away with Richard to New York, Elizabeth is racked with guilt for her promiscuity; yet, the couple lacks the economic stability to consider marriage since "northern opportunity" is an oxymoron for Black migrants: Elizabeth works as a maid, Richard as an elevator operator. After Richard is misidentified as a crime suspect and then beaten in police custody, he is utterly broken and takes his own life. Elizabeth, who felt that Richard, in his weakened state, couldn't bear the news of an unexpected pregnancy, never told him she was pregnant. After losing Richard, "Elizabeth, one night, had become an old woman and was half mad with fear and grief"[25]: as a single mother, she watches her son John during the day and works as a domestic at night, thus relying upon a drunk neighbor within

20. Even when John articulates that he cannot know the depths of his mother's heart, he is closer to seeing her than the church women who speak in hackneyed biblical phrases and who judge a mother by whether her children are faithful or not.

21. Baldwin, *Go Tell It on the Mountain*, 14.

22. Baldwin, *Go Tell It on the Mountain*, 28.

23. Baldwin, *Go Tell It on the Mountain*, 76.

24. Baldwin, *Go Tell It on the Mountain*, 168.

25. Baldwin, *Go Tell It on the Mountain*, 205.

earshot acting as babysitter. Desperate for a husband and father figure, but a scrap of her former dignity, Elizabeth marries the Deacon Gabriel Grimes, the despised brother of her friend and co-worker.

Gabriel imprisons Elizabeth by constantly, hypocritically reminding her of her sexual shame and by slighting her son John.[26] Even when Elizabeth carries a fourth child for Gabriel, she can do nothing to earn her husband's or God's favor. When her husband touches her, she fantasizes about Richard but tries to convince herself to live in the present. Evident in Elizabeth's fear of Gabriel and of a male God is a critique of the ways in which theology and practice have perpetuated the martyrdom, silence, and asexuality of mothers. Throughout his novels, Baldwin reflects on his own experience of false spiritual comfort: "And the passion with which we loved the Lord was a measure of how deeply we . . . avoided and despised ourselves."[27] Elizabeth, a weary southern matriarch, reverberates with this kind of self-hate and skepticism, illuminating the impact of intersectionality in women's migration experiences.

Baldwin's southern matriarchs who occasionally speak out against Gabriel are beaten physically, mentally, and/or emotionally, or left to die for having a voice. Throughout the novel, these characters echo a Black feminist outcry against religious patriarchy. From the "harlot" Esther, who professes the novel's best line to Gabriel's rotting soul, "I guess it takes a holy man to make a girl a real whore,"[28] and then dies in childbirth, to Elizabeth, the holy helpmate of a second-fiddle "kind of holy handyman"[29] who rarely preaches but tinkers with broken appliances in a storefront church, these women resist the spiritual and sexual tyranny of feckless men. Gabriel's chief power is to change light bulbs and to feign spiritual illumination so as to guilt others and thereby conceal his own shame. As Baldwin reveals in, "Come out of the Wilderness," about an imbalanced couple, Gabriel knows all too well that "to

26. Elizabeth does not know of Gabriel's grotesque past filled with hypocrisy so criminal in scale as to have made him the indirect cause of three people's deaths. Gabriel is responsible, directly or indirectly, for the deaths of the following women: the first wife, Deborah, who he mistreated and betrayed; the mistress he impregnated and abandoned, Esther; and his and Esther's child, Royal, whom he never claimed as his own.

27. James Baldwin, *The Fire Next Time* (New York: Vintage, 1991), 41.

28. Baldwin, *Go Tell It on the Mountain,* 154.

29. Baldwin, *Go Tell It on the Mountain,* 46.

enforce his power over her, he had only to keep her guilt awake,"[30] and in this story, Baldwin testifies to women's creative resistance.

Baldwin gives to Florence hard-won insights about gender such as "It sometimes came to her that all women had been cursed from the cradle; all, in one fashion or another, being given the same cruel destiny, born to suffer the weight of men,"[31] or "I don't believe the nigger's been born what knows how to treat a woman right. . . . Look like ain't no woman nowhere but ain't been dragged down in the dirt by some man, and left there, too, while he go on about his business."[32] Since Florence doesn't divulge Gabriel's secret past to Elizabeth, the two women are preempted from forming an alliance that might challenge patriarchy or simply carve out a safe space. Nonetheless, Florence takes a lead role in the text and offers one way of understanding the ominous, ambiguous pronoun in the novel's ironic title, *Go Tell It on the Mountain*. Florence confronts Gabriel, and it's as if Baldwin's title and John's whisperings to starlet Bette Davis in the movie theater, "Go on, girl,"[33] could be redirected in urging Florence to proclaim not salvation but its many perversions: "I'm going to find some way . . . to rise up and tell it, tell everybody, about the blood the Lord's anointed is got on his hands."[34]

John, like his aunt, "longed for the power to cut his father down"[35] because he too seeks a balance of affirmation and revenge that culminates in self-worth. All he wants is one safe space: but he finds in the church "there was no speech or language, and there was no love; no one to say: You are beautiful, John; no one to forgive him, no matter what his sin; no one to heal him, and lift him up."[36] The women in John's family mirror these same feelings regarding their own invisibility. Interestingly, the kind of God and church community John imagines sounds more like womanist theology than patriarchal Christianity, more like God Our Mother than Our Father. Tragically, John doesn't find such a great, equalizing love, and instead asserts his male privilege. On the one hand, Baldwin empathetically exposes one of

30. James Baldwin, "Come Out of the Wilderness," *Going to Meet the Man* (New York: Dial Press, 1965), 215.

31. Baldwin, *Go Tell It on the Mountain,* 78.

32. Baldwin, *Go Tell It on the Mountain,* 183.

33. Baldwin, *Go Tell It on the Mountain,* 33.

34. Baldwin, *Go Tell It on the Mountain,* 292.

35. Baldwin, *Go Tell It on the Mountain,* 199.

36. Baldwin, *Go Tell It on the Mountain,* 271.

the church's chief problems: Black male clergy who imitate aspects of White, enslaving Christianity in dominating over Black women, the so-called pillars of the church, like property. In this sense, Baldwin's novel predates what James Cone would poignantly observe, "It is truly amazing that many Black male ministers, young and old, can hear the message of liberation in the gospel when related to racism but remain deaf to a similar message in the context of sexism."[37] On the other hand, Baldwin focuses the novel on John's reclamation of his masculine agency and glorifies John's dream of usurping the very power that he condemns in Gabriel, thus leaving the question of Elizabeth's servility acknowledged but not yet altered. While John is motivated to come to spiritual ascendance to please his mother while subversively conquering his stepfather, John ends up feeling more estranged from his mother through his identification with the patriarchal church. John is free to testify to God's mercy and to proclaim his own spiritual rebirth whereas Florence, Deborah, Rachel, Esther, and Elizabeth "have been expected to bear all and tell nothing . . . in a kind of loyalty that does not allow one to air 'dirty laundry'" in all its forms, from shame to silence to abuse in the home and church.[38] Yet, John's internal world screams to the mountaintops of all that he intuits in his mother's identity and history in her face, her quietude, her weeping, her praying, her shame, and her photographed, distant happiness—but ironically, without ever knowing her story, which is also in large part, his own.

Harlem, Part 2: On Ellison's Mary Rambo and the Nameless Migrant

Ellison presents the Invisible Man as a kind of orphan, whose parents are mentioned only superficially, whose grandmothers are not mentioned at all, and whose grandfather's dying words echo with cynical mystery throughout the novel. Due to a series of "bad choices," the Invisible Man is spat out from the womb of a historically Black college. Following his slapdash, forced migration to Harlem, the Invisible Man meets a mother figure named Mary Rambo. A Harlem transplant from the south, Rambo accosts the Invisible Man not merely with her hospitality but her iconography. Rambo is a hyper-visible representation of southern matriarchy within Harlem—from her formidable physique; her role as the maternal landlady of new migrants; her rambling, preaching, blues-singing voice; to her Biblical name, Mary, the

37. James Cone, *Speaking the Truth: Ecumenism, Liberation, and Black Theology.* (Grand Rapids: William B. Eerdmans Publishing, 1986).

38. Elaine Brown Crawford, *Hope in the Holler: A Womanist Theology* (Louisville, KY: Westminster John Knox Press, 2002), 74.

suffering servant, and mother of God. The Invisible Man can do nothing but follow Rambo, an affable stranger, home. With the simple act of carrying her groceries inside at the first meeting, he begins his formative, but brief sojourn in her boarding house. The Invisible Man is as skeptical of his mother figure as he is confused by her, yet all the while connected to her through psychological space. Snippets of her blues music and the presence of a racist coin bank are emblems of Black southern resistance and trauma. While the migrant refusal to commune physically with Rambo beyond the span of a few days illustrates the rejection elements of his southern past and one figuration of a southern mother, he nonetheless negotiates internally with an ancestral past she evokes.

Scholarly discussion of Rambo as a southern matriarch addresses both Ellison's novel and an excised chapter, published as a stand-alone story entitled "Out of the Hospital and Into the Bar" (1961) and tends to either identify Rambo as a sexist stereotype or to celebrate Rambo as an identity touchstone.[39] In either articulation, as martyr or moral guide, Rambo is primarily seen to be "the preserver of Black life who helps carry on a Black tradition"

39. Rambo can be seen as an asexual, Black mother figure, whose primary role in the novel is to support the narrator's self-discovery; thus, the invisible mother is even more dramatically unseen than the invisible protagonist. Many scholars discuss the motif of Ellison's stereotyped, and therefore, invisible Black mother figure, Mary Rambo. See Carolyn W. Sylvander, "Ralph Ellison's *Invisible Man* and Female Stereotypes," *Negro American Literature Forum* 9, no. 3 (1975): 79; Yolanda Pierce, "The Invisible Women in Ralph Ellison's *Invisible Man* (1952)," in *Women in Literature: Reading through the Lens of Gender*, eds. Jerilyn Fisher and Ellen S. Silber (Westport, CT: Greenwood, 2003), 158; James Smethurst, "'Something Warmly, Infuriatingly Feminine': Gender, Sexuality, and the Work of Ralph Ellison," in *A Historical Guide to Ralph Ellison,* ed. Stephen C. Tracey (Oxford: Oxford University Press, 2004), 120; Mary Rohrberger, "'Ball the Jack': Surreality, Sexuality, and the Role of Women in *Invisible Man*," in *Approaches to Teaching Ellison's* Invisible Man, eds. Susan Resneck Parr and Pancho Savery (New York: Modern Language Association, 1989), 130; Ann Folwell Stanford, "He Speaks for Whom? Inscription and Reinscription of Women in *Invisible Man* and *The Salt Eaters*," *MELUS* 18, no. 2 (1993): 17, 21–24; Lisa Maria Hogeland, "*Invisible Man* and Invisible Women: The Sex/Race Analogy of the 1970s," *Women's History Review* 5, no. 1 (1996): 31–53; Isiah Lavender III, "Invisible Women in *Invisible Man*," *ANQ: A Quarterly Journal of Short Articles, Notes and Reviews* 27, no. 3 (2014): 149–50. Along similar lines, Keith Byerman discusses the lack of agency in women characters who populate Ellison's short stories in "'I Did Not Learn Their Name': Female Characters in the Short Fiction of Ralph Ellison," *American Studies* 54, no. 3 (2015): 101–102, 113.

and who "typifies down-home maternalism that is evident in the extended family of African Americans."[40] Farah Jasmine Griffin views Rambo's boarding house as "a safe space" and Rambo as "the ancestor [who becomes] a site of negotiation for the construction of [the migrant's] new self,"[41] whereas Griffin reads the Invisible Man's rejection of Rambo as evidence of his hubris in "shun[ning] those elements that bind him to a racial past."[42] I interpret the migrant's ambivalent vacillations as essential to his identity struggle, a fact broadcast by his namelessness across a nearly six-hundred-page epic. The migrant's search for interiority requires temporal rejection from the southern matriarch, Rambo, as representative of the "stifling provinciality of race,"[43] but the omnipresence of Rambo in the narrator's psyche suggests a dynamic struggle with southern matriarchy.

Rambo is as troubling as she is affirming, and the relationship between her and the Invisible Man is one of ongoing consternation—the only thing "preserved" is the language with which to define and redefine "a Black tradition" and the contesting of what exactly a southern matriarch can preserve for a community in flux. Whereas Ellison once commented that Rambo was the type of woman responsible for helping countless young Black men find their way in Harlem,[44] the Invisible Man demurs Rambo's use of the collec-

40. *The Concise Oxford Companion to African American Literature,* eds. William L. Andrews, Frances Smith Foster, and Trudier Harris (New York: Oxford University Press, 2001), s.v. "Mary Rambo."

41. Farah Jasmine Griffin, *"Who Set You Flowin'?": The African American Migration Narrative* (New York: Oxford University Press, 1996), 7.

42. Griffin, *"Who Set You Flowin'?,"* 131.

43. Griffin, *"Who Set You Flowin'?,"* 131.

44. In the author's note to the excised Mary chapter of *Invisible Man,* entitled "Out of the Hospital and Under the Bar," Ellison writes, "For those who desire more than the sheer narrative ride, who hunger and thirst for 'meaning,' let them imagine what this country would be without its Marys. Let them imagine, indeed, what the American Negro would be without the Marys of our ever-expanding Harlems" (243). Ellison refers here to Mary as "a woman of the folk, who helped release the hero from the machine" (243). Citing limitations of space, Ellison expresses sorrow that he was not able to include the longer chapter in the published novel (243). I am treating the excised chapter as a separate text rather than a missing puzzle piece: in the longer chapter Mary feeds the narrator while he is in the factory hospital and administers a remedy that came from her 103-year-old mother who got it from her mother; this medicine cures the narrator and brings him to the point of saying, "I'm freeing me," (265) as he successfully escapes captivity and makes his way to Mary's

tive "we"[45] of southern Black folk in favor of the self-discovery and mobility associated with urban beginnings. Layering one southern migration within another, Ellison emphasizes not a stop-and-shop tradition bearer in Rambo but a site of communal engagement where mutual recognition and defamiliarization are an essential, ongoing process.

Rambo exhorts the Invisible Man to become the kind of leader she imagines he should be: echoing Mahalia Jackson's rendition of "Move on Up a Little Higher," Rambo says, "You go to lead and fight and move us all on up a little higher."[46] Rambo lumps him into a collective "us," and imposes upon the Invisible Man the task of racial uplift. Immediately, upon meeting her, the narrator notes his invisibility in her presence:

> There are many things about people like Mary that I dislike. For one thing, they seldom know where their personalities end and yours begins; they usually think in terms of "we" while I have always tended to think in terms of "me."[47]

Tongue in cheek, Ellison reveals that the Invisible Man has, in fact, committed a similar crime of perception by referring to Mary as a "they" and categorizing her as a southern matriarch along with "people like Mary." Thus, the odd couple of southern mother figure and son begin a relationship based on a host of misperceptions, some of which will be resolved.

Ellison ironizes the way the migrant inwardly rebukes Rambo's understanding of the Black community yet outwardly appropriates Rambo's rhetoric in his first important speech. Directly after Rambo's pep talk about racial uplift and the call to southern Black male migrants, the Invisible Man dramatically protests the eviction of an elderly Black couple and starts nothing short of a revolution in advocating for the rights of the formerly enslaved couple while citing maternal legacy as deeply significant. References to women called "Big Mama," "quilts and broken-down shoes," "an old breast pump

---

boarding house. Mary plays a more explicit role as a folk-healer and mentor-ancestor in the stand-alone chapter; however, in the novel more so than in the chapter, Ellison toes the line between homage and parody, and Mary is not simply a magical martyr, because her expectations greatly irritate and inspire the narrator. See Ralph Ellison, *Invisible Man* (New York: Vintage International, 1995).

45. Ralph Ellison, *Invisible Man* (New York: Vintage International, 1995), 316.

46. Ellison, *Invisible Man*, 255.

47. Ellison, *Invisible Man*, 316.

fall[en] in the snow" and a card addressed to "Dear Grandma" situate the speech as a rallying cry not just for equal housing rights, social justice, or civil disobedience, but also for racial pride through the figure of the southern matriarch.[48] In his first political speech, the narrator refashions the concepts Rambo suggested to him of a common Black family: "They're our people, your people and mine, your parents and mine."[49] The contradictory safe space of Mary's boarding house becomes integral to the Invisible Man's dynamic ideas about community and individuality.

Even when the Invisible Man does leave Rambo's apartment, he oft thinks of his mother figure and imagines a kind of hero's return to his southern mother in Harlem. Rambo represents the symbolic South to which he cannot return, or at least not as recognizably the same person. In a totalizing statement, the Invisible Man brings Rambo, his childhood home, the college, and the Brotherhood together, because they all represent ownership: "I realized I couldn't return to Mary's. . . . I had been as invisible to Mary as I had been to the Brotherhood. NO, I couldn't return to Mary's, or to the campus, or to the Brotherhood, or home."[50] To pursue personal growth, the Invisible Man opts to keep running, beyond geography, to run, as it were, in his mind.[51]

Yet even in exile, he holds onto a vestige of the baggage born by southern matriarchy; he unwittingly breaks and absconds with a racist coin bank from Rambo's apartment. The racist iconography of the bank comprises a crudely drawn Black man with full lips, his "grinning mouth"[52] agape to receive the coin from an extended hand; and the abject red T-shirt that reads "FEED ME;"[53] the bank evinces the ongoing cultural appropriation of the Black body.[54] That potent bequest, "FEED ME" evokes not only the grinning slave fed, prostrate, on his knees at the master's pig trough but also the mammy's teats, free for everyone's taking. The Invisible Man blames Rambo for the presence of the bank in

48. Ellison, *Invisible Man*, 277.

49. Ellison, *Invisible Man*, 278.

50. Ellison, *Invisible Man*, 571.

51. See Ellison, *Invisible Man,* 534, where the migrant says, "I ran through the night, ran within myself. Ran," suggestive of the hibernation to come.

52. Ellison, *Invisible Man*, 319.

53. Ellison, *Invisible Man*, 321.

54. For instance, in the 1930s and 1940s, the "happy darky" slave reappears in blackface minstrel shows in the forms of urban Black figures, whether the fetishized tap-dancing dandy or the unscrupulous lawyer, as seen in the popular, long-running radio-turned-TV show, *Amos 'N' Andy*, now widely recognized as grotesquely racist.

her boarding house—Rambo's tolerance, passivity, ignorance, and servitude he assumes have permitted the presence of the garishly racist memorabilia. Then, he, too, shares in the conspicuously hidden nature of the bank, which makes it to his underground cave and suggests a psychological fight for an unfettered identity, for a name that doesn't reek of property.

While Rambo's bank shrapnel and coins remain even in exile as a reminder of suffering, the narrator burns the documents that comprised various racial identities, thus anticipating the notion of race as a social construct, namely that "race clearly has a biological element—*because we have awarded it one.*" The last pages of the novel float the blues, flashing a memory of Rambo's own maternal voice, which cannot be burned like a document or made illegible like the bank's splintered mantra. The blues snippet awakens the narrator's awareness of the "lower frequencies"[55] of his own voice and of the possibility of meaningful interpersonal connections. Seeing Rambo as an access point to blues ideology, Ed Pavlić interprets Rambo as embodying "the folk image of the black community as 'briar patch,' a place of physical and existential 'hiding' from historical capture and psychological pain."[56] I would draw attention not to a ready-made safe space, particularly not to a woman as an objectified hideout, but to the collage effect of the polyvocal, fragmented consciousness of the narrator in the moment of improvisation. Rather than merely using Rambo as a means to self-enlightenment, by the end of the novel, the narrator acknowledges the complexity of individuality and the call-and-response mutuality of community. In hearing Rambo sing, the migrant wondered "who 'articulated her grievances'" and confessed that he "had really never seen her" because he had "been acting like a child, not a man."[57] He remains wary of collective identity that might erase individuality, his or Rambo's, but is nonetheless drawn to ideals about social responsibility, evoking Rambo's first exhortation. The symbolic "briar patch" of the Black community is not literal so much as emblematic of modern Black interiority, of contemplative quietude that remains awake to formative resonant voices like Rambo's. During his first "period of quietness"[58] in Rambo's boarding house,

55. Ellison, *Invisible Man*, 581.

56. Edward Michael Pavlić, *Crossroads Modernism: Descent and Emergence in African-American Literary Culture* (Minneapolis: University of Minnesota Press, 2002), 91.

57. Pavlić, *Crossroads Modernism,* 297. See Pavlić, *Crossroad Modernisms,* 128–29 for an important discussion on the way the Invisible Man perceives Rambo's struggles intuitively through the blues and the familiar smell of cabbage.

58. Ellison, *Invisible Man,* 258.

the Invisible Man acknowledges the "nebulous hope"[59] within his heart as an imprint of his southern mother, the only piece of his given identity he wishes to keep in constructing a new self.

Motherless Harlem

Through symbolic and literal inherited traumatic narratives, son-protagonists John Grimes and the Invisible Man absorb the positive and negative attributes of maternity, simultaneously clinging to and forsaking the matrilineal pain and resistance that shapes them. Through a connection, mostly internalized, with a southern matriarch, the Invisible Man and John maintain an empathetic, conflicted perspective that acknowledges the interiority of Mary Rambo or Elizabeth Grimes, respectively, despite the ways in which male privilege provides the freedom to reconstruct a new identity. Even in their rebirths, the son-protagonists situate themselves in relation to their mother's homes, songs, bodies, doorways, hearts, as if to suggest there are ways in which these men do not want to be estranged. And even in their exiles, whether the physical internment of the Invisible Man, or John's spiritual ascent up to the mountaintop, there is an acknowledgment, if not an homage, to the woman who has been doubly exiled, the very source of everyone else's home who herself is not at home anywhere, least of all Harlem.

Bibliography

Alinia, Minoo. "On Black Feminist Thought: Thinking Oppression and Resistance Through Intersectional Paradigm." *Ethnic and Racial Studies* 38, no. 13 (2015): 2334–340.

Andrews, William L., Frances Smith Foster, and Trudier Harris, eds. *The Concise Oxford Companion to African American Literature.* New York: Oxford University Press, 2001.

Baldwin, James. "Come Out the Wilderness." In *Going To Meet the Man,* 195–225. New York: Dial Press, 1965.

———. *The Fire Next Time.* New York: Vintage, 1991.

———. *Go Tell It on the Mountain.* 6th Edition. New York: Dell Books, 1981.

59. Ellison, *Invisible Man,* 258.

———. "Previous Condition." In *Going to Meet the Man: Stories,* 81–100. New York: Vintage International, 1995.

Benjamin, Shanna Greene. "There's Something about Mary: Female Wisdom and the Folk Presence in Ralph Ellison's *Invisible Man.*" *Meridians* 12, no. 1 (2014): 121–48. https://doi.org/10.2979/meridians.12.1.121.

Byerman, Keith. "'I Did Not Learn Their Name': Female Characters in the Short Fiction of Ralph Ellison,' *American Studies* 54, no. 3 (2015): 101–14.

Coates, Ta-Nehisi. "What We Mean When We Say 'Race Is a Social Construct.'" *The Atlantic.* May 15, 2015. www.theatlantic.com/amp/article/274872.

Cone, James H. *Speaking the Truth: Ecumenism, Liberation, and Black Theology.* Grand Rapids: William B. Eerdmans Publishing, 1986.

Crawford, Elaine Brown. *Hope in the Holler: A Womanist Theology.* Louisville, KY: Westminster John Knox Press, 2002.

Ellison, Ralph. *Invisible Man.* New York: Vintage International, 1995.

———. "Out of the Hospital and Under the Bar." In *Soon, One Morning: New Writing by American Negroes, 1940–1962,* edited by Herbert Hill, 242–90. New York: Knopf, 1963.

———. "Twentieth-Century Fiction and the Black Mask of Humanity," *Shadow and Act,* 24–44. New York: Vintage Books, 1972.

Grant, Jacquelyn. "Black Theology and the Black Woman." In *Words of Fire: An Anthology of African-American Feminist Thought*, edited by Beverly Guy-Sheftall, 320–336. New York: The New Press, 1995.

Griffin, Farah Jasmine. *"Who Set You Flowin'?": The African American Migration Narrative.* New York: Oxford University Press, 1996.

Harris, Trudier. *Black Women in the Fiction of James Baldwin.* Knoxville: University of Tennessee Press, 1985.

———. *Saints, Sinners, Saviors: Strong Black Women in African American Literature.* New York: Palgrave, 2001.

———. "This Disease Called Strength: Some Observations on the Compensating Construction of Black Female Characters." *Literature and Medicine* 14 (Spring 1995): 109–26.

Harris-Perry, Melissa V. *Sister Citizen: Shame, Stereotypes, and Black Women in America.* New Haven: Yale University Press, 2011.

Hogeland, Lisa Marie. "*Invisible Man* and Invisible Women: The Sex/Race Analogy of the 1970s." *Women's History Review* 5, no. 1 (1996): 31–53.

Kinnamon, Keneth. "The Pastoral Impulse in Richard Wright." *Midcontinent American Studies Journal*, 10, no. 1 (Spring 1969): 41–47.

Lavender, Isiah III. "Invisible Women in *Invisible Man.*" *ANQ: A Quarterly Journal of Short Articles, Notes and Reviews,* 27, no. 3 (2014): 146–151.

Morrison, Toni. "The Kindness of Sharks." *Playing in the Dark: Whiteness and the Literary Imagination*, 60–91 New York: Vintage, 1993.

Pavlić, Edward Michael. *Crossroads Modernism: Descent and Emergence in African-American Literary Culture.* Minneapolis: University of Minnesota Press, 2002.

———. "Syndectic Redemption: Above-Underground Emergence in David Bradley's *The Chaneysville Incident.*" *African American Review* 30, no. 2 (1996): 165–84.

Pierce, Yolanda. "The Invisible Women in Ralph Ellison's *Invisible Man* (1952)." In *Women in Literature: Reading through the Lens of Gender*, edited by Jerilyn Fisher and Ellen S. Silber, 157–59. Westport, CT: Greenwood, 2003.

Rich, Adrienne. *Of Woman Born: Motherhood as Experience and Institution.* New York: W. W. Norton, 1976.

Rohrberger, Mary. "'Ball the Jack': Surreality, Sexuality, and the Role of Women in *Invisible Man.*" In *Approaches to Teaching Ellison's* Invisible Man, edited by Susan Resneck Parr and Pancho Savery, 124–32. New York: Modern Language Association, 1989.

Stanford, Ann Folwell. "He Speaks for Whom? Inscription and Reinscription of Women in *Invisible Man* and *The Salt Eaters*," *MELUS* 18, no. 2 (1993): 17–31.

Smethurst, James. "Something Warmly, Infuriatingly Feminine': Gender, Sexuality, and the Work of Ralph Ellison." In *A Historical Guide to Ralph Ellison,* edited by Stephen C. Tracey, 115–40. Oxford: Oxford University Press, 2004.

Spillers, Hortense J. "In the Time of the Daughters and the Fathers." In *Black, White, and in Color: Essays on American Literature and Culture,* 230–50. Chicago: University of Chicago Press, 2003.

Sylvander, Carolyn W. "Ralph Ellison's *Invisible Man* and Female Stereotypes," *Negro American Literature Forum* 9, no. 3 (1975): 77–79.

Tate, Claudia. "Notes on the Invisible Women in Ralph Ellison's *Invisible Man.*" In *Ralph Ellison's* Invisible Man*: A Casebook,* 253–66. New York: Oxford University Press, 2004.

Walker, Alice. *In Search of Our Mothers' Gardens: Womanist Prose.* San Diego: Harcourt Brace Jovanovich, 1983.

Wright, Richard. "Big Boy Leaves Home." In *Uncle Tom's Children*, 16–61. New York: HarperCollins, 1991.

Hannah Baker Saltmarsh's book of literary criticism, *Male Poets and the Agon of the Mother: Contexts in Confessional and Postconfessional Poetry,* concerns gender, confession, and mother-son relationships. Saltmarsh's first book of poems, entitled *Hysterical Water,* is forthcoming from University of Georgia Press in 2021. Saltmarsh lives in Hyattsville, Maryland, with her husband and their three children.

Kiese Laymon's Matriarchs
Grandmothers for Our Times

Kristy McMorris

Over the last decade, Kiese Laymon has emerged as an important voice in contemporary southern and African American writing. Much of Laymon's writing explores and interrogates Black masculinity. Yet while his primary characters include adolescent Black boys and nonfictional portrayals of himself, all of these personas are deeply embedded within complex social and familial networks. Central to these networks are women.

Raised by his mother and additionally nurtured by his grandmother and aunt, many of Laymon's original and enduring frames of reference were borne out of his relationships with these women. In his book of essays, *How to Slowly Kill Yourself and Others in America* (2013), Laymon writes letters to them conveying the impact that they have had on his life. In a letter to his mother, he writes, "I hope you can read this book and know that I listened and I watched. I want you to be proud of the teacher, writer, and worker that I've become. Thank you for being my first teacher."[1]

Laymon deeply explores his relationship with his mother in his personal writing. In fact, his most recent book, *Heavy: An American Memoir*, is addressed to his mother.[2] However, Laymon's grandmother is also key to his self-formation. In *Heavy*, the author describes how he spent his holidays

1. Kiese Laymon, "Epilogue: My First Teachers—A Dialogue," *How to Slowly Kill Yourself and Others in America* (Chicago: Agate Bolden, 2013), 145.

2. In his review of *Heavy*, Saeed Jones writes, "Laymon's memoir is written as a direct address to his mother, a single parent who raised him in Mississippi while completing her postdoctoral work and passionately engaging in black activism with the hope of saving not just her family but the lives of black people throughout the state. . . . By directly addressing his mother and by portraying her as a nuanced and complicated character, Laymon illuminates the fierce love and deception that define his relationship to the woman who made him." (*New York Times,* November 13, 2018).

growing up with his extended family at his grandmother's house. In the novel *Long Division*, one of the teenaged protagonists travels from Chicago to Mississippi to spend every spring break with his grandmother. While she certainly provides needed childcare to her single-parent daughter, the grandmother also offers a much-needed lens through which Laymon and his characters see both themselves and the world. Laymon is not only invested in honoring these matriarchal figures in his life, he is also deeply invested in reimagining the discursive and social terrain that these women inhabit. Part of that work is to imbue these matriarchal figures with all of the authority that they exercise in their households and beyond despite the social and political constraints to which they are subjected by racist and patriarchal ideologies.

In this essay, I focus on Laymon's portrayals of the grandmother figure as they serve to illuminate the worlds that Black women inhabit while transgressing the boundaries of those worlds and pointing the way to better futures. In this way, Laymon's textual grandmothers interrogate patriarchal and racist structures in order to be responsive to the specific social and political demands of the twenty-first century. To frame my discussion of the grandmother figure in Laymon's texts, I will consider these characters vis-à-vis Black feminist analyses of frameworks for Black women's identities, which will serve to contextualize these grandmothers and their desires both within the texts and beyond.

Grandmas' Portrayals

Laymon presents the social and political demands of the contemporary period rather obliquely in the first part of *Long Division*. As readers get to know the protagonist, City Coldson, he is preparing to compete in a nationally televised contest, "Can You Say That in a Sentence?" On the surface, City and his classmate and schoolyard nemesis, LaVander Peeler, both of them young Black males, have earned their place in the spotlight, representing Mississippi before the nation. While this scene looks like an earnest opportunity and exhibition of Black excellence, moments around the contest shed light on the structures of exclusion and discrimination that yet impact the boys.

These invisible barriers of the country's racial history become palpable in City's first (and only) round as a contestant. While the competitors are generally asked to correctly place a relatively far-flung vocabulary word like "lascivious" or "cacodoxy" in a dynamic sentence, City is flummoxed when the first word that he must use is "niggardly." As a young Black man growing up in Mississippi, he views the linguistic proximity between the n-word and "niggardly" with suspicion that quickly turns to anger. His rage in this moment fuels his tirade before the judges, his fellow contestants, and the whole viewing audience on this live televised program. City goes from whispering into the microphone, "My insides hurt when you say that word," to declaring, "I mean, even if I used the word right, I still would've lost. . . . That's messed up, man."[3]

Subsequent to his televised outburst, City walks off the stage and then walks a few miles home where he expects to walk into the punishment that his mother would have for him after her long day at work. He anticipates her "legendary back beating" for the way he conducted himself on television. Upon his return to his empty home, he anticipates his mother's telling him "why what I did was wrong for me, wrong for black people yet to be born, and wrong for the globe. Mama would tell me this, I figured, while crying and giving me the legendary beating of my life."[4] However, the "legendary beating" does not come; instead, "she barely said a word to me."[5] In contrast with City's tumultuous night, his mother remains silent in this scene. Rather than vocalizing her disapproval, "[s]he just folded up in her bed and kept crying on the phone."[6] She is emotionally unable to face her son but instead channels the shame and confusion he had felt onstage as she pleads to her own mother, "'I'm so sorry, Mama. I'm so, so sorry.'"[7] In this moment, America's racial history as crystallized in City's moment on the stage breaks down all communications between the protagonist and his mother creating an effective gulf between them, thus illuminating the ways that the specter and the reality of racism hinders individuals in their efforts to sustain meaningful and supportive communication and relationships.

Contrasting with the mother's silence, the first maternal voice that readers hear in the novel belongs to Grandma, as City's mother has arranged to send him away to spend a week in the country with his grandmother. When she sees City get off the bus, she greets him warmly. With this greeting, Grandma makes a number of key interventions within City's lived experience. When City is first introduced as a character, he is in the middle of a schoolyard battle to roast his rival, LaVander Peeler, who derides him for his weight. Grandma, on the other hand, embraces his "husky" body—"My baby's still

3. Kiese Laymon, *Long Division* (Chicago: Agate Bolden, 2013), 38–39.

4. Laymon, *Long Division*, 45.

5. Laymon, *Long Division*, 45.

6. Laymon, *Long Division*, 45.

7. Laymon, *Long Division*, 45.

husky."[8] Similarly, unlike the silence between City and his mother, Grandma both validates and reassures her grandson. Even without his saying anything, Grandma affirms and accepts City as a person as well as his performance at the contest. Throughout his bus ride to Melahatchie, Mississippi, City was learning of the world's reactions to his outburst at the contest via social media, and the alternating praise and condemnation of the world had left him anxious and confused. So when Grandma tells him, "You look so intelligent. I don't care what none of them folks say," she establishes that City is entering a nonjudgmental space where all of the aspects of his personhood matter.[9] In this way, Grandma offers him loving guidance to be able to chart his own pathways to growth.

Yet, the affirming space that Grandma fosters is not only manifested in the way that she validates City, but he also validates and admires her. In fact, the bulk of the page where the text introduces Grandma is comprised of concrete details of her physical appearance. Entitled "Thick Parts," the narrator frames the section with a brief assessment of his grandmother, whom he describes as "thick and perfect-looking."[10] Truly, Grandma was so "thick" that City would have "bet my original wave brush that Grandma was probably the thickest, finest grandma in all of Mississippi, Alabama, Arkansas, and Louisiana."[11] As City introduces her, he expresses his praise, both for her affirming presence as well as for her physical beauty. Thus, not only does he find refuge with her, but within that space of refuge, Grandma gives City the tools to recognize and reconfigure the landscape of what constitutes aesthetic value. The book juxtaposes City's capacity to see his grandmother as "thick" and "fine" while she admires his growing "husky" body. In doing so, the author offers a vision of community, appreciation, and acceptance within Black families, and of all the interactions that readers encounter in the book, this scene with Grandma represents the first time that difference is held up as beautiful and needing to be protected and sustained.

However, Laymon's portrayal of Grandma in the novel—pointing to her admirable physical, intellectual, and empathetic qualities—is best understood within a broader consideration of perceptions of Black women in American society. In *Ar'n't I a Woman?*, a historical analysis of Black women's experience on the plantation, Deborah Gray White describes archetypal narratives of Black American women which continue to show up in present-day

8. Laymon, *Long Division*, 78.

9. Laymon, *Long Division*, 78–79.

10. Laymon, *Long Division*, 79.

11. Laymon, *Long Division*, 78.

perceptions of Black women's identities. Of these archetypes, "one of the prevalent images of black women in antebellum America was of a person governed almost entirely by her libido, a Jezebel character."[12] Through this stereotype, Black women were viewed as "exceptionally sensual,"[13] ruled by their overwhelmingly prominent and voluptuous corporeal bodies. It is thus significant that Grandma's attractiveness and physical attributes have a prominent place in her portrayal. This foregrounding of the body echoes the centrality of the body in historical and societal perceptions of Black women.

Even though racist and patriarchal ideologies have historically condemned the Jezebel figure for her supposed sexuality and bodily appeal, Gray White also interrogates the archetypal figure of the Mammy who would appear to exist on the other end of the spectrum of Black women's identities. Gray White identifies the mammy as "a woman completely dedicated to the white family, especially to the children of that family. She was, in short, surrogate, mistress and mother."[14] An important "feature about Mammy was her advanced age. . . . However, Mammy's age might also be a metaphor for the asexuality attributed to her."[15] The Mammy figure's asexuality would point to ways in which her role functions as disembodied. She was not seen as a woman who conceived and gave birth to her own children; her body and sexuality were generally disregarded. Instead, she was required to be an asexual being whose only desire was to nurture others. Taken together, the Jezebel and the Mammy figures point to the contradictory discursive space in which Black women have been made to exist within American society—on one hand, hypersexual ruled by her sensual desire, on the other hand, asexual, transcending her worldly and corporeal existence. Both archetypes hinge upon the violent erasure of Black women's experiences and a total denial of Black women's desire. Any attempts to shape others or oneself within the constraints of these archetypal narratives generally reveal themselves to be the discursive prisons that they are, offering Black women no hope of existing in their full humanity.

Yet in this early scene in *Long Division*, Grandma complicates this Mammy/Jezebel dichotomy. Indeed, she is a nurturer serving as a "friend and advisor" to her grandson.[16] While his mother pushes him to display excellence

12. Deborah Gray White, *Ar'n't I a Woman?: Female Slaves in the Plantation South* (New York: W. W. Norton, 1999), 28.

13. Gray White, 28.

14. Gray White, 60.

15. Gray White, 60.

16. Laymon, *Long Division*, 49.

unceasingly and punishes him when he falls short, City describes his Grandma as "one of the only people who would know what it was like to be up there on that stage."[17] His time with her throughout his life has taught him to expect unwavering empathy and acceptance, belonging and community within his grandmother's home. In this way, Grandma's work to nurture others is a vital part of her identity.

Yet unlike the Mammy archetype, Grandma's acts of nurturing are not disembodied from her physical presence. She is a woman who has loved and married, conceived and raised children, and to let her grandson tell it, still maintains her sexual appeal. Rather than inhabiting either end of Mammy/Jezebel dichotomy, Grandma inhabits a complex spectrum of Black womanhood embodying her sensuality, her intellect, and her maternal perspective and expression. In this way, Laymon reconfigures the discursive space through which Black American women have been viewed historically to illuminate a more complex and multidimensional rendering of Black women's humanity.

In her essay in the 1970 anthology, *The Black Woman*, activist and performer Abbey Lincoln offers a more contemporized analysis of the discursive space in which Black women are conventionally relegated within American society. She argues, "We are the women . . . whose nose is 'too big,' whose mouth is 'too big and loud,' whose behind is 'too big and broad,' and whose suffering and patience is too long and enduring to be believed. Who're just too damned much for everybody."[18] The tendency toward excess and extremes within these societal perceptions that Lincoln captures echoes the excessive sensuality of the Jezebel archetype and the extreme asensuality and selflessness of the Mammy archetype. Embodying "just too damned much," Black women can never simply achieve equality with other women or men, and these perceptions of excess are instead used to other Black women, as Lincoln describes. Considering the continual erasure and disavowal of Black women's humanity, Shannon Barber captures the societal perceptions that aim to entrap Black women: "Within the culture, we are praised for our strength and shamed if we are 'too' strong."[19] Indeed, the Black woman's being is always positioned as condemnable.

17. Laymon, *Long Division*, 79.

18. Abbey Lincoln, "To Whom Will She Cry Rape?" *The Black Woman*, ed. Toni Cade Bambara (New York: New American Library, 1970), 186.

19. Shannon Barber, "From Black Men to White Women: Black Women Ain't Real to You," *Wear Your Voice*, May 31, 2018, https://wearyourvoicemag.com/identities/black-women-aint-real-to-you.

Yet these ideas of excess can alternatively be embraced as plenitude. Within Laymon's depiction of the grandmother, the fact of her abundance is central. Her body is impressive in its size and attractiveness—at almost six feet tall, "the thickest, finest grandma" across four states—but she is in no way associated with excess in her grandson's eyes. She is perfection incarnate. In this way, Laymon challenges the contradictory perceptions of Black women both within American society and within the Black community. As Grandma takes the countercultural position to live fully as a big and beautiful Black woman who lovingly affirms her "husky" and dissident grandson, she remains an embodied figure whose corporeal reality informs her intellectual and affective relationship with the world around her. Her goodness, according to her grandson, lies at the intersection between her empathy, her intellect, and to quote the text, her "thick parts."

Grandma in Context

Thus, in many ways, Laymon portrays Grandma with beauty and strength. In this way, she appears almost invincible, but Laymon does not allow readers to rest easy in Grandma's transcendence. Rather, she is a human who is placed within a particular sociopolitical context, as a Black woman in post-Jim Crow Mississippi. In fact, immediately within a page of introducing Grandma in all her "fineness," readers develop a deeper understanding of her through her encounters with others in her community.

City and Grandma's first errand after she picks him up from the bus station is a trip to Walmart to buy a wig. Grandma knows exactly what she is looking for. But in order to get her new wig, she must pass a White saleswoman who functions as a gatekeeper of sorts within this scene. Projecting a colonial and segregationist mindset, the saleswoman directs Grandma's attention to products that have been set aside for Black people. "Hey. Hello'ew there! . . . We want y'all to know'ew that today we've got a special on our Wigs4Blax brand."[20] From City's perspective, he quickly identifies the "Wigs4Blax" as "the raggedy looking wigs on the sale rack." In this scene, the White saleswoman is embodying an authority though she aims to control Grandma, in this case relegating the grandmother to purchase a subpar wig. Examining the subtle politics of this scene, readers see echoes of segregation and racial apartheid, as resources and options for Black people are shown to be separate and unequal. While this moment is initiated by Grandma's pursuit of what *she* wants, it ends with the White saleswoman *telling Grandma what she wants*,

20. Laymon, *Long Division*, 80.

directing her desire to be more aligned with the sociopolitical practices of contemporary racism.

Still, in addition to the segregationist politics that are on view within this scene, the saleswoman also conveys a colonial mindset as she positions herself as an authority on Blackness and Black people's choice of wigs. Certainly, she demonstrates that authority in the way she pushes Grandma toward the Wigs4Blax, but as her sales pitch continues, her sense of authority grows as she expresses even more expertise about Black hair and Black life. She aims to persuade Grandma by offering her a deal: "If you buy one of those Gary curl wigs, y'all get a free year subscription to the new Ebony magazine."[21] Although the woman speaks from a place of authority, her actual knowledge in this situation is questionable. Certainly, Laymon assumes that at least some of his readers will know that *Ebony* magazine is far from "new," as it began publication in 1945. However, additional contradictions in this scene are especially impactful for City. Having just admired his grandmother for her impressive strength and beauty, he senses that in having to face this White woman, "Her voice, her body, everything shrunk. It was like she wasn't even Grandma anymore."[22] Given his interactions with her and everything he knows about her, City portrays Grandma with the authority of expertise: "The rumor was that Grandma actually brought the Jheri (not 'Gary') curl to Melahatchie from Milwaukee back in the early '80's," thereby establishing Grandma's long-standing expertise on the hairstyle as a trailblazer and trendsetter, thus deconstructing the power dynamics of this scene.

Perceiving the destabilized power dynamics between Grandma and the saleswoman clearly puzzles the narrator, and he quickly becomes angry due to the false displacement of authority in this scene and the seemingly automatic association between authority and Whiteness.

Despite the nearly totalizing nature of anti-Black racism, Grandma frames her silences vis-à-vis the saleswoman in terms of her own agency. When, later that afternoon, City expresses his admiration of the stories she tells of his grandfather, the young man asks, "Would you tell that story at the mall in front of that White lady, with the same dynamic sentences?"[23] Her response reveals her acts of discernment rather than her subjection to racism. "First of all, that wasn't no story. And I don't know nothing about no dynamic

21. Laymon, *Long Division*, 80.
22. Laymon, *Long Division*, 81.
23. Laymon, *Long Division*, 82.

sentences. . . . That's the truth. And the truth ain't got a thing to do with that damn white woman, City." Given her clear understanding of the political landscape in which she lives and the character of the people she encounters, Grandma does not share her insight or her perspective with the saleswoman, and her framing that decision in terms of her agency is a vital part of understanding the many dimensions of this character.

Grandma and the Movement for Black Lives

As a Black woman living in Mississippi in the twentieth and twenty-first centuries, Grandma has clearly experienced racist discrimination; however, she has also suffered great loss due to the quotidian nature of violence within a regime of anti-Blackness. Only by way of a complete reading of the novel can readers deduce that Grandma is a widow after her husband drowned trying to save a White child in a nearby lake. One of the great ironies of the novel is that the rescued child grows up to become a White nationalist who re-enters the life of the Coldson family when he assaults City in a racist attack. In this way, the violence that Grandma experiences mirrors the everyday violence of anti-Black racism for people of African descent in the United States and elsewhere around the globe.

In July of 2013, the Black Lives Matter movement was born immediately following the acquittal of George Zimmerman for the killing of Trayvon Martin. Born as a social media hashtag, Black Lives Matter soon became an international movement whose guiding principles include restorative justice, collective value, loving engagement, and a commitment to women, the LGBTQ community, and an unapologetic Blackness.[24] In the organization's statement on "What We Believe," the writers speak to the circumstances that catalyzed the movement:

> Black Lives Matter began as a call to action in response to state-sanctioned violence and anti-Black racism. Our intention from the very beginning was to connect Black people from all over the world who have a shared desire for justice to act together in their communities. The impetus for that commitment was, and still is, the rampant and deliberate violence inflicted on us by the state.[25]

24. Black Lives Matter, "What We Believe," 2018. https://blacklivesmatter.com/what-we-believe/.

25. Black Lives Matter, "What We Believe."

Much of *Long Division* is an exploration of the state-sanctioned violence and anti-Black racism to which Black people have been subjected within this country. The novel interrogates the extremely disproportionate violence and suffering experienced by African Americans throughout the twentieth and twenty-first centuries, from lynching to disenfranchisement and all manner of racial antagonism in between. That Grandma would lose her husband as he sacrificed his life to save a White child is a clear instance of tragedy while it is also an apt metaphor for all of the ways that Black America, whom Nikole Hannah-Jones describes as the "perfecters of this democracy," has suffered sacrifice and loss again and again for this nation.[26]

The repetition of anti-Black violence plays a structural role in Laymon's novel. On his second day in Melahatchie with his grandmother, City leaves her home with friends only to be beaten and tormented by Pot Belly (the White child who was saved from drowning decades earlier by Grandpa Tom Henry). Having seen City's outburst on the televised contest, Pot Belly and his friends target the protagonist for his outspokenness against racism. The attack on City illustrates how the freedom of the White American citizen is predicated on the pain inflicted on the Black body. Pot Belly commits these acts of violence against City because he can, because he will not face any repercussions from the state, and because Black boys cannot have outbursts on television where they interrogate the nation's racial order and their place in it. City's outburst upends the stability of that racial order, and Pot Belly steps in to restore the status quo.

When Grandma sees her injured grandson, he is still processing his encounter with Pot Belly: "All I could do after getting my chest smashed into the ground and being called [the n-word] by those white men was hope it all stopped hurting. That was it."[27] Upon seeing him, Grandma immediately asks "what was wrong," and "What happened to your lip, baby?"[28] Although City does not disclose much information about his afternoon, the protagonist's reticence does not prevent the sequence of consequences that will soon befall Pot Belly.

26. Nikole Hannah-Jones, "Our democracy's founding ideals were false when they were written. Black Americans have fought to make them true," *The 1619 Project: New York Times Magazine,* August 18, 2019.

27. Laymon, *Long Division,* 96.

28. Laymon, *Long Division,* 98.

Rage and Retribution

In a 1961 article, "The Negro in American Culture," James Baldwin states, "To be a Negro in this country and to be relatively conscious, is to be in a rage almost all the time."[29] In her book, *Eloquent Rage: A Black Feminist Discovers Her Superpower*, Brittney Cooper reclaims the seemingly stereotypical image of the Angry Black Woman to consider rage and its utility in the project of striving for liberation and social justice within the overlapping oppressions of racism, patriarchy, and capitalist disenfranchisement of Black women and their families. Cooper's exploration of rage offers a needed framework for understanding Grandma within *Long Division*.

Shortly after Grandma discovers City's injuries, one of his friends casually mentions that Pot Belly is in the work shed behind Grandma's house. When City investigates this for himself despite his disbelief, he discovers that his attacker has indeed been beaten, bound, and gagged, silenced and made immobile in the abandoned work shed. While the protagonist's affective response to Pot Belly's situation ranges from suspicion and anger to sadness and sympathy, he also comes to understand that the project that his family has undertaken is one of collective retribution and therefore must have priority over his growing sympathy toward his attacker.

Retribution. Conceptually, the word retains a discursive opening through which disenfranchised people have been able to envision power despite the perception that the power of the state and its agents is all-encompassing. But living in a place where state-sanctioned violence against Black people has been woven so deeply into its formation and history, Grandma knows that the state won't provide her any recourse for the beating of her grandson. Unlike the subordinate role Grandma may seem to embody in various moments in her life, she directly commits this act of retribution against Pot Belly. When she suffered the loss of her husband, there was nothing to make up for his loss. Any desire she may have had for recompense was left unfulfilled. So, when she sees her injured grandson, Grandma doesn't take the chance of leaving retribution in anyone else's hands.

Retribution, in many ways, mirrors the idea of vengeance in the way that it acknowledges an individual or collective desire to channel one's agency to right a wrong. However, there is a fundamental difference between retribution and vengeance. When one seeks vengeance, one acts in response to a

29. James Baldwin, Emile Capouya, Lorraine Hansberry, Nat Hentoff, Langston Hughes, and Alfred Kazin, "The Negro in American Culture," *CrossCurrents* 11, no. 3 (1961): 205–24. http://www.jstor.org.ezproxy.simons-rock.edu/stable/24456864.

prior wrong, but there is no evocation within the word itself of that which happened before, of that which precipitated this act of vengeance. Certainly, vengeance occurs within a "back and forth" of discrete actions, but the word itself does not witness this underlying dialectic. Vengeance, on some fundamental level, stands on its own, as the intention there is to outmatch and destroy the opponent, thus ending the dialectic.

Retribution, on the other hand, does a different kind of work. Though it echoes vengeance on a conceptual level, the "re" that prefaces the root word offers a clear acknowledgment of that which happened before. Unlike vengeance, retribution does not stand alone; it may not be the last word. Perhaps instead it may always stand in an uneasy tension with an opposing force.

As a Black woman who has lived all of her life in Mississippi, through the civil rights movement, through the Southern Strategy, through the murders of Emmett Till and James Craig Anderson, Grandma has a deep understanding of what it means to live in an uneasy tension with opposing forces. She has learned how to survive in a White supremacist society. When Grandma imprisons and beats Pot Belly in the work shed behind her house, she expresses the rage that she feels in response to the continuous assaults of White supremacist violence. As the White man groans on the grandmother's property, readers as well as City himself must reckon with the reality before them. Pot Belly will not be allowed to go free; Pot Belly will not allowed be to post bail; Pot Belly will not have the opportunity to be tried before a jury of his peers who have repeatedly proven themselves antagonistic to Black survival and freedom. Grandma takes this act of retribution into her own hands because the stakes of Black survival and freedom are too high to leave to chance.

Rather than delivering the death stroke to White supremacy, Grandma resettles the score as retribution, signaling something that is cyclical, a return to a kind of balance between multiple forces, a balance that we have not yet achieved in this country. In this way, *Long Division* reclaims Grandma, the matriarch, as a fundamental site of power that channels our collective energy toward the valuing and sustaining of Black life, past, present, and future.

Bibliography

Baldwin, James, Emile Capouya, Lorraine Hansberry, Nat Hentoff, Langston Hughes, and Alfred Kazin. "The Negro in America." *Cross-Currents* 11, no. 3 (1961): 205–24. http://www.jstor.org.ezproxy.simons-rock.edu/stable/24456864.

Barber, Shannon. "From Black Men to White Women: Black Women Ain't Real to You." *Wear Your Voice*. May 31, 2018. https://wearyourvoicemag.com/identities/black-women-aint-real-to-you.

Cooper, Brittney. *Eloquent Rage: A Black Feminist Discovers Her Superpower*. New York: St. Martin's Press, 2018.

Gray White, Deborah. *Ar'n't I a Woman?: Female Slaves in the Plantation South*. New York: W. W. Norton, 1999.

Hannah-Jones, Nikole, Mary Elliott, Jazmine Hughes, and Jake Silverstein. *The 1619 Project: New York Times Magazine*, August 18, 2019.

Laymon, Kiese. "Epilogue: My First Teachers—A Dialogue." *How to Slowly Kill Yourself and Others in America,* 141–45. Chicago: Agate Bolden, 2013.

Laymon, Kiese. *Long Division*. Chicago: Agate Bolden, 2013.

Lincoln, Abbey. "To Whom Will She Cry Rape?" In *The Black Woman*, edited by Toni Cade Bambara, 182–189. New York: New American Library, 1970.

Kristy McMorris, PhD, hails from McComb, Mississippi. Having been raised blocks away from her grandmother, her childhood church, and key stops on the Mississippi Blues Trail, family, culture, and geography are central to her writing and research. Dr. McMorris has a bachelor of arts in English and African American literature from Howard University in Washington, DC, and a master of arts and doctor of philosophy in Comparative Literature and Africana Studies from New York University.

Representing a third generation of educators within her family, Dr. McMorris was not only taught the importance of education, but she grew up fully immersed in the lives of teachers. As an educator, Dr. McMorris has focused her career on expanding the mission of higher education serving as a professor, and later as the founding director of an early college program for young people in Harlem, New York. Dr. McMorris is currently the dean of studies at Bard Academy and Bard College at Simon's Rock in western Massachusetts.

The essay published in this volume is dedicated to the mothers, grandmothers, and other ancestral matriarchs that have paved the way for her journey today.

Auntie and Mama Zuma

Cheylon Woods

Throughout his career, Dr. Ernest J. Gaines wrote strong female characters who led their communities during an era when women are not allowed the levels of autonomy we see today. These characters evoke memories of southern women who not only had a deep understanding of the oppressive society around them, but held a certain type of kindness and sternness to ensure that the ones they loved went out into a cold, harsh world knowing that there were people who cared and supported them. Dr. Ernest J. Gaines has given many interviews in which he discussed his Aunt Augusteen and how she inspired his work, how she served as a muse for the way he understood Black southern femininity, especially during the Jim Crow era.

The following section is not an essay but an edited transcription of oral interviews with Dr. Gaines and two of his siblings about their aunt, Augusteen Jefferson (Auntie), and their grandmother, Julia McVay (Mama Zuma). These interviews were conducted in 2017 with the purpose of documenting their memories of these women as the matriarchs of their family. All changes made to the original transcript were for readability and clarity, and I strived to preserve the tone and cadence of Dr. Gaines and his siblings. Original transcripts and recorded interviews are housed in the Ernest J. Gaines Center at the University of Louisiana at Lafayette.

This section is a tribute to Auntie and Mama Julia from Dr. Ernest J. Gaines, Norbert Colar, and Lois Young.

Augusteen Jefferson (Aunt Augusteen or Auntie)

Ernest J. Gaines: Well, you know Auntie was crippled. I don't know exactly how it happened. Whether she was born that way or whether it happened when she was a small child. But she was crippled all the years I knew her and my siblings knew her. I am the oldest. She would crawl over the floor as a child, five or six months old, would do. We lived in a house that was built during slavery for slaves. We lived in those homes from the 1940s to the

1960s. The floor was made of rough cypress. You would not want to walk on those floors in bare feet, still, Auntie crawled on the floor with no gloves on her hands or anything on her knees.

She did everything for me and my siblings . . . my brothers and sisters. She cooked for us, she washed our clothes, she ironed our clothes. She could cook well. We didn't have the greatest (quality) food, but it was cooked well. We had a wood-burning stove and she sat on a little bench by the stove. We had the wood on the floor that she could reach and put in the stove. She had another little bench in front of her. We would bring the ingredients, the rice or beans or whatever she was cooking, and she would prepare the food up on that little bench. We had fresh food because we had a garden and raised chickens and a couple of hogs a year. On occasion a farmer, a guy, would raise cattle, butcher it and come down the quarter and sell the beef on a Sunday. Everybody had their rice and beans, corn, peas, or okra. We didn't eat too much leafy vegetables . . . we did eat leaf vegetables, but they were cooked. We didn't eat much lettuce. She would move closer to the stove so she could pick up the food and put it into the pots on the stove. Besides cooking for us, she also washed clothes. We brought her the clothes and the tub of water, she would soak the clothes for a while, and she would brace herself on the rim of the tub to wash the clothes. Washing, washing, washing. Her arms were extremely strong. All of her strength went to her arms. We took the clothes and hung them on the line outside, and when they were dried, we brought them in, and the clothes were ironed. We brought the little bench back to her and the iron. She had to put the iron on the stove in order to heat the iron. Then she would spread out her clothes on the bench and iron them.

She also disciplined us. We had corporal punishment, we had to get our own switch. We had to break our own switch, because she couldn't do these things, and bring them back to her. This didn't always happen in the kitchen; it could be out in the front room or out on the porch. The switch had to be the proper length and the proper size and we had to get down on our knees to take our punishment. We were supposed to do this, and we did it.

Auntie could also crawl out into the yard, to the vegetable garden. Most of the homes there on those plantations had a vegetable garden beside or behind the house. We had potatoes, cabbages, mustard greens and collard greens, okra, cucumbers, peas, different types of produce at all times. Auntie had a little short handle hoe and she would just chop among the vegetables She would always like to put her hands into the earth too, she would pull little grass sprouts up and would work around her plants or whatever she had in the garden at that time of year. She liked to do that and she always liked to put her hands in that dirt. She liked to come down and just feel the earth, feel that little hoe, that little short handled hoe. We could grow it all. I learned how to plant seeds and how to train snap beans so they would grow on the poles. She would say something like "put the pole close together so the beans can climb up (on the pole) She knew a lot and I learned a lot of things, I had to. We also had pecan trees in our backyard. She would crawl over the floor, through the kitchen, down the steps, and across the yard to the pecan trees that were roughly twenty to thirty feet away from the house. She would pick pecans out of the grass and put them in a sack she brought with her. Then she would come back inside and make pralines or cookies with those pecans.

We never did feel sorry for Auntie. Everything she did was as natural to us as anybody else walking. The other people in the Cherie Quarter never felt sorry for her. Most of the people there lived on the plantation and were neighbors. Everybody treated Auntie just like she was one of them, they didn't show any pity I think, there was no need to. Auntie did everything, and she could do as much as others were doing. Her only problem was that she couldn't walk. Auntie kept people's children because most people worked in the fields. If they had a baby, they would pay Auntie 50 cents a day, and she would have a couple of little children she would look after. They [the community] used to visit Auntie all the time because she couldn't go to their place. Old people would talk and talk, she had someone visiting every day. They would sit around and talk. They would visit her and they never felt sorry for her. If she was out there picking pecans, some of the people would come by. An old man or woman would stand around and talk to Auntie while they did the same thing. If she was in the garden, they would do the same thing, stand around and talk, and she would talk to them.

Another thing they used to do, Auntie and some of the older women . . . when I say older women, I mean Auntie's age. Auntie was in her forties at that time I suppose, forties or fifties. I think she died when she was sixty years old. . . . They would make quilts. They would make quilts sitting on the floor. Auntie was already sitting on the floor and the other women would sit there and they would work on these quilts. Maybe it would be three or four of them working together.

And, of course, many of these people made their own clothes: aprons, dresses, or some other kinds of clothes. I don't think they made pants for us, but a dress or apron, they could do things like that. I know Auntie did a lot of patching on our clothes because we were always tearing them. She would put a little piece of cloth and patch it up. Often it didn't match the other clothes, but it covered up the holes.

We could hear the people singing in the church up the quarters. We lived about a hundred or two hundred yards from the church, and we could hear them singing. Auntie would sing along, those little songs. We could hear them praying and preaching, Auntie would know who was singing or praying by their voices. She made sure we went to church too. She made us go to church. You couldn't sing any blues on Sundays, you had to respect the Lord's Day on Sunday, be nice little boys on Sundays. They would bring her the sacrament on sacrament day, say a little prayer or something. They bought the sacrament from church, I remember that.

When I was about thirteen or fourteen years old, I was washing dishes at a restaurant after school and the owner would bring me home at night. Auntie would already be in bed but she would get up to unlatch the door, with a broomstick or something, and get back in bed again. I left in 1948 because my family wanted me to continue school. I had gone to school as far as I could in my parish, and I didn't go to high school because there were no high schools for Blacks at this time in Pointe Coupee Parish. We went to school five and a half months out of the year. I didn't have family in any other part of Louisiana with whom I could stay to go to school. My Auntie wanted me to stay in school; when I moved to California, she told me to be sure to study.

My mother and stepfather had moved to California during the war, as many Black and White people were doing at that time. They were leaving the plantations and going to the West Coast and the East Coast where there were more opportunities for jobs. By then the machinery was taking most of the farming jobs, so all these people had to leave and find work in the cities up north and to the west. I joined my folks in 1948.

I remember the day I left. I left on a Sunday and Auntie had cooked fried chicken for me to eat on my way to California. I had some fruit, I guess. The older women had bought me some things, some sandwiches, to take with me. I know it was difficult for me to finish packing. I had a hard time packing because I didn't want to leave, and I knew I had to go. It took me a long time to pack up my one little suitcase then tell Auntie goodbye. I couldn't cry there, just couldn't cry. I would cry later. The old people were sitting out on the porch while I was inside. A couple of my brothers and other kids played while I packed. When it was time to go, they followed me to the road to catch the bus. I remember just bending over Auntie as she sat on the floor, I took her hand and she took mine, I said "Auntie I am going now, I have to go" and she just shook her head. She gave me advice: "Be good. You came from good people now you be good up there." I said, "Yes, Ma'am," and she said "Okay. Be good."

So I said goodbye to all of them. I had written letters for some of these people, because they could not write, and read their letters when they received mail. They all said goodbye to me, and my brother, Lionel and some other kids followed me to the road to catch the bus. A Trailway bus took me to New Orleans, and from New Orleans I caught a train to California. I was fifteen years old. I have never done anything like that in my life.

I used to write back to Auntie telling her how my grades were going and I was doing all right and all of that sort of thing, and how much I missed home. About two years after I had gone [to California] I had a chance to come back and visit. I think I spent two or three weeks, no, the entire summer here, I think. The people treated me the same way they treated me before. Always wanting me to do something, then cooking something special for me. I did all the things young guys would do that summer of '50 or '51. Fishing, hunting with BB guns . . . we would kill some birds and bring them back, and Auntie would make gumbo or fix something with whatever we brought home. Then I went back to California.

Mardi Gras Day 1953, Auntie died, and we didn't have enough money for me to come back. We only had enough money for Mama to come back, so I couldn't come to the funeral, which was probably the worst day of my life. I was closer to Auntie than I had been to anybody, closer to her than I was to my mother, but I could not go back to the funeral. I wrote letters to different people explaining how I felt, but they could not help me. I didn't go back to Louisiana until I finished college. I visited the cemetery where Auntie was buried. They told me she was buried by the pecan tree in the center of the graveyard. The tree was there but there was no marker for her grave. My brothers, Lionel and Eugene, are buried close by the tree to keep her company. Auntie was buried there but there is no mark or anything like that, no mark at all. When my two brothers, Lionel and Eugene, died I had them buried by that tree because I wanted a mark there for Auntie, so I had them buried and that's where they are buried now. But exactly where Auntie is in that exact space, I know within five or six feet, maybe ten feet, I know she is in that area. But exactly, to know exactly where it was, I don't know because by the time I came back, the grave sunk in a bit, the dirt sunk so I couldn't tell exactly where the grave was. I know it was in an area over by twenty feet, or something in that diameter. I still miss my aunt; as a matter of fact, I think of her every day, every day of my life I think of Auntie.

Norbert Colar: Aunt Augusteen was our foster mother. From the time I was just a young child, she always seemed to have been there. She couldn't walk, I never really knew exactly what her total condition was, I supposed she must have had something like . . .

Lois: Polio or something like that?

Norbert: Something of that nature because she didn't have the strength in her legs to stand at all, but she would move around the house effortlessly. She had a wheelchair that she didn't care to use. In those days the wheelchairs were built like this chair right here (points to a dining room table chair). Auntie was a fairly short woman, so it would have been a hassle getting in and out of that wheelchair all the time, and she preferred not to even use it. Even though she couldn't walk, she had full control of the home and all of us children. From my oldest brother to the youngest, we did whatever she wanted us to do and she was just a very loving, caring, stern kind of person that made sure that everything went the way it was supposed to. The range of things that she was able to do was just incredible. Like when it came to laundry. Auntie would have us bring two #2 tubs right near the bench, fill them with water, and she would start to wash the clothes on the washboard. She would wring out the laundry and put it down into the water to be rinsed. Once the clothes were washed, Charles, Lois, and I go out into the backyard and hang it up on the line; you know, the old type clothesline where you had clothespins and a big prop to hold the wire up so the clothes didn't touch the ground. I never saw it as a job. I was just doing what she needed to be done to get the clothes washed.

The same thing happened when she was preparing dinner. Auntie knew how to prepare anything you could find, from wild game to domesticated animals (cows, chickens, pigs), and all kinds of vegetables. She did all the cooking in the house. The way she could use that stove; I mean she baked bread; both the yeast bread that rose to just regular biscuits and other bread you could cook right on top of the oven as well as in the fireplace. When it was inclement weather, like when you had rain and coldness, she would cook at the fireplace. On regular, warm days she would crawl into the kitchen, get up on the bench and have me bring her whatever she needed so that she could wash, clean, and prepare the food for cooking. After she lit the stove, she would send me out into the garden for ingredients. Say, for instance, if she wanted a head of cabbage, I just went out and cut a head of cabbage and bring it back, and she would wash it, prepare it and get it ready for cooking. I did the same thing if she was preparing chicken or something out of the backyard. When I was five or six, she taught me how to catch a chicken. I would drop corn near my feet and all the chickens would come running. She would select the chicken to cook and I would catch the chicken and wring its neck so that my aunt could then take the hot water and pull the feathers out and everything. I would help her do that. Everything that needed to be done was done by hand and with her directions.

Whether it was feeding the chickens, feeding the hogs, or whatever it was going on, she would just supervise and we would go out and do it.

Auntie was like a parent. She gave everybody a job. We would get up in the morning, and one of us would go out and would get the kindling or anything that needed to be bought inside, like cutting wood. Others would be making up beds and taking out the chamber pots and cleaning them. Just getting things done, and after breakfast in the morning, somebody washing the dishes. Somebody always had some little chore to do. The same thing happened when we came home from school, it was always some kind of chore that we all had to do. We all took part in working in the garden. We all took part in cleaning the front yard. As a matter of fact, in those days, especially during the summertime, we would have to sweep the yard. There were no lawns, but we cut like a trench around the rose bushes and the other flowers in the yard and keep that watered and the rest of the yard would be as clean as the porch and the house was. Everything was just swept up nice and neat. It was something else.

When I was little, I would watch her crawl down the steps, into the yard, and out into the garden to show us how to do things. As we got older, she would crawl out on the porch, sit on its edge, and just tell us what she wanted us to do. Auntie used to order these seeds from a catalog, from the Sears catalog, flower seeds, all types of vegetables. Learning how to garden from Auntie was a fun little thing we did together. We took care of the plants, and when the vegetables matured, we would sit around and shell peas and beans so we could dry them in this little storage room my dad built in the backyard. So you would take things like beans, pinto beans, and put them in burlap sacks and hang it so it could dry. And then things like garlic . . . remember we used to braid those, Lois, and hang them up in the kitchen?

Lois: Yeah.

Norbert: We also had a little grinder in the storage shed, and we used it to grind dried corn and other kinds of feed for the chickens and hogs. It just all worked. Everything just seemed so well structured.

Auntie was very kind, but If she told us to do something and we didn't do it or we started arguing or fighting with one another, we took that long walk out into the front yard and got a switch off the peach tree. You bought it back in and knelt down if she felt that we needed a couple of hits to get us to understand that when she said no, she meant no, and she didn't want us fighting among one another. It was something that we did and a few minutes later we were playing and laughing and talking and doing everything else we were supposed to do. She was, there was no doubt, in control of everything. It was just a good environment, very safe and loving.

Once we got all the things she wanted to be done done, we could go out and play as long as we wanted to or until she told us to come back into the house. At that time, those old houses sat on pillars and so we could also go under the house to play as well as in the yard and out in the pastures. It was just a lot of freedom of movement. Charles and Lois and I would just go outside and pick berries and go looking for crawfish in the big ditches and stuff like that. It was just fun going out around the countryside, and Auntie felt comfortable allowing us to do those things. We walked all around through the fields and everything. The people working in the fields would say, "Your aunt, does she know you are out here?" and we would say, "Hello," and go back home. Most of the time we bought the berries, muscadines, and all kinds of stuff we would find, home. It was just a fun way to live. There was no stress in terms of feeling like we didn't have the things we thought we needed or was looking for something we thought we would have. None of that was going on. It was just a very good environment to live in. I had no idea, in terms of economics, what our status was because we were always comfortable.

Although we freely played throughout the Quarters, Aunt Augusteen always put restrictions on how far and where she wanted us to go, especially when Charles was given a bicycle by a family friend named Lester Simon. When that old bike came to Charles, I thought the greatest thing going.

We would go to New Roads with our Aunt Octavia, Uncle Horace's wife, and every time we went to New Roads, Charles would buy one of these little tiny cans of paint. They only sold black and white paint, so one week the bicycle was black and about a week or two later the bicycle would be painted white. Then we started to realize that you could mix it, make it gray and we painted the bicycle gray. Naturally, it was just a fun thing to do.

Our aunt didn't want us to get in trouble riding the bike somewhere where we might have an accident or something. She would always tell us, "Okay don't pass the railroad track." Near the graveyard [Mount Zion Cemetery] there used to be a railroad track just before the graveyard, and she didn't want us to go across the railroad track. Going up toward the river (False River), she didn't want us going any further than near the land where our grandmother lived, which was probably about a half a block from the main road or highway (False River Road). I would sit on the handlebars and Charles would start pumping the bicycle, you know pedaling the bicycle. We would start riding nice and fast and Charles would say, "Hey man, let's go over the railroad tracks," and I would say, "Auntie told us we can't go over the railroad tracks." He would say, "Yeah but nobody is going to know," and I would say, "Yeah, but she told us don't go over the railroad tracks."

So we would ride over the railroad track and the next thing we know we are headed toward the sugar mill and then we'd get about halfway down and I'd say, "Man, we got to go back," and so we would turn around and start coming back. Charles was pumping away and sometime later we would get back and she would say, "How far did you go? Did you go over the railroad track?" and we would say, "Oh no, no." "Did you go over the railroad track?" and I had a hard time not telling her the truth, so I would go on and confess and Charles would just look at me. Next thing you know we are going over to the peach tree to get a switch and bringing a switch back to Auntie. There was a network between the older people in the quarters, where they had messages going up and down the Quarter with one another that was always ahead of us. We knew she couldn't follow us, but she always knew what was going on when we got home or the following day. I guess somewhere along the line she was talking with the neighbors and telling them to look out for us on the bicycle and everything, and that's how she knew we went over the tracks. It took us a while to figure out that people were paying attention to what we were doing and letting her know. It was a learning process that worked out good, it was a lot of fun.

Auntie was very strict regarding the children and weapons. All of the women in my family were. I remember one time Charles and I went to the carnival with Aunt Octavia. Charles and I were naturally enjoying things like the carousel, Ferris wheel. We must have had about a dollar or so to spend and Charles decided to take this picture in a photo booth. I think it cost a nickel or a dime; you go in and get a photograph, a little black and white picture. Before taking the picture, Charles played a game and won this little pocket knife, and he decided that he was going to take a picture with it. So he takes this picture, and he is holding this knife in front of him like he is a warrior or something. . . . It was kind of neat, I mean you read the Tarzan comic books and Prince Valiant and all that, all of these guys knew how to handle a knife and stuff so that was kind of heroic to see that. We would watch these films on the weekends. This is all due to the influence of comic books. . . . Anyway, to Charles it was a great picture. To me, it was a pretty nice picture, but Auntie didn't appreciate that a bit. When we got home, once again, Charles took that walk out to the peach tree and got a switch. She wore Charles's butt out. That was the last we saw of the picture.

She didn't want Charles to believe that brandishing a knife was a positive thing. Charles was holding it like in a stabbing position. She didn't go for that at all, because, number one if you brandish a knife toward someone else you might end up hurting them or getting hurt. Number two, once you have a knife, you now have an edge. And this makes you a little bit more than the next guy, a lot more menacing or whatever it meant. Usually, adults that were drinking, they would get angry and the first thing they thought about was the weapon they were carrying, the same as today. So she didn't want any of that in our paths, especially at that age (between eight and ten). But it was all about not getting in trouble and not having that thought in your head. At that particular time, segregation was in full force and she just didn't want anything to happen to any of us. I know she didn't approve of it at all and I am sure that was the reason that she didn't want him to get in trouble someday, so she took the knife away and the picture.

The same thing happened to me. We got these BB guns, little air rifles, and Charles and I used to go hunting and pretending we were in the Old West and stuff. We would shoot at birds and everything very seldom hit anything but it was just fun going around the countryside. We were always told not to point these rifles, these air guns at one another. We had a rifle in the house to hunt deer, we had a shotgun also. We knew that weapons were dangerous and we were told to never point it at anybody, but as long as we were out shooting at little targets it was okay.

We had these little stationary bull's-eye targets that we used to put on a fence. Charles and I would sit down and shoot at the targets. After we shot at a target, we had to go and get the target to see if you actually hit it because those little BBs were really small. Sometimes they made just a little indenture on the bull's-eye, you could barely tell if you had done anything. One day, our friend from a few doors down, Sam Bebin (Buck), came into the yard to play and shoot targets. Buck takes his shot and goes out to the gate to see if he hit the target. Before he could come back to the porch, I was aiming at the target and I accidentally hit him on the back of the neck. Buck comes back and lays on the porch face down. My mother comes out and she goes, "What's the matter with you, Buck? What you doing down there?" (Buck says) "Oh, Jr. shot me." [Laughter.] I didn't mean it, but I shouldn't have been shooting the gun while he was down there by the target. That was another walk to the peach tree. And then they took the BB gun, put it up on the wall and I was restricted from using the BB gun for the next month or two. It was a long time before I touched that thing again. We learn our lessons from making mistakes as well as being told.

You know, years later I am in the military and they are saying the same thing. Never point a weapon toward anyone and never discharge a weapon if someone is in the area where a weapon is being fired. Those kinds of messages stay with you, they don't leave you. As a matter of fact, I became a weapons instructor in the military. I always thought about that little situation. Sam and I today, every now and then, he is living out in San Francisco, we talk about once a month on the phone and we'll talk about that. He and I will laugh and talk about it. Cost me a pretty good butt whipping.

Lois: There is just one thing he [Norbert] didn't cover and that's I would like to talk about we called her Auntie (Ain-knee) and she smoked a pipe. She was a big pipe smoker and she would save the bottom of the goo, we called "pompe." I am not sure how you spell it, P-A-U-P-E-E?

Norbert: I think, P-O-M-P-E.

Lois: It was the substance in the bottom of a pipe that was sticky and whatever. But she would save this pompe and we would wrap it in like little balls and then the people would come by or we would deliver it to different people and they would put it in their mouth. It was straight nicotine, if you wanted a high, that was it. Also, a lot of the individuals would come by and spend time with Auntie. They would sit on the porch and talk to her and pick up their pompe. I always . . . that was amazing to me. I would watch the whole process. I would watch her smoke the pipe every day, save this stuff in little round things, and wrap it in little paper. I just thought the process was most unusual. I was spellbound by it. Especially they put it in their mouths and I was thinking about their teeth and gums . . . but they seemed to really enjoy it very, very much. She smoked her pipe every day.

Julia McVay (Mama Zuma)

Lois: Oh yes, I have a couple of stories about Mama. I lived with my grandmother, Julia McVay, and she worked at the big house which you have seen on Cherie Plantation. Our place was very close to the big house. She would work just about every day. Every weekday I would get up in the mornings and get ready. I would go down to the Quarters to be with the boys and Auntie while Mama Julia would go to work in the big house. In the evenings, in the afternoons I would go back to the big house, to Mama Julia's, but I would spend the day down with Auntie and the boys.

I learned to cook very early. Yeah, I started cooking when I was about six and she had a little stool made for me. I would step on, step up so I can be high enough for the stove. She would tell me what to put in the pot. We would cook everything. Our favorite was the tomatoes and corn. What was that called, tomatoes and corn?

Norbert: Succotash.

Lois: The other thing with Mama Julia was I would go fishing with her. She was a great fish person, woman. I'm telling you and with an old rod, old cane rod and she had the hip boots and she bought me some boots too you know. I was so proud, there we go, we just had to cross and be right there at the river. There were no houses or anything there when I was living with her. So we would just cross the road and go down to the river to do our fishing. She would catch more fish, I wouldn't catch any. I would catch maybe a little one. But she would yank them out, I am telling you she was a real fish person. She just knew how to work with that rod. Then of course we would go home and clean the fish and fry them.

I remember one time the great story about Mama Julia was I had my chores. We started doing chores very early in our lives and one of mine was to mop the bedroom. I don't know if you have seen in some of the old places the beds are really high and the bedspreads would go all the way down to the floor. She told me to mop the bedroom. So I came in and did my little mopping. But when it came to the bed, I took the mop and went all the way around. I thought I was finished so I went to bed. She woke me up about one or two o'clock in the morning and she said, "Get up." I said, "What's wrong Mama?" She said, "Did you mop?" I said, "Yes." "Did you mop everything, the whole floor?" I said, "Yes." She said, "I want you to get up and finish because you didn't mop under the bed." Here at one or two o'clock in the morning, I am getting up, getting the bucket, the mop and everything.

But I tell you I am one person that will not cut a corner today. I mean when I do something, I do it thoroughly. It may take me long because I am really slow but efficient. I never will forget that. She got me out of bed in the middle of the night, the middle of the morning to finish that chore. What a lesson that was. There is no way I halfway do anything anymore.

Norbert: Julia McVay, we used to call her Mama Zuma. Years later I found out that the name Zuma was a nickname a lot of the slaves used for different people. So I don't know how she went from Julia to Zuma, but we used to call her Mama Zuma.

It is a great thing about having an auntie and a grandmother like ours. My mother was a straight-up disciplinarian, she didn't let us get away with anything, but when you have a loving aunt and loving grandmother around, boy they can just take away the harshness. They would pet us and tell us how nice we are and say the same thing our mother was saying but in a much gentler way and you don't repeat that behavior. Whenever I was around my grandmother or around my aunt I always felt really comfortable around them, even when they scolded me about something I shouldn't do. They were very kind . . . they wouldn't let us get away with anything . . . they would just tell you things that made you want to do what they said.

After college I worked in probation and counseling. I worked with juveniles for a long time. The way you express behavior and explain to them how to deal with it has a lot to do with whether or not they listen to you. Much of my approach with the kids I worked with was influenced by the way they talked to me when I was a child. As a counselor, I could sit there and let them say all they wanted to say and a lot of them just wanted to get stuff off their chest, maybe straighten out a few issues here and there. I often wonder if part of my comfort with being a counselor had a lot to do with my aunt. People would come in and just spill their guts about all sorts of things, and she would just sit there and talk to them. She wouldn't tell them what to do or how to do it, she would just sit there and listen to them. When they had said all they wanted to say they would get up and take off. I found out that years later when I started working in probation I started dealing with addicts and other types of people. I had no problem dealing with them.

Lois: I think we all have such fond memories of growing up and not even thinking about being poor. My little . . . I don't have any pictures, I am sure they must be some pictures somewhere, but I would have these big ribbons in my hair. My little dresses would be starched and I was just a little clean princess, I am telling you, mostly because of Mama Julia and Auntie. To this day you care about your appearance, what you look like, how you look like and from a little girl I was brought up that way so it just stuck with me. What fond memories of such wonderful strong women. They were just amazing.

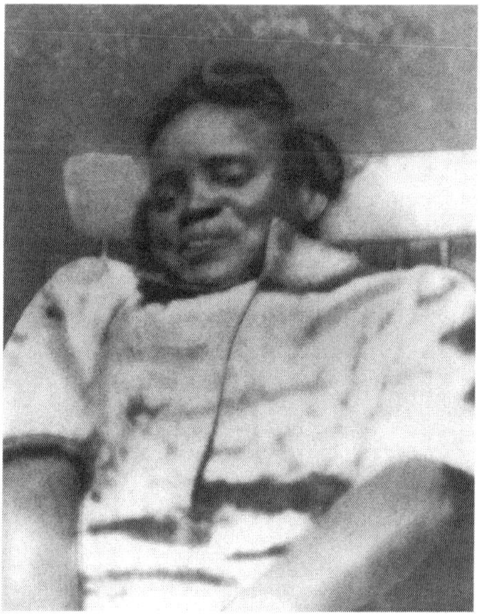

Courtesy of the Ernest J. Gaines Center, University of Louisiana at Lafayette

Cheylon Woods is an assistant professor and the archivist/head of Ernest J. Gaines Center. She actively worked with communities and prominent figures in the region to fill in information gaps related to African American history in South Louisiana. Cheylon received a dual BA degree in history and political science from Louisiana Tech University. She later received her master's degree in heritage resources from Northwestern State University in Natchitoches, Louisiana, and her master's in library and information science from Louisiana State University. Between her two master's degrees, Mrs. Woods was awarded a fellowship through the Institute of Museum and Library Services at the Alabama Department of Archives and History. As a fellow, Cheylon worked with the staff of the Alabama Department of Archives and History to work with Black communities throughout the state document and preserve their histories. Mrs. Woods has presented on the work of Dr. Ernest J. Gaines nationally since 2015 and continues to publish works on Black historical collections, Dr. Ernest J. Gaines and his work, and the preservation of rural Black communities through folklore and archives. She is a member of Phi Alpha Theta, Society of American Archivists, Louisiana Library Association, Society of Southwest Archivists, and Association of the Study of African American Life and History.

Part V

The Matriarch Outside Fiction

"We Were All We Had"
Transcending Race and Forging a Community of Mothers in the Post-Civil Rights Era South

Marco Robinson

"During that time colored folks and white folks had to figure out a way to stick together . . . we were all we had."

—Alice Mae Lipford

A central part of the southern experience that has been situated along the periphery of the regional narrative is the valiant stories of the women of the Southland. During slavery, times of war, and even times of immense social change, women came to the helm as central players, contributors, and political actors in shaping the destiny of the American South. Historian Glenda Gilmore asserts, "Women were integral components of economic gain, generational change and ultimately civic participation."[1] Moreover, the social upheavals of the mid-1900s placed both Black and White southern women in a conundrum. On the one hand, women saw the transformation of the public and private spheres after World War II as an opportunity to seek an education and become more active leaders in their communities. On the other hand, in many instances, women of both races were catapulted into positions where they became community mediators and played pivotal roles in re-establishing equitable race relations in their communities. Alice Mae Lipford, a Black domestic and mother of four in DeSoto County, Mississippi, recalled, "During that time colored folks and white folks had to figure out a way to stick together . . . we were all we had."[2]

1. Glenda Gilmore, *Gender and Jim Crow: Women and the Politics of White Supremacy in North Carolina, 1896–1920* (Chapel Hill: University of North Carolina Press, 1996), 1–10.

2. Alice Mae Lipford, interview by Marco Robinson, 2000.

Lipford's observation embodies the optimism and even uncertainty Black and White women felt during and after the height of the civil rights era in the South. Jason Sokol argues, "When the civil rights movement tore through the southern landscape in the 1950s and 1960s, it challenged the attitudes of many, undermined their customs, and upended their ways of life."[3] Notably, in DeSoto County, local women's lives were profoundly changed by social developments resulting from the civil rights movement and the economic changes that occurred in the area after World War II. Many women in the area left the domestic sphere and found work outside the home. Most importantly, many women of both races sought opportunities to obtain a college education. As a result of local women entering into these public spaces, the traditional racial and gender hierarchies within the communities in DeSoto County were given a face-lift, especially in the town of Hernando.

Black and White women living in Hernando's incorporated city limits and immediate outer lying areas were among the first individuals in the county to confront the realities of school integration, primarily due to many of their roles as teachers, administrators, and most importantly mothers. The mothers of Black and White school children in Hernando were on the front lines of the school desegregation process and their reactions, good and bad, set the tone for the whole town. Central to Hernando's integration story are the efforts of Black and White female school administrators who served as mediators and community bridge builders during this critical time of transition. The life experiences of Gemenie Bowdre (a Black woman) and Carolyn Cleveland (a White woman), both female administrators in the DeSoto County School District during the integration period, are examined in this chapter to bring light to their roles in smearing the color line and uniting mothers in Hernando.

The oral histories that I conducted with local women in Hernando revealed a myriad of issues related to place, gender, class, power, and race. Consequently, as Glenda Gilmore argues, "Place assembled the current concepts of class and race into a stiff-sided box where southern whites expected African Americans to dwell."[4] Likewise in DeSoto County, as it relates to gender roles, during the early to mid-1900s, both Black and White women

3. Jason Sokol, *There Goes My Everything: White Southerners in the Age of Civil Rights, 1945–1975* (New York: Vintage Books, 2006), 1; Note: DeSoto County is the farthest northwestern county just south of Memphis, Tennessee, and Hernando is the county seat.

4. Gilmore, *Gender and Jim Crow,* 1–10.

were mainly relegated to the domestic sphere, had limited educational opportunities, and played minimized roles in public affairs. This storyline is profoundly altered by the social and economic changes that occurred during the post-World War II years in the county. The archival records used and oral testimonies that follow illuminate DeSoto County's tumultuous racial history, place women as central figures in promoting change in the county's post-civil rights era history, and present scholars and lay-readers alike with a different narrative that begs them to reconsider the roles of southern women in American culture and history.

Segregated DeSoto County: The Worlds of Black and White Women as Witnessed Through the Eyes of Gemenie Bowdre and Carolyn Cleveland

Gemenie Bowdre's and Carolyn Cleveland's experiences growing up in Jim Crow era DeSoto County were profoundly shaped by the racial order and caste system created during Reconstruction. Black progress threatened what (White) southerners called "place."[5] Therefore, post-Reconstruction era DeSoto County was characterized by segregationist public policies, racial discrimination, and the lack of economic equality for Blacks. During the early 1900s, a bold color line was drawn between the races that relegated most Blacks to sharecropping situations and deprived them of participating in the local political processes. Then too, class structures within DeSoto County's White community stratified land-owning Whites above landless poor White farmers. As it relates to poor Whites, Wayne Flynt asserts, "After the [Civil] war, poor whites assumed many aspects of a caste system, their status became more rigid, and their alienation from the general political order more intense."[6]

The racial and class hierarchical structures existing in DeSoto County during the early 1900s were maintained through violence and promoted by local educators. The origins of this racial strife can be found during the antebellum period where slave owners sought to maintain control over the large slave population in the area and after the Civil War due to their desire to relegate emancipated Blacks to second-class citizenship in order to maintain White social, economic, and political dominance. Julius Thompson concludes, "No state was more severe in terms of lynching than Mississippi, which holds the

5. Gilmore, *Gender and Jim Crow,* 1–10.

6. Wayne Flynt, *Dixie's Forgotten, New Edition: The South's Poor Whites* (Bloomington: Indiana University Press, 2004), 33.

record for the highest number of lynching victims in the United States from 1865 to 1965, at more than 500 out of a total of at least 5,000 victims since Reconstruction."[7] The lynching data collected by Thompson revealed that DeSoto County was in the top five counties where lynchings occurred and Hernando was one of the top five destinations where vigilante justice was carried out.[8] In March of 1934, an unidentified *Pittsburgh Courier* correspondent reported the lynching of three African American boys in Hernando. The account described included the boys begging for their lives to be spared and the crowd singing "I'll be glad when you're dead and bye bye black blackbirds."[9] The public spectacle and statistics of violence in DeSoto County described above created an atmosphere of terror and supported White dominance in the area. This same message was interwoven into the writings of local school administrators in DeSoto County, namely Edwin Henderson Randle.

Edwin Henderson Randle, founder and principal of Randle University School, a local private school for Whites located in Hernando, wrote widely on "the Negro Problem" and in support of White supremacy. Randle was also an ex-Confederate soldier, former slave owner, and local leader in the Methodist Church. His three seminal works are *The Characteristics of the Negro* (1910), *The Plurality of Human Race* (1911), and *Antagonism of Forces in Nature Universal* (1912). In these works Randle promoted Southern White male paternalism, Black subservience to White authority, and the superiority of the White race based on religious and scientific evidence. Glenda Gilmore maintains, "In the segregated South, Whites invented a past for posterity by making up on a daily basis a multitude of justifications and rationalizations for racial oppression."[10] Randle wrote, "The negroes had more liberty without freedom than they now have with freedom and truly one of the Negroes most serious losses in the changed condition is in no longer having their children partly raised by white people."[11] Many White southerners at the turn of the twentieth century could

7. Julius Thompson, *Lynchings in Mississippi: A History, 1865–1965* (North Carolina: McFarland & Company, 2007), 1.

8. Julius Thompson, *Black Life in Mississippi: Essays on Political, Social and Cultural Studies in a Deep South State* (Lanham, Maryland: University Press of America, 2001), 62–69.

9. *Pittsburgh Courier*, March 22, 1934; Note: The boys were accused of attacking a White girl in Holly Springs, Mississippi, a nearby town.

10. Gilmore, *Gender and Jim Crow,* 1–10.

11. E. H. Randle, *Characteristics of the Southern Negro* (New York: Neale Publishing Company, 1910); E. H. Randle, *Plurality of Human Race* (Nashville: Publishing

work themselves into a frenzy when it came to questions of social equality between the two races.[12] The idea that Black people in the South were a serious liability instead of a valuable labor source surfaced shortly after the issuance of the Emancipation Proclamation.[13] Moreover, and arguably, Randle's assertions regarding race and White supremacy had a profound impact on shaping many members of DeSoto County's White community's ideas on race and place due to his influence as an author, educator, and community leader.

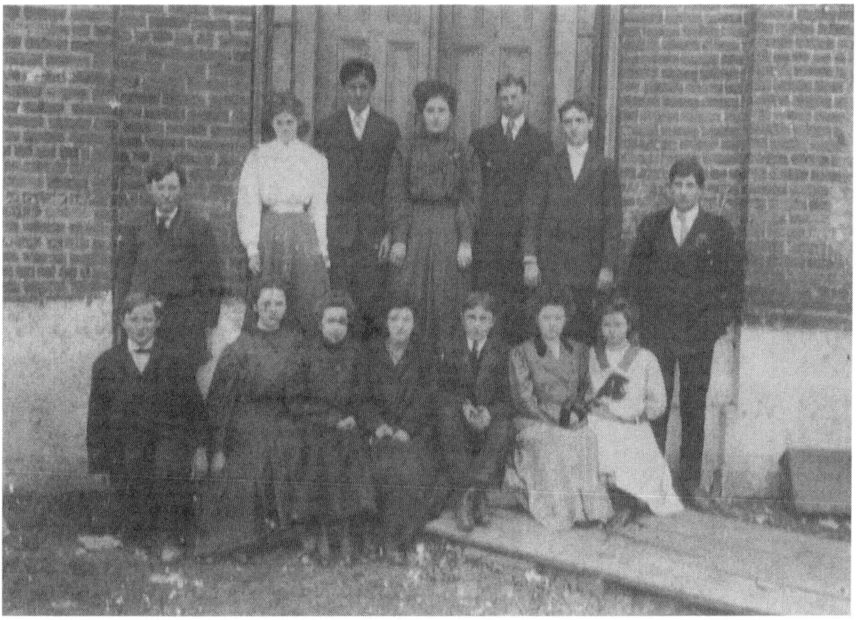

Fig. 1: Picture of students at Randle University School, c. 1900, courtesy of DeSoto County Museum

House of the Methodist Episcopal Church South, 1911); E. H. Randle, *Antagonism of Forces in Nature Universal* (Nashville: Publishing House of the Methodist Episcopal Church South, 1912); Randle, 1, 58–59.

12. James Hollandsworth, *Portrait of a Scientific Racist: Alfred Holt Stone of Mississippi* (Baton Rouge: Louisiana State University Press, 2008), 3.

13. George Fredrickson, *The Black Image in the White Mind: The Debate on Afro-American Character and Destiny, 1817–1914* (Hanover, NH: Wesleyan University Press, 1971), 324–25.

During the late 1800s and early 1900s, the socioeconomic conditions surrounding race and place in DeSoto County created a historical vacuum that had suction on the lives of all residents. Both Bowdre and Cleveland's lives were thrust into the intersection of these community race and class dynamics. They both were born into a racially segmented society shaped by White male authority. Using education as their vehicle, Bowdre and Cleveland learned to navigate and reshape the boundaries of their worlds. The fact that they were both females further complicated the social and economic terrain which they had to traverse to be successful. Most DeSoto County women, both Black and White, were still confined to working in their homes, assisted their families on small farms, could not vote, and received limited opportunities to get a college education. According to Cheryl Greenberg, "Fully fifty-five percent of black women in the United States reported having a job in 1910, compared with twenty percent of white women."[14] Following World War I, in 1920, DeSoto County's population was just over 25,000, of which over 18,000 of the residents were Black. Black voter repression and economic discrimination ensured the Black majority in the county would not enjoy any political or economic influence. The threat of violent reprisal, in the minds of local Blacks, represented a line of demarcation in the county which they dare not cross.

Gemenie Bowdre was born July 1, 1928, a year before the stock market crash that brought the country into the Great Depression. James and Julia Pope-Bowdre, her parents and landowners, weathered this turbulent time by holding fast to their faith and working hard on their farm. James and Julia Bowdre instilled a strong work ethic in their three children, engaged in a Christian lifestyle, and promoted belief in one's self. Bowdre remembered, "My parents taught me that I could become whatever I wanted to be." Although the Bowdres were farmers, they understood that more doors would open for their daughter if she had an adequate education.[15] They paid for all of their children to attend high school. The untimely death of Bowdre's father when she was seven years old had a profound impact on her life. She recalled, "Following daddy's death everybody was responsible for working."[16]

At an early age, Bowdre was confronted with discouraging ideas regarding her sex. She recalled, "There was an instance in my Sunday school class at

14. Cheryl Greenberg, *To Ask for an Equal Chance: African Americans in the Great Depression* (Lanham, MD: Roland & Littlefield, 2009), 5.

15. Gemenie Bowdre, interview conducted by Marco Robinson, 2000.

16. Bowdre, interview, 2000.

church where the male parent of a boy I beat in a memorization competition told his son not to let a girl bet him . . . boys are smarter than girls."[17] This incident left an indelible mark on Bowdre and she worked to overcome male chauvinistic ideas and transform traditional gender roles ascribed to women in her community. Tera Hunter asserts, "African American women were central to public discourse about race, gender and they fought for dignity and self-respect and won small gains, moments of reprieve, and symbolic political victories."[18] Academic pursuits were an essential part of Bowdre's formative years.

Bowdre received her education in a one-room school house located at Morgan Grove Baptist Church. During this period, churches supported "community church schools" in the immediate area. The majority of DeSoto County's community church schools went through the eighth grade and students of all ages were integrated into one classroom. Bowdre recollected, "When I became a teacher at Morgan Grove I had grades one through eight . . . It was a very difficult task teaching." [19] During the Jim Crow Era, there was no public-supported high school in DeSoto County for African Americans. Following completing the eighth grade, Bowdre began her studies at Baptist Industrial College High School, a private high school established by the Black Baptist churches in northwest Mississippi.

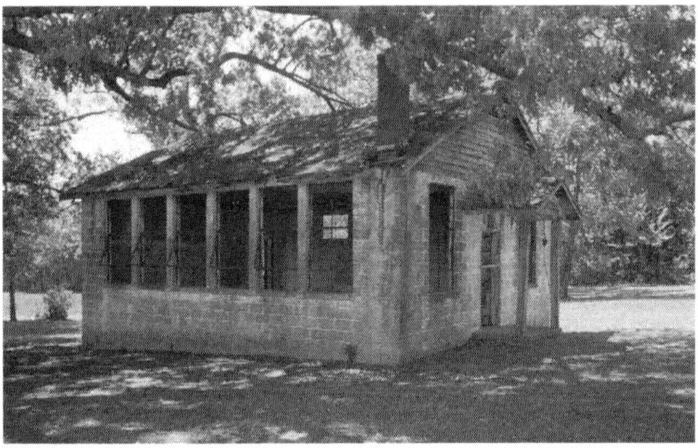

Fig. 2: Picture of the Morgan Grove School, courtesy of Gemenie Bowdre

17. Bowdre, interview, 2000.

18. Tera Hunter, *To 'Joy My Freedom: Southern Black Women's Lives and Labors after the Civil War* (Cambridge, MA: Harvard University Press, 1997), viii.

19. Bowdre, interview, 2000.

The Black Baptist church played a significant role in the African American community in DeSoto County, particularly as it relates to education. In 1885, the Pleasant Hill/Hammon Hill Association, an organization composed of Black Baptist churches in DeSoto County and neighboring counties, was organized for the expressed purpose of raising money to build a high school for Blacks living in northwest Mississippi. During the late 1800s and early 1900s, the closest high school to DeSoto County residents was at Rust College in Holly Springs, Mississippi, located over twenty miles away. Bowdre entered Baptist Industrial College High School (BICHS) during the early 1940s in order to become a teacher.[20] James Anderson contends, "The teacher training courses also included ample time for agriculture, gardening, cooking, sewing, housekeeping, canning and similar tasks."[21] All of which were a part of the BICHS curriculum.

While at BICHS, Bowdre blossomed as a student and leader. She was active on campus as well as in the community. In 1948 Bowdre wrote "The Need for Better Education," a poem which illustrates her support for education and eliminating the discriminatory plight of Black people:

> There are so many people
> With an indigent occupation
> They could have a better job
> If [they] had a better education
> We are Negroes as a race
> Given the back seat in every place.[22]

Nurturing instructors and the wholesome learning atmosphere at BICHS prepared her to become a teacher and, even more, a leader in her community. Although the school ran on an industrial education model, the faculty instilled confidence in the students and issued them the challenge of solving the problems in their communities. Due to having to work on her family's farm and having to save money for tuition, Bowdre didn't graduate BICHS until 1948.

20. Bowdre, interview, 2000.

21. James Anderson, *The Education of Blacks in the South, 1860–1935* (Chapel Hill: University of North Carolina Press, 1988), 144.

22. Baptist Industrial College High School Yearbook, 1960, Hernando Public Library Archive.

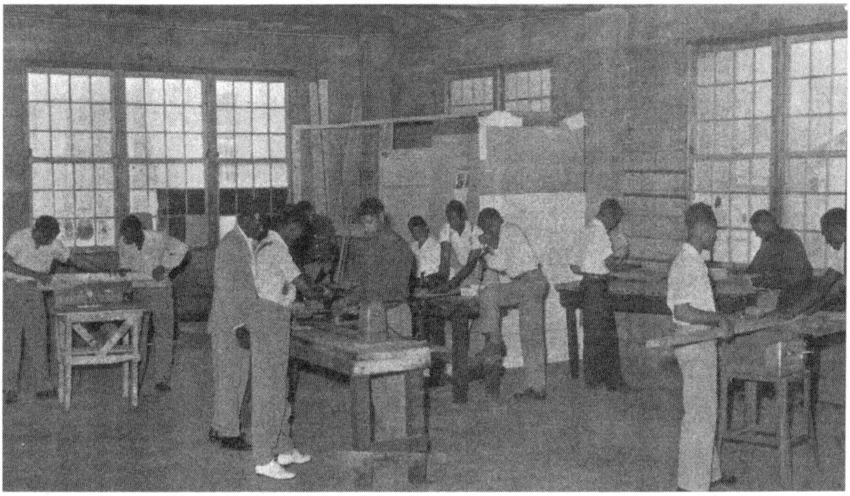

Fig. 3: Picture of students at Baptist Industrial High School, early 1900s, courtesy of Hernando Public Library

She proudly represented the seniors as their vice president and was the valedictorian of her class.[23] Following leaving BICHS, Bowdre attended Rust College to become a teacher and later returned to DeSoto County to teach during the school integration process.

On the other hand, Cleveland, although she was White, did not enjoy overwhelming privileges as most non-Blacks. She had to endure the rigors of being poor and working-class, which confined her to grueling work on her family's farm and often excluded her from some educational opportunities extended to wealthy White children.[24]

Carolyn Cleveland was born July 29, 1943, in the middle of World War II at Wadsworth Medical Clinic in Hernando. Her parents, Charles and Bernice Pickle, were small farmers and resided in the Love Station Community south of Hernando. Cleveland remembered, "We were so poor and my seven siblings and I had to work so hard."[25] During Cleveland's early years her family engaged in small farm ventures in the Love Community and were often

23. Bowdre, interview, 2000.

24. IPUMS National Historical Geographic Information System: Version 12.0 [Database]. Minneapolis: University of Minnesota. 2017.

25. Carolyn Cleveland, interview conducted by Marco Robinson, 2017.

assisted by Blacks. She recalled, "My family and I worked closely with blacks in our community, and in many cases, the help they provided was essential to our crop turning out good."[26] Cleveland's upbringing and sense of tight-knit community shaped her worldview that "all people are created equal." Race relations in her immediate circles were more fluid than static. Historian C. Vann Woodward concluded, "The determination of the [Blacks'] place took shape gradually under the influence of economic and political conflicts among divided white people."[27] Woodward's reference to "divided white people" is directly reflective of the White community in DeSoto County where not all Whites on an individual or collective level identified with the tenants of White supremacy or felt compelled to maintain the system through their actions. Nonetheless, local Whites' inaction, concerning Black equality, would later be called into question during the post-civil rights era.

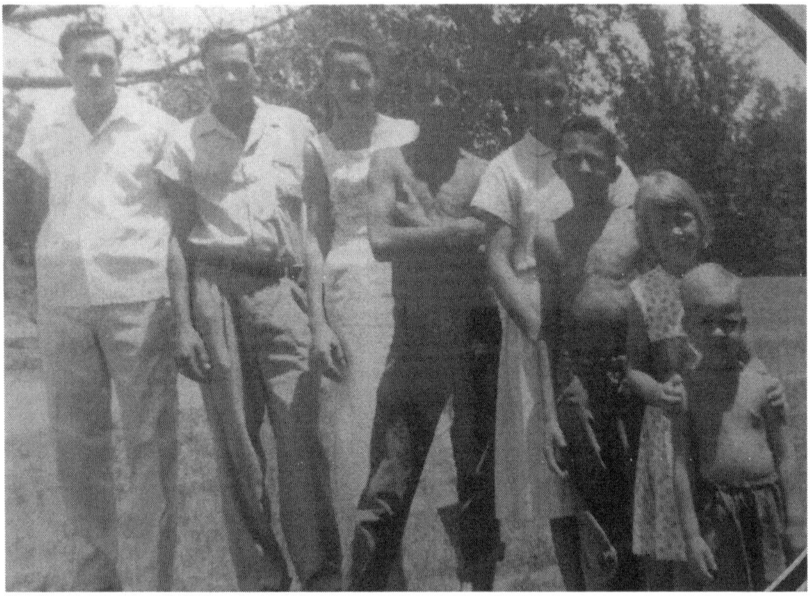

Fig. 4: Picture of Cleveland and her siblings (She is fourth person from the right), c. 1950s, courtesy of Carolyn Cleveland

26. Cleveland, interview, 2017.

27. C. Van Woodward, *The Strange Career of Jim Crow* (New York: Oxford University Press, 2001), 1–3.

By 1950, the socioeconomic dynamics of both the Black and White communities were changing due to the growth of the national economy during World War II and the mechanization of local farming practices. As a result, the Cleveland family shifted their efforts from primarily cotton farming to running a dairy farm. Still, according to 1950s Census data, 19,977 of DeSoto County's residents lived on farms (total county population 24,599).[28] Likewise, the gender-specific division of labor in the county reflected these numbers. Seventy-five percent of males in the county were employed in agriculture compared to 40 percent of the county's working females. Many women, more Black than White, worked as domestics. Approximately 185 women in DeSoto County were employed as private household workers. Additionally, in 1950, 12,000 of the residents were between the ages of fifteen and sixty-four, and there were 8,000 people employed as identified in Census records.[29] Reflecting on the changes to the local economy, Cleveland lamented, "My family and I woke up at 4:00 am every morning and milked sixty to eighty cows . . . the work was extremely hard."[30]

Along with the socioeconomic changes, Cleveland also experienced how members of the White community perceived her belonging to a poor, working-class family. She remembered, "Although I was smart my teachers always called on the children who belonged to the more affluent families in Hernando."[31] Being passed over because she was not wealthy left an inerasable memory in Cleveland's mind, and she resolved that whenever she became a teacher, she would be fair and provide an opportunity to all her students regardless of their social class. Once Cleveland graduated from all-White Hernando High School in 1961, she went on to Northwest Mississippi Junior College and Memphis State University and obtained degrees in education.

Neil Foley asserts, "Whiteness thus fractured along racial as well as class lines distinctions . . . and whites were worried that their race had become vulnerable to pollution by the growing population of poor whites on cotton farms." [32] Likewise, the White community in DeSoto County and Hernando

28. IPUMS National Historical Geographic Information System: Version 12.0 [Database]. Minneapolis: University of Minnesota. 2017.

29. IPUMS National Historical Geographic Information System: Version 12.0 [Database]. Minneapolis: University of Minnesota. 2017.

30. Cleveland, interview, 2017; Marco Robinson, "Hernando, Mississippi: A Tale of Managed Integration" (master's thesis, Jackson State University, 2003), 11–15.

31. Cleveland, interview, 2017.

32. Neil Foley, *The White Scourge: Mexicans, Blacks, and Poor Whites in Texas Cotton Culture* (Berkeley: University of California Press, 1997), 39.

was not monolithic in economic status or ideas regarding race. DeSoto County's White community was composed of individuals with various socio-economic statuses ranging from large and small landowners, tenant farmers and sharecroppers, small business owners, and merchants. Additionally, local Whites' ideas varied in regards to race. During the late 1940s and early 1950s, not all Whites that experienced the desegregation of the military after World War II joined the White supremacist calls for action and resistance. Nonetheless, class dynamics and struggle are under-discussed issues within the historical literature on White communities in the southeastern portion of the United States, but had a profound impact on these White communities, especially in DeSoto County. The fissures within and solidarity of the White population would soon be put to test with the issuing of the *Brown v. Board of Education* ruling.

Neil McMillen contends, "Although World War II did not diminish the South's mythological status—indeed, it enhanced it—the social changes it brought to the region were vast and far reaching."[33] No other social change galvanized every rung of southern society as did the United States Supreme Court ruling that "separate but equal" educational facilities was unconstitutional in 1954. As in many communities across the South, the White community in DeSoto County received the ruling with apprehension and uncertainty. Many Whites wondered what was to become of their way of life now that the highest court in the land looked upon racial segregation unfavorably. Segregation served not only to remind Black people of their inferior civil status, but also to allow White people disproportionate access to public monies.[34] Now that there were legal measures in place to ensure educational equity and equal funding to Black schools, the leaders of the White community in DeSoto County had to respond and confront the growing movement to obtain civil rights for Black Americans.

The Civil Rights Era, School Desegregation, and Social Change in DeSoto County and Hernando

The civil rights movement altered race relations, overturned ingrained practices, subverted traditions, ushered in political change, transformed institutions, undermined a way of life, and even turned cities upside down.[35]

33. Neil McMillen, ed., *Remaking Dixie: The Impact of World War II on the American South* (Jackson: University Press of Mississippi, 1997), xv.

34. Greenberg, *To Ask for an Equal Chance*, 5–10.

35. Sokol, *There Goes My Everything*, 4.

DeSoto County and Hernando were not excluded from these social and political transformations. With the systematic exclusion of Black people from the polls through literacy tests, poll taxes, grandfather clauses, fraud, and intimidation, Whites controlled the government at the municipal, state, and federal levels and therefore determined the allocation of public spending.[36] The *Brown* ruling required all White school districts to integrate, but to stall the desegregation process many districts engaged in "equalization plans." DeSoto County's equalization program consisted of building three schools in the county for African Americans. The Black community welcomed the construction of Hernando Central, East Side, and Delta Center High Schools, but the construction of new schools in the county still did not create "educational parity." Historian Charles Bolton contends, "The elimination of Mississippi's dual educational system occurred largely on white terms."[37]

An examination of Mississippi's educational equalization program of the 1940s and 1950s shows that it did little to improve Black education in the state and ultimately demonstrated the need for the establishment of a unitary school system.[38] The funding that DeSoto County's all-White school board funneled into the new Black schools was not adequate. In 1954, Mississippi school districts spent an average of $6.16 on each Black student and a total of $47. 95 on each White students annually. White teachers in Mississippi were paid $220.00 per month while Black teachers were only paid $130.00 on average.[39] Geraldine Johnson-Patton, a student at Delta Center High School, recalled, "We had to use second-hand textbooks passed down to us from the white schools in the county." In addition, teachers at the all-Black schools taught overcrowded classes and had little to no funding for instructional materials. Gemenie Bowdre experienced these circumstances during the 1960 school year, when she was a third grade teacher at Hernando Central. Bowdre remembered, "I taught a class of sixty-five third graders and we had old books and limited resources."[40] In addition, the students wanted the curriculum to include more Black history. Leslie McLemore, a student at Delta Center, recollected, "We protested in order to have black history included in what we

36. Greenberg, *To Ask for an Equal Chance,* 5–10.

37. Charles Bolton, "Mississippi's School Equalization Program, 1945-1954: A Last Gasp to Try to Maintain a Segregated Educational System," *The Journal of Southern History* LXVI, no. 4 (2000): 781.

38. Bolton, "Mississippi's School Equalization Program," 783.

39. Bolton, "Mississippi's School Equalization Program," 781.

40. Geraldine Patton, interview conducted by Marco Robinson, 2010.

were taught at school."[41] Ultimately, the allure of the new school buildings did not alleviate the realities of limited funding for books, instructional resources, and diversifying the curriculum.

R. E. Rutherford, DeSoto County superintendent of education, worked closely with the Mississippi State Sovereignty Commission, a state government agency created to subvert civil rights activities and delay efforts toward school desegregation. In April of 1962, Rutherford gave agency investigator Tom Scarbrough an update on civil rights activities in the county. Rutherford stated, "All of his teachers, both white and colored, were required to sign the loyalty oath as well as make a sworn affidavit listing the organizations to which they now or have belonged to for the past five years."[42] Bowdre's name was on the list of teachers who had taken the oath and she submitted the affidavit. Rutherford gave Scarbrough the documents, assuring Scarbrough that none of his teachers were members of the National Association for the Advancement of Colored People (NAACP) or any other civil rights organizations.

Bowdre, like many other African American teachers and administrators in DeSoto County, was under constant surveillance and faced the possibility of being fired if their names were associated with any civil rights activities. The White male leadership of the DeSoto County schools resolved that they would be proactive and give their best efforts to stop the inevitable integration. By the 1960s, most White communities in Mississippi formed local all-White citizens councils, state-wide organizations that were instrumental in organizing all-White private academies to spearhead their efforts in stopping school integration and the desegregation of public accommodations.[43] In most instances, in contrast to the profiles of members of other White supremacist groups, the citizens council's leaders and members were well educated and affluent landowners. The organization's primary goal was to circumvent any efforts at Black social and racial equality. However, there still was no consensus within DeSoto County's White community on who should lead the "resistance" due to, arguably, issues related to class.

On one visit, DeSoto County Chancery Clerk Jimmy Tipton informed Scarbrough that "there was no Citizens Council in DeSoto County" and that

41. Dr. Leslie McLemore, interview conducted by Marco Robinson, 2008.

42. Mississippi State Sovereignty Commission, Memorandum composed by Tom Scarbrough, April, 1962, SCRID# 2-130-0-19-1-1-1, Series 2515: Mississippi State Sovereignty Commission Records, 1994-2006, Mississippi Department of Archives and History.

43. Bolton, "Mississippi's School Equalization Program," 781–85.

when they met to organize one, "those present on that occasion were not of the right caliber of people, so it was decided to make an investigation and decide later."[44] Tipton's comments illustrate the complex intra-racial class politics at work within the White community in DeSoto County during the 1960s. Jason Sokol emphasizes, "White southerners' racial attitudes and behavior frequently revealed a confused and conflicted people, at times divided within and against themselves."[45] As civil rights activities intensified all over the American South, the White male officeholders of DeSoto County did their best to organize all rungs of White society in the interest of preserving White supremacy.

Although changes were occurring in the local schools in DeSoto County, the area was not exempt from the buildup of civil rights activity that was happening elsewhere in the state and country. During the 1960s, the White citizens of DeSoto County watched the growth of the civil rights movement with much apprehension and braced themselves for the inevitable changes to the local social order. The White community in Hernando was not hospitable to any suspected civil rights workers or activities. As utilized by many White communities in Mississippi, violence and intimidation were two of their primary means of resisting the social and political changes brought by the national movement for Black equality. However, the use of these tactics was not exclusively against Black activists and agitators.

During the summer of 1960, Alton West, a White dairy farmer residing in the Lake Commorant area of DeSoto, was run out of town and his house burned because allegedly he was allowing NAACP meetings to be held on his property. [46] Additionally, in August of 1965 Betty Cartwright, a Caucasian woman from Memphis, Tennessee, wrote Dr. Martin Luther King Jr. a letter detailing an incident where local Whites in Hernando, Mississippi, assaulted her, her fiancé, and a friend because they were mistaken for civil rights workers.[47] Regardless of the dissension over leadership among different factions within DeSoto County's White community, the goals and directives

44. Mississippi State Sovereignty Commission, Memorandum composed by Tom Scarbrough, August, 1960, SCRID #2-130-0-4-2-1-1.

45. Sokol, *There Goes My Everything,* 14.

46. I. F. Palmer, "White Farmer Flees Mississippi Racists After House Burns Down," *Tri-State Defender*, 1960. Letter wrote to Dr. Martin Luther King by Betty Cartwright, Department of Justice Files, 1965.

47. Letter wrote to Dr. Martin Luther King by Betty Cartwright, Department of Justice Files, 1965.

were the same—stop Black equality at all costs. Vigilance in regards to resisting Black equality was maintained at all costs, even if it meant chastising members of the White community.

Local Whites in DeSoto County also issued their retribution to Black residents who challenged the racial status quo. The White community knew racial equality was possible following the passage of the Civil Rights Act of 1964 and the activities that had transpired in Mississippi related to the Freedom Summer. Local White leaders were issued a red alert that called for using any measure necessary to prevent the extinction of White economic and social supremacy. In 1965 Mr. and Mrs. Haywood Wilkins, Black residents of Hernando, were told by the local welfare office that their checks were being held up because their grandchildren enrolled in a previously all-White school.[48] African American residents who were movement participants or seen as sympathetic to the movement became targets. The local White political and business leaders of DeSoto County, in most cases, used economic leverage to curtail Black activism. However, this did not always work, as in the case of Leslie McLemore.

McLemore lived in the Walls area of DeSoto County and his grandfather was a landowner. Leslie and his brother Eugene attempted to attend the service of the local all-White Catholic Church in Walls. The parishioners objected and threatened that the boys should leave town for their safety. McLemore recalled, "My grandfather was one of the biggest taxpayers in town and no one was going to threaten him by telling his grandsons what to do."[49] McLemore's grandfather's economic status protected him from White reprisals. Leslie went on to graduate from Rust College, become active in the movement through the Student Non-violent Coordinating Committee (SNCC), and obtain a doctorate degree from the University of Massachusetts Amherst. Members of the Black community in DeSoto County had to navigate the tumultuous racial and social landscape where racial hostilities were further exacerbated by the passage of the Voting Rights Act of 1965. The passage of this monumental legislation and the growing momentum of the national civil rights movement culminated to produce the circumstances around one of the most notable civil rights era events that occurred in the nation and DeSoto County during the 1960s.[50]

48. Department of Justice Memorandum, Report from the Mississippi State Department of Welfare, 1965.

49. McLemore, interview, 2008.

50. Fred Powledge, *We Shall Overcome: Heroes of the Civil Rights Movement* (New York: Atheneum Books, 1993), 104–108.

In June of 1966, White tensions in DeSoto County were flaring over the activities of James Meredith, an Air Force veteran and the first African American student to graduate from the University of Mississippi. Meredith staged a "March Against Fear," which passed through DeSoto County en route to Jackson, the state's capital city. James Meredith commented, "I had gone there to talk to Negroes, to explain that the old order was passing, that they should stand up as men with nothing to fear."[51] Meredith's plea to Blacks in DeSoto County to become active in the movement had little appeal. Only one person from the local Black community joined him during his trek through DeSoto County. As local and state law enforcement trailed Meredith, he was shot by Aubrey Norvell, a tri-state area White male, outside of the city limits of Hernando. Meredith barely survived the ordeal, but regained his health and continued the march accompanied by Dr. Martin Luther King and Stokely Carmichael. The Meredith March and his subsequent attempted murder transfixed the minds of both Blacks and Whites in DeSoto County on seriously considering the current possibilities of changes in the local racial order.[52]

Time magazine featured a photo of Meredith shot on the ground as their picture of the year. The silhouette of this image was ingrained in the minds of millions worldwide and, on a local level, this horrendous act gave DeSoto County a place among the pantheon of White communities in the South committed to "massive resistance." Clive Webb asserts, "After *Brown*, southern whites abandoned tried-and-true evasive techniques that for decades had successfully nullified the constitutional rights of blacks, in favor of outright defiance."[53] The incident signaled a call to action for the African American community in DeSoto County. Many Blacks who were traumatized by this event channeled their energies into getting the first Black elected official into office during the 1980s. Moreover, this incident along with the *Alexander vs. Holmes* ruling, in which the United States Supreme Court ordered school desegregation in all Mississippi school districts by 1970, paved the way for substantive changes in race relations in DeSoto County.

51. Aram Goudsouzian, *Down to the Crossroads: Civil Rights, Black Power and the Meredith March Against Fear* (New York: Farrar, Straus, and Giroux, 2014), 16–20; *Royal Oak Michigan Tribune*, June 7, 1966.

52. Goudsouzian, *Down to the Crossroads*, 34.

53. Clive Webb, ed., *Massive Resistance: Southern Opposition to the Second Reconstruction* (Oxford: Oxford University Press, 2005), 34.

Throughout the 1960s, the DeSoto County Board of Education used "freedom of choice" as a tactic to deter school integration. In 1967–68 school year, Peggie Dobbins was the first Black female to attend Hernando High under the freedom of choice policy. Dobbins remembered, "Our parents wouldn't let us go and march with James Meredith and after he was shot all I thought about was what can I do." [54] With the issuing the Supreme Court ruling and local Blacks becoming more assertive, the DeSoto County Schools administrators' backs were against the wall. School leaders had to produce an integration plan to be implemented during the 1970–71 school year. By this time, Carolyn Cleveland had taught a year at Southaven Elementary (1965) and now was a stay-at-home mom raising her son. The inevitable came, and now the White male leadership of DeSoto County had to foster social change. Local Black and White women, like Gemenie Bowdre and Cleveland, became an intricate part of this process. Therefore, "When tranquility settled over the sites of the civil rights movement, the work of adjusting to life in a new world finally began."[55]

DeSoto County's School Desegregation Plan and Forging a Community of Mothers in the Post-Civil Rights Era South

The South in the 1970s was a society remarkably similar to that of Jim Crow times in some respects, yet fundamentally transformed in others.[56] Coupled with the ensuing social changes, DeSoto County underwent a drastic population shift during the 1960s. DeSoto County's population grew into close to thirty-six thousand by 1970. During this year, the White population became the majority in the county for the first time since the antebellum era. However, this trend accompanied Black migration out of the county. The majority of Blacks who migrated out of the county moved to nearby Memphis in search of better economic and educational opportunities. During the previous thirty years, between 1940 and 1970, seven thousand African Americans migrated from DeSoto County.[57] Black migration from the county later impacted racial reforms in electoral politics. African American candidates had to have White votes to be elected to office. Nonetheless, in 1970 the entire community's focus was on school desegregation and implementing the school board's plan.

54. Peggie Dobbins, interview conducted by Marco Robinson, 2014.

55. Sokol, *There Goes My Everything,* 18.

56. Sokol, *There Goes My Everything,* 18.

57. IPUMS National Historical Geographic Information System: Version 12.0 [Database]. Minneapolis: University of Minnesota. 2017.

At first glance, one could conclude that the DeSoto County Board of Education's desegregation plan met all of the criteria set by the Supreme Court and federal government in facilitating racial integration. Although all of the legalities were addressed, where the rubber met the road was in both the Black and White community's morale regarding the process. The plan was crafted in a manner to expedite the integration process, to thoroughly explain implementation procedures, and so that personnel changes were equitable. School board leaders fully understood that the federal government would enforce funding sanctions if the process did not meet federal guidelines. To address transparency, the school board implemented a media policy where "All citizens of [the] DeSoto County District will be fully informed about the legal requirements and details of this Desegregation Plan through news releases, making copies of the plan available in school libraries, county office[s], and through public meetings."[58] School leader's openness regarding the plan was to avert White "backlash" incidents such as the one created in Grenada, Mississippi, where the majority of the White community protested school integration in the face of federal sanctions.[59]

The redistribution of students and staff to assure racial integration was at the center of the plan. The DeSoto County Board of Education consolidated several of the all-White and all-Black schools to facilitate this process. Due to the large number of Whites who moved into DeSoto County during the 1960s, there were not enough educational facilities to house students during the 1970–71 school year. The district administrators identified school overcrowding as a significant issue that the district needed to address within the confines of the integration process. As it relates to hiring and dismissing staff, the school board developed a "non-racial objective criteria" to be used in selecting personnel, although this policy did not ensure racial parity in the selection and releasing of Black principals and teachers.[60] Leslie McLemore remembered, "DeSoto County lost some of its best black teachers and administrators due to integration."[61] Historian Adam Fairclough asserts, "The integration of school faculties had a disproportionate effect upon black teachers and desegregation plans tried to create majority white/minority-black ratios

58. "The Desegregation Plan," 1970, the DeSoto County Board of Education, Hernando Public Library Archives.

59. Robinson, "Hernando, Mississippi," 34–36.

60. Desegregation Plan, 1970.

61. McLemore, interview, 2008.

in individual schools."[62] Numerous issues stifled racial equality during the integration process in DeSoto County, but there was one notable story that unfolded at Hernando Elementary in 1974.

At the time of the implementation of the 1970 Desegregation Plan, Bowdre was still teaching at all-Black Hernando Central and Cleveland was about to come off maternity leave. Both ladies were key players in the integration process going smoothly at newly built Hernando Elementary. In 1976, the duo came to work with each other under seemingly precarious circumstances. Bowdre, a Black woman, was selected principal and Cleveland, a White woman, was selected as assistant principal at Hernando Elementary. Both women were propelled into a situation where they had an opportunity to promote more harmonious race relations in DeSoto County and provide a model for their respective communities to follow during the crucial times of the post-civil rights era. Most important, breaking away from DeSoto County Schools' standing tradition of all-White male administrators, Bowdre and Cleveland were among the first women chosen for leadership positions in the history of the district. Their actions were instrumental in ushering in a new era of educational reform and race relations.

The impact of the civil rights movement differed from person to person, family to family, town to town.[63] Without a doubt, Bowdre and Cleveland's educational experiences and upbringings prepared them to facilitate integration at the elementary school, but this task was a challenge. Their activities inside and outside of school proved pivotal to their success. Their success was based on the superb working relationship that they developed with each other. Cleveland recalled, "Ms. Bowdre was a super nice person to work for and to work with." The good working relationship that they developed was contagious and in turn was emulated by the faculty and staff. "Hernando had good administrators and faculty both black and white," Cleveland exclaimed.[64]

The daily operations of the school were often demanding due to policies handed down by the DeSoto County School District. Student grade placement in relation to their level of academic preparation was a significant issue. The district engaged in a policy of "ability grouping," which did not always place students fairly. In many instances, the prevailing assumption was the majority of the students who came from the Black school were underprepared. Bowdre

62. Adam Fairclough, *A Class of Their Own: Black Teachers in the Segregated South* (London: Belknap Press, 2007), 394.

63. Sokol, *There Goes My Everything,* 4.

64. Cleveland, interview, 2017.

conceded, "In some cases students were not prepared because of the lack of resources they had available to them at the former black schools, but they were willing to work hard to get on their correct grade level."[65] The ability-grouping policy did allow for many of these underperforming students to get caught and they were retained in a lower grade. Cleveland stated, "I worked with one of the lower performing groups and we did our best to get them to their level." [66] Meeting this challenge, Bowdre and Cleveland relied on their motherly instincts and embraced their students as if they were their own children.

Cleveland exclaimed, "I loved my children . . . I didn't care if they were black, white, Mexican, or oriental."[67] The student's mothers noticed Bowdre and Cleveland's adoration for the students at Hernando Elementary and how they took care of them as their own. Alice Lipford, a local Black woman and mother of one their students, recalled, "I wasn't worried about my child while she was under their care because I knew they were going to be a real mother to them." The strong sense of community Bowdre and Cleveland cultivated at the school united Black and White mothers together. Lipford stated, "I had never attended a parent meeting until then and I was able to connect with a number white folks." [68] Bowdre and Cleveland's efforts to "forge a community of mothers" went beyond school.

Day in and day out, both Black and White mothers in Hernando crossed the fading color line that once divided their community as they dropped off and picked up their children from school. The relationships they developed were instrumental in uniting women from all races and economic backgrounds in Hernando. Bowdre said, "My staff and I did our best to engage parents and the general community in bonding and developing friendships."[69] Cleveland and Lipford's friendship extended beyond the schoolyard. They both were regulars at the local thrift store and they identified items for each other. Cleveland remembered, "I ran into a lot of my student's parents at the Goodwill and Alice Mae was one of my good friends."[70] Hernando mothers were among the first individuals in Mississippi to enter into what was formally racially divided and contested public space in order to usher in a new age of racial toleration in their

65. Bowdre, interview, 2010.
66. Cleveland, interview, 2010.
67. Cleveland, interview, 2017.
68. Lipford, interview, 2000.
69. Bowdre, interview, 2010.
70. Cleveland, interview, 2017.

communities. Bowdre's and Cleveland's example of inter-racial cooperation, being motherly role models for their students, and their relationships with their student's mothers represent a chapter in southern women's history that is one of the least discussed by researchers. Hernando's community of mothers sought to make connections in their community across racial lines and, in turn, distance themselves from their tumultuous past.

The legacy of racism in DeSoto County runs deep and the persistent issues surrounding racial inequality are an inherent part of the social fabric in the county. Even in those cases where the civil rights movement succeeded in changing Whites' attitudes and altering their lives, nothing was simple or straightforward about those transformations.[71] Although Bowdre and Cleveland were able to help "forge a community of mothers," there were still issues related to race persisting in the DeSoto County School System. The selection of a set of separate Black and White homecoming kings and queens lasted until 1998. Strikingly, there were several cases brought against the school system regarding the disproportionate suspension rates of Black to White students. Notwithstanding these issues, in 1987 Bowdre was elected to the DeSoto County School Board and became the first African American elected to public office since Reconstruction. Bowdre died in 2017 following a fifty-year career as a teacher, administrator, and board member in DeSoto County. Cleveland is retired and currently resides on her farm in Hernando. Bowdre's and Cleveland's experiences provide a unique perspective of southern history and culture through mama's eyes.

Bibliography

Anderson, James D. The Education of Blacks in the South, 1860–1935. Chapel Hill, NC: University of North Carolina Press, 1995.

Bolton, Charles C. "Mississippi's School Equalization Program, 1945–1954: 'A Last Gasp to Try to Maintain a Segregated Educational System.'" *The Journal of Southern History* 66, no. 4 (2000): 781–814. https://doi.org/10.2307/2588011.

Fairclough, Adam. *A Class of Their Own: Black Teachers in the Segregated South.* London: The Belknap Press, 2007.

Flynt, J. Wayne. *Dixie's Forgotten People: The South's Poor Whites.* Bloomington: Indiana University Press, 2004.

71. Sokol, *There Goes My Everything,* 15.

Foley, Neil. *The White Scourge: Mexicans, Blacks, and Poor Whites in Texas Cotton Culture*. Berkeley: University of California Press, 1999.

Fredrickson, George M. *The Black Image in the White Mind: The Debate on Afro-American Character and Destiny, 1817–1914 [by] George M. Fredrickson*. New York, Harper & Row, 1971.

Gilmore, Glenda Elizabeth. *Gender and Jim Crow: Women and the Politics of White Supremacy in North Carolina, 1896–1920*. Chapel Hill: University of North Carolina Press, 2019.

Greenberg, Cheryl Lynn. *To Ask for an Equal Chance: African Americans in the Great Depression*. Lanham, MD: Rowman & Littlefield, 2011.

Hollandsworth, James. *Portrait of a Scientific Racist: Alfred Holt Stone of Mississippi*. Baton Rouge: Louisiana State University Press, 2008.

Hunter, Tera W. *To 'Joy My Freedom: Southern Black Women's Lives and Labors After the Civil War*. Cambridge, MA: Harvard University Press, 1999.

McMillen, Neil R. *Remaking Dixie: The Impact of World War II on the American South*. Jackson: University Press of Mississippi, 1997.

Powledge, Fred. *We Shall Overcome: Heroes of the Civil Rights Movement*. New York, Antheneum Books, 1993.

Randle, E. H. *Antagonism of Forces in Nature Universal; the Genesis of the Fittest, Applications to Evolution*. Nashville, TN: Pub. House of The M. E. Church South, 1912.

———. *Characteristics of the Southern Negro*. New York: The Neale Publishing Company, 1910.

———. *Plurality of the Human Race, According to the Teachings Both of the Bible and of Science*. Nashville, TN: Smith, 1911.

Robinson, Marco. "Hernando, Mississippi: A Tale of Managed Integration" Master's thesis, Jackson State University, 2003.

Sokol, Jason. *There Goes My Everything: White Southerners in the Age of Civil Rights, 1945–1975*. New York: Vintage Books, 2007.

Thompson, Julius Eric. *Black Life in Mississippi: Essays on Political, Social and Cultural Studies in a Deep South State*. Lanham, MD: University Press of America, 2001.

———. *Lynchings in Mississippi: A History, 1865–1965*. Jefferson, NC: Mcfarland & Company, 2007.

Woodward, C. Vann. *The Strange Career of Jim Crow*. New York: Oxford University Press, 2006.

MARCO ROBINSON is a native of north Mississippi and writes on various aspects of the Black experience in the American South and throughout the African Diaspora. Robinson's research employs the use of qualitative methods, archival research, community studies, and focuses on the use of digital tools for historic preservation. His scholarship delves into pedagogical approaches to the aforementioned topics and bringing light to the lived experiences of obscure individuals or groups. Robinson is an assistant professor of history at Prairie View A&M University and he currently resides with his family in Houston, Texas.

Women in the Shadows

Lynda Frese

The long arc of history, with its gorgeous and infernal twists, has always informed my interest in matriarchal stories. Early in my career as a visual artist I was moved by the Venus figures of prehistory (small portable sculptures, rock engravings, and cave paintings) and comforted by the images of the Madonna I grew up with as a Catholic White girl on the East Coast. I wondered about the origins of these holy images and began to see the ways they are connected. In an early body of work called *Immagini Pagane* (*Pagan Images*), largely completed in northern Italy, I drew upon the way depictions of the Madonna had been borrowed from the early goddess myths, noticing how icons of the Virgin Mary are often found in womb-like caves and watching religious rituals along the Ligurian coast, in which her statue emerges triumphant from the sea. We may say the ultimate matriarchal figure is Mother Nature herself—the nurturing and life-giving aspect of the natural world personified. Indigenous peoples in South America call her *Pachamama*, but there is no specific iconic image associated with her. She is invisible, and yet she is everywhere. The religious, ethical, and spiritual dimensions of our being in this world of nature are ongoing themes for me in my work as a visual artist.

Early pagan mythologies honoring the sacredness of nature (polytheistic, not patriarchal or hierarchal, and endlessly open to interpretation and modern discovery) became a kind of bedrock subject material for my work. However, the images from prehistory can resist interpretation. There is no text that accompanies them, but nonetheless it is still a history. Like all histories, there are parts that are hidden by our own blind spots. I think the history of the goddess cults has always been hidden in plain sight. The eternal story of the feminine divine has been adapted and revered, but also concealed and vilified. Grand churches, synagogues, and mosques have been built over (and built with) the stones of her ancient temple sites. These early configurations of matriarchal ideals informed my approach to examining the history of women in Louisiana—women in the shadows, women who had done great (or terrible) things, and whose stories I believed had not been covered or needed to be uncovered again in new ways.

In the collaborative project *Reconstituting the Vanished: Gender, Memory and Placemaking in the Delta South* (1994–1997), a series of my constructed early digital images was presented with an interpretive text by Dr. Barbara Allen. The series examined the lives of four Louisiana women of note using photographs and narrative to retell their story in a public display format. "We used physical places as the common ground of these women's lives. We wanted to extend a new feminist reading of these women's pasts and the places they built to recover and reconstruct a new gender-inclusive public memory."[1]

One of our subjects was Marie Thérèse Coincoin (1742–1816), a freed slave and slave owner, *médicine* (healer), plantation owner, businesswoman, and mother of ten children whose descendants established a historical Creole community in a colonial outpost of French Louisiana. There are no photographs of this woman, who died before the advent of photography. In the series, a portrayal of her is called *Bewitchment.* The digital collage includes photographs of a vintage colonial house with its dirt floors and *bousillage* (building material that mixes mud and Spanish moss), antique shoes, human hair, and stone and glass vessels symbolic of motherhood and fertility. Another image called *Treehouse* includes quilts, family photos of her descendants, and the oak tree in front of her Isle Brevelle home.

In 2014, two decades later, I began work on the series *Art & Shadows* about a South Louisiana sugarcane plantation and the generations of families who lived and worked there.[2] I spent a year working on-site as an artist-in-residence at the Shadows-on-the-Teche, an extraordinary property in New Iberia, Louisiana. William Weeks Hall, the final owner of the Shadows,

1. Barbara Allen, *Reconstructing the Vanished: Memory, Gender and Placemaking in the Delta South,* Perspective Gallery, Virginia Polytechnic Institute and State University, Blacksburg, VA, February 28–May 16, 2015 (National Capital Region Campus).

2. The *Art & Shadows* series, comprised of twenty-two artworks, was created during a yearlong residency at Shadows-on-the-Teche in New Iberia, Louisiana. It was part of a pilot program for one visual artist and one musician and supported by grants from the National Trust for Historic Preservation and the National Endowment for the Arts; its goal was to demonstrate how innovative arts programming at historic sites can enhance their role as community assets and increase cultural and economic impacts in their neighborhoods and regions.

bequeathed this estate and its historical collections to the National Trust in 1958. It was their first Gulf South site.

As with the *Reconstituting the Vanished* series, I encountered the beauty and struggled with the pain of the narratives revealed in the archives. They were described in love letters, evoked in family photographs and paintings, or told in the business ledgers that addressed crop production and inventory, including human inventory—at its height, the plantation had 164 enslaved workers in the fields and in the big house. I wanted to embed these complex narratives in the art somehow, leaving interpretation open for viewers.

Near the end of the Civil War, Yankee soldiers bivouacked at the Shadows while the matriarch Mary Weeks was still living there; largely because of these circumstances, the contents of the house were left intact in the chaotic aftermath of the war. Antique clothing was preserved in pristine condition. Pottery shards, coal, and children's marbles were later excavated from the soil under the old slave quarters, now demolished; some of these objects can be seen scattered in the foreground of the artwork *Two Sides of Mary*, which shows the main house in the background and a cornerstone of the slave quarters in the foreground.

Selected images from the site's archives were combined with my own photographs of interior domestic spaces, household objects, and textiles—from embellished ball gowns to enslaved children's clothing. I made photographs in the Shadows' iconic gardens (where ancient trees are named after family members, such as the oak in *Two Sides of Mary*) and in the surrounding cane fields and bayous. The land itself is a subject. Each picture in the series features a plant, bringing its own associations for the viewer. In these constructed images, connections between the layers of history, memory, and the natural world are uncovered.

It was seeing the personal clothing items, especially of the children, that first gave me an idea about how to proceed with a complex narrative project about plantation life. A small enslaved boy's vest, a little White girl's dress, trousers of a field hand—they were so intimate, they evoked my compassion and curiosity. The textiles brought forth stories for me that could be woven into the art. One could imagine the personal histories of individuals and their family relations, all vividly existing within the larger scope of antebellum Louisiana history. I placed the garments in contexts with other objects in the collection, in environments that were a little surreal: they float in the fields and over the Bayou Teche, they hover in the parlor and bedroom. In the photo collages, I explored how the size and placement of images can shift meaning in a narrative and create new hierarchies. "Inner domestic spaces and the sugar cane fields that surround them—these images construct a narrative of parallel lives, as writer Toni Morrison would observe, and suggest the complex ecologies of southern plantation life."[3]

Spending time looking at the vintage photographs at the Shadows (stored in a bank vault closed to the public) was a rare opportunity during my yearlong residency. I was drawn to these older treasures, and especially as a photographer, to the unusual stereoscopic pictures from the 1850s. There is one of women and children in front of the Grand Côte slave quarters and another of wash day, where a small child leans up against her pregnant mother—images I've never forgotten.

But in general, there is a dearth of photos of the enslaved population, and while pictures of the White people had names and dates attached, pictures of Black people rarely did. (There were no pictures of people laboring in the fields; these kinds of work scenes were uncommon in early photography.) As in the series *Reconstituting the Vanished*, I wanted to somehow portray people who had never had their portraits made. *The Rocking Chair* features a child's dress ca. 1845, a piece of hand-hewn furniture from the slave quarters, archival boxes from the Shadows' attic, and red camellias from the garden. It evokes the maternal bond between the unseen mother and child— the caring and attention, the absence and longing.

The director of Shadows-on-the-Teche, Pat Kahle, wrote about the toil of the sugarcane grinding season on the Weeks Plantation at Grand Côte, making "Beautiful Sugar":

> [On] a Louisiana sugar plantation from October through December, during the grinding season when cane was harvested, hauled to the mill, and made into sugar, it was not uncommon to work sixteen or more hours a day, seven days a week. This is the main reason for the familiar fear of being sold "down the river to Louisiana." Slaves often worked half the night, every night, in addition to their daywork. Once the sugar mill was fired up at the beginning of harvest, it kept going twenty-four hours a day until grinding was complete, as it still is today. Not all of David Weeks's 164 slaves worked the cane fields or sugarhouse. Some made clothes, usually two sets of clothes a year for each slave. Others did laundry, prepared food, or were personal servants for the Weeks family.[4]

3. Dr. Mary Ann Wilson, "Introduction," *Lynda Frese: Holy Memories & Earthly Delights* (Lafayette: University of Louisiana at Lafayette Press, 2018), 2.

4. Patricia Kahle, *Shadows-on-the-Teche: Preserving a "Picture of the Life,"* (Lafayette: University of Louisiana at Lafayette Center for Louisiana Studies, 1996), 23.

Imagine having only two sets of clothes for the year. These details impress upon us the significance of each garment. Who created these garments, who wore them, how did they signal status, privileged comfort or utilitarian need?

Clothing was so precious. While making one particular artwork I was absorbed by Sue Monk Kidd's novel *The Invention of Wings,* about an urban enslaved woman in nineteenth-century Charleston, South Carolina, in which the plot involves a stolen dress. In the piece *Her Other Dress*, a nightgown from the textile collection floats between the rich interior of the Shadows' carpeted and wallpapered parlor and the wilderness of the bayou, where some slaves fled. As I recall, this item is labeled "slave woman's gown." It is likely one of two garments she owned.

At one point a friend pointed out that my *Art & Shadows* project was mostly focused on the women and children, and that I might be missing something. . . . This made me laugh! We all have our lenses for understanding history and personal narratives that influence our creative work. It is true that the early history of the Shadows-on-the-Teche is female-centered in my work, and often addresses the relationships of children and mothers. The matriarchal story is one of the grand designs of history and of art.

LYNDA FRESE is a visual artist based in south Louisiana and professor emerita at the University of Louisiana at Lafayette. Frese has been an artist-in-residence at the Rockefeller Foundation Bellagio Center, the Bogliasco Foundation, the American Academy in Rome, and other rural residencies in Italy. Her work has been widely exhibited and published and is found in private and public collections including the Houston Museum of Fine Arts; the San Francisco Museum of Modern Art; the Ogden Museum of Southern Art; the Center for Photography at Woodstock, New York; the High Museum of Art; the Mississippi Museum of Art; and the Hilliard Art Museum in Lafayette, Louisiana. Ms. Frese received Artist of the Year at the 2016 Louisiana Cultural Awards for her sustained work celebrating the culture and history of the South. A recent monograph, *Holy Memories & Earthly Delights,* was published by UL Press.

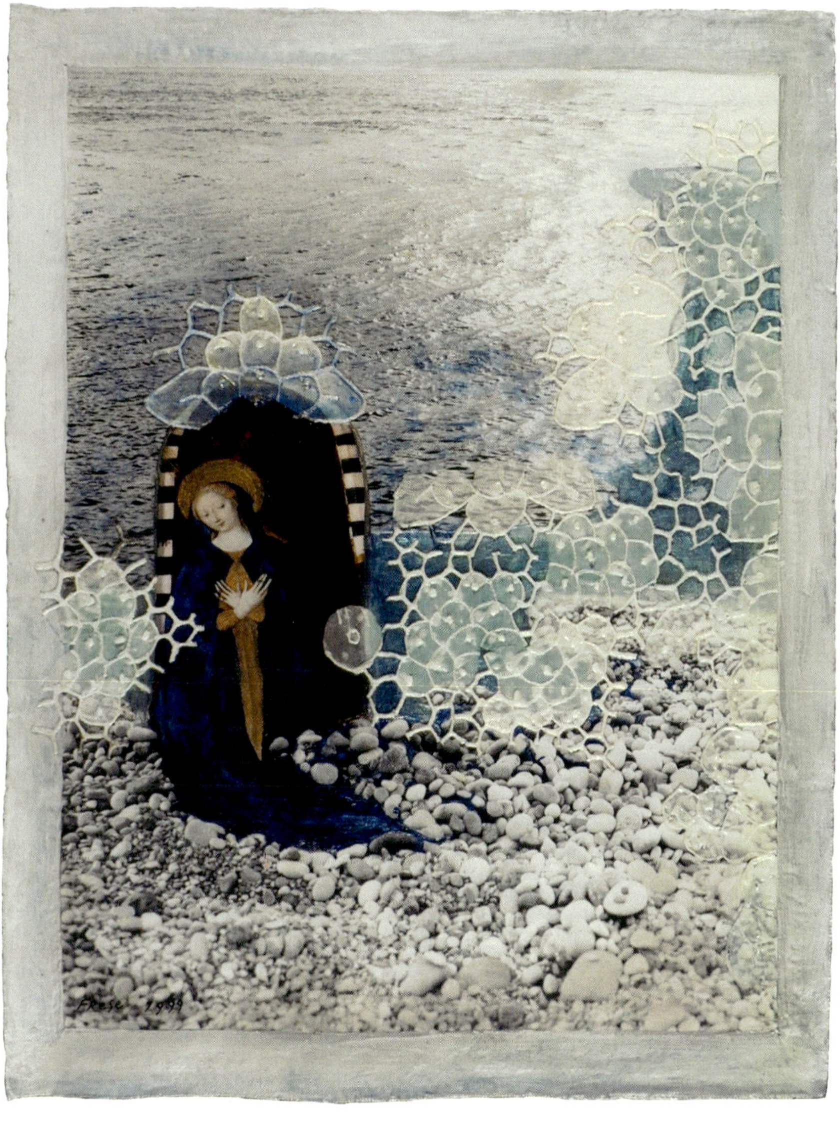

Stella Maris (Star of the Sea)

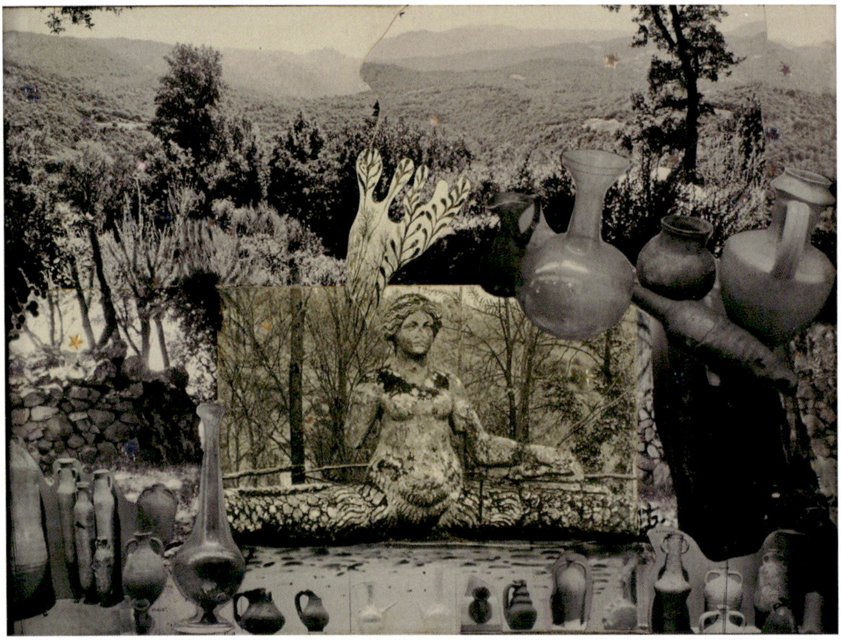

Stone Yogi

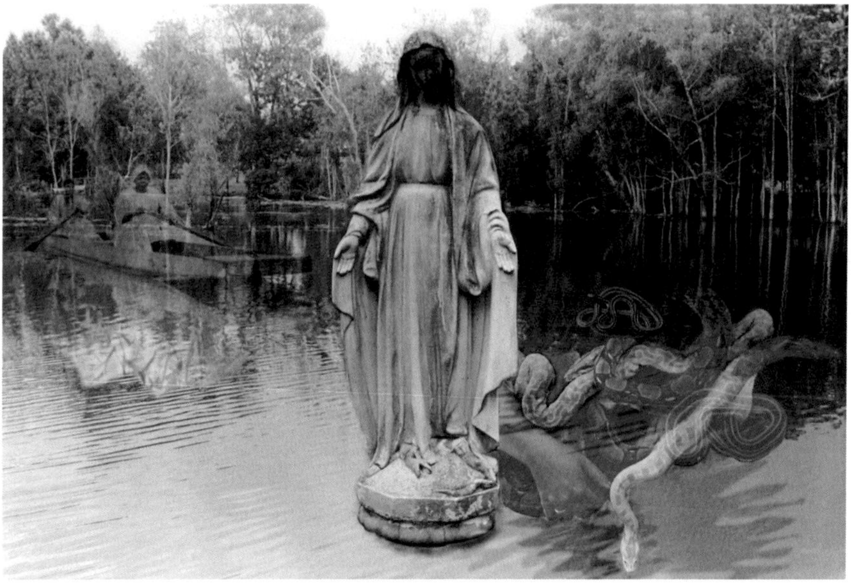

Cane River (from the series *Reconstituting the Vanished*)

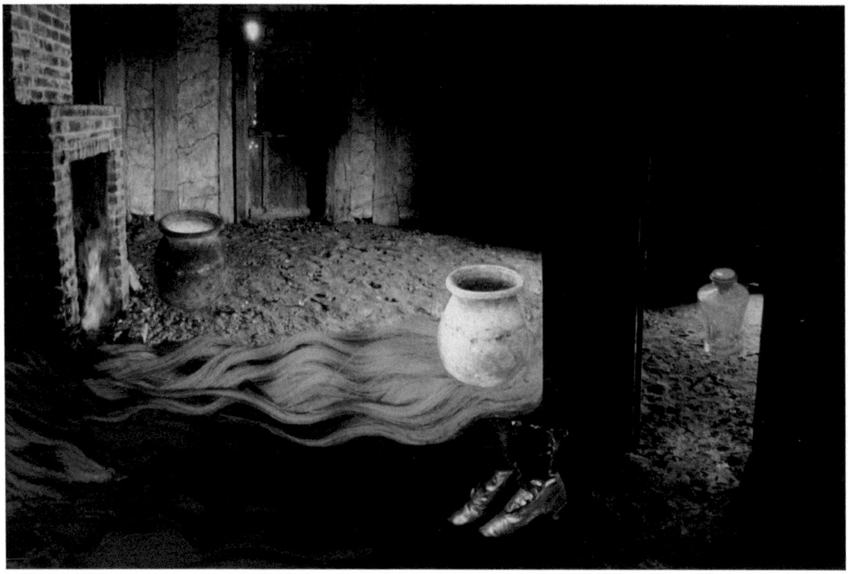

Bewitchment (from the series *Reconstituting the Vanished*)

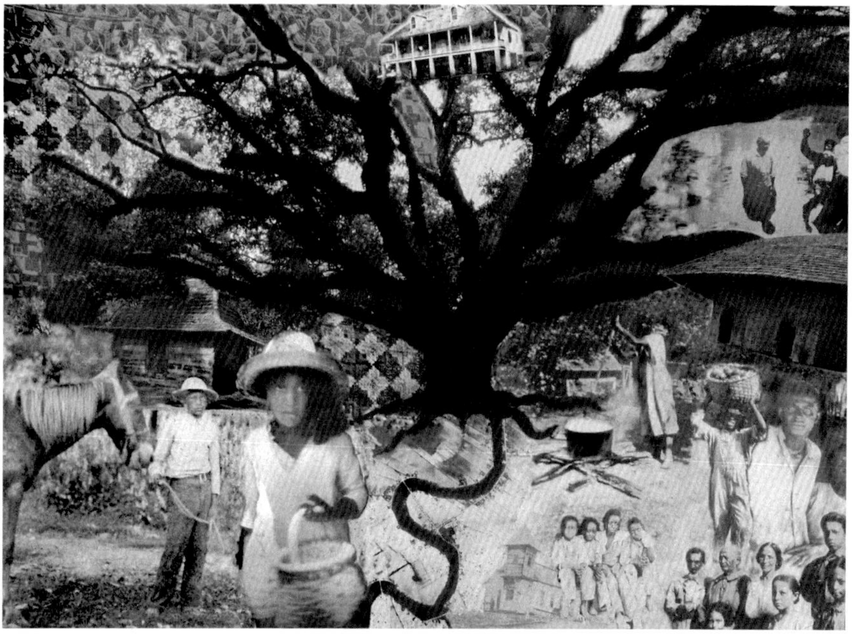

Treehouse (from the series *Reconstituting the Vanished*)

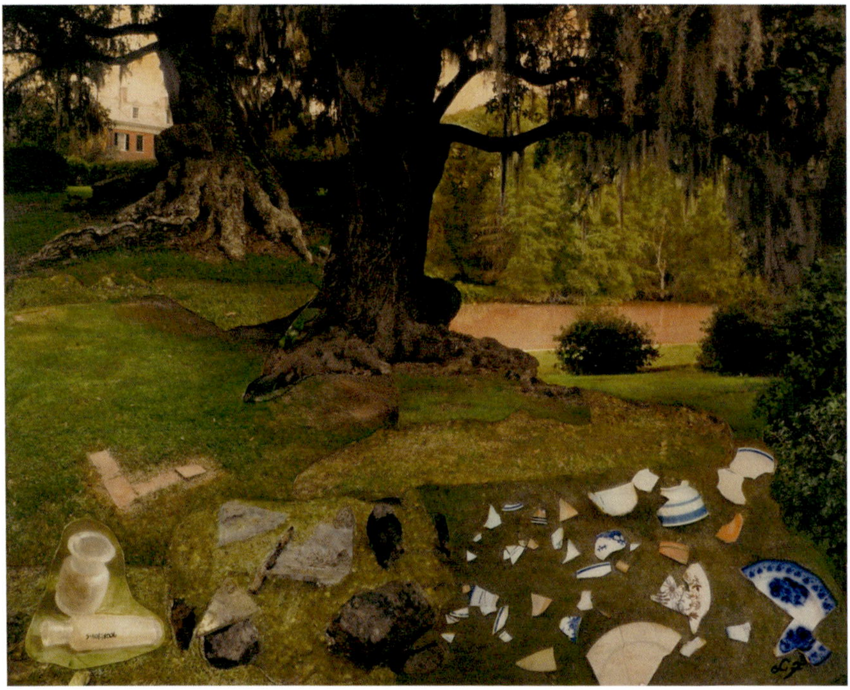

Two Sides of Mary

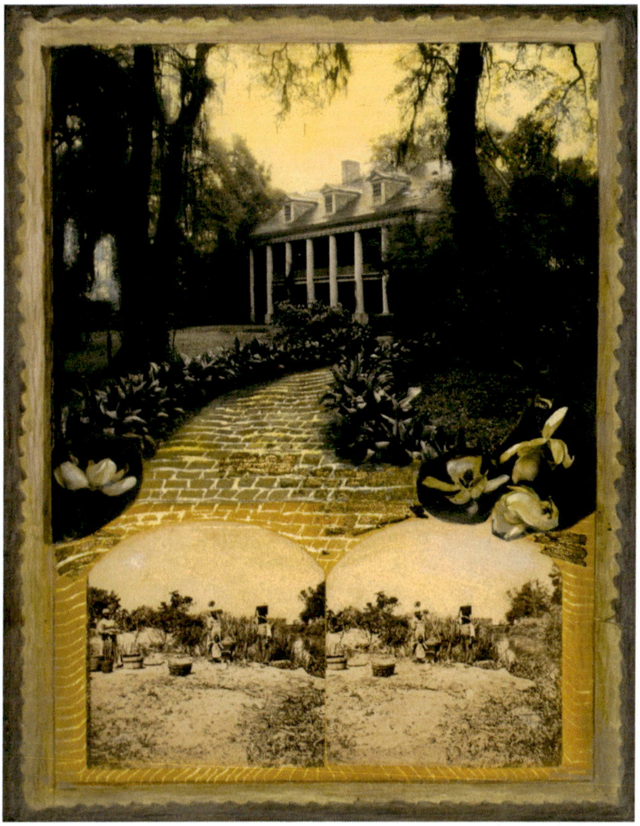

Above: *House and Field*
Right: *Field* detail (wash day)

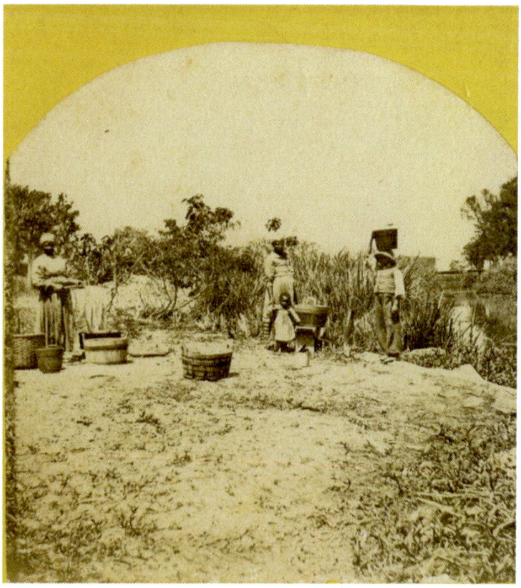

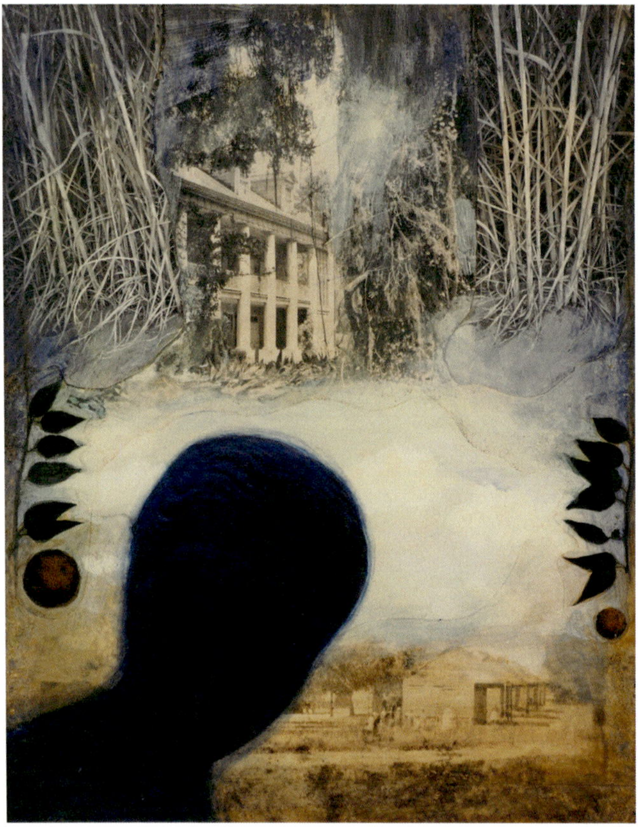

Above: *Gimlet Eye*
Right: *Gimlet Eye* detail (Grand Côte)

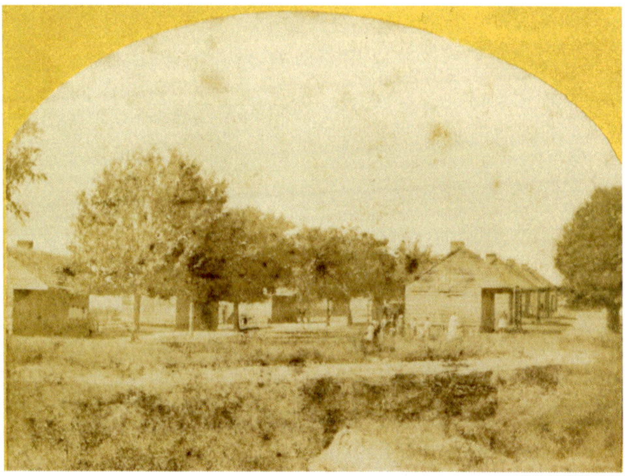

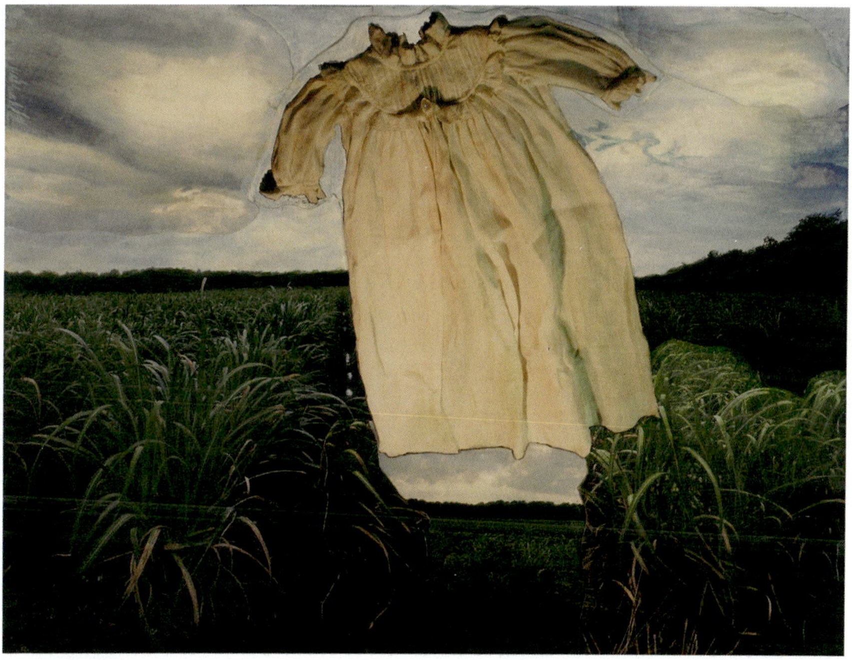

The Planter's Daughter

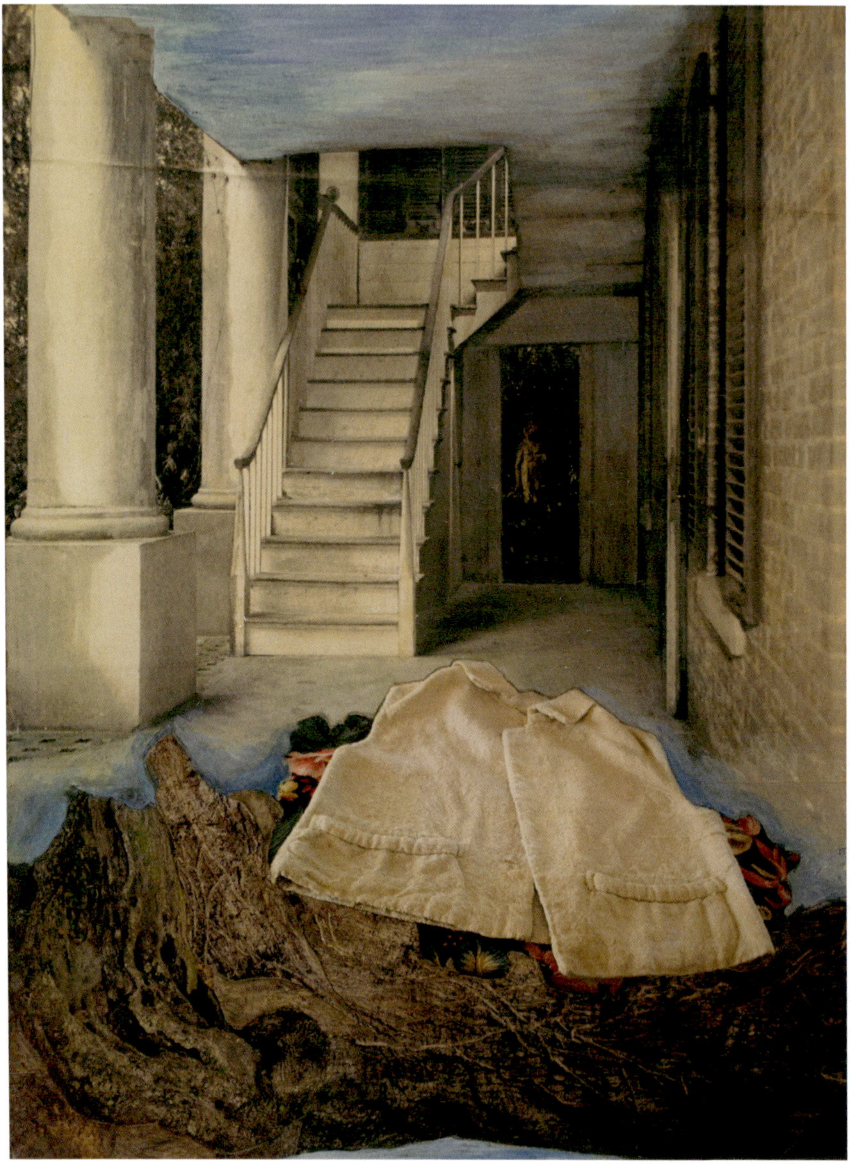

The Worker's Son

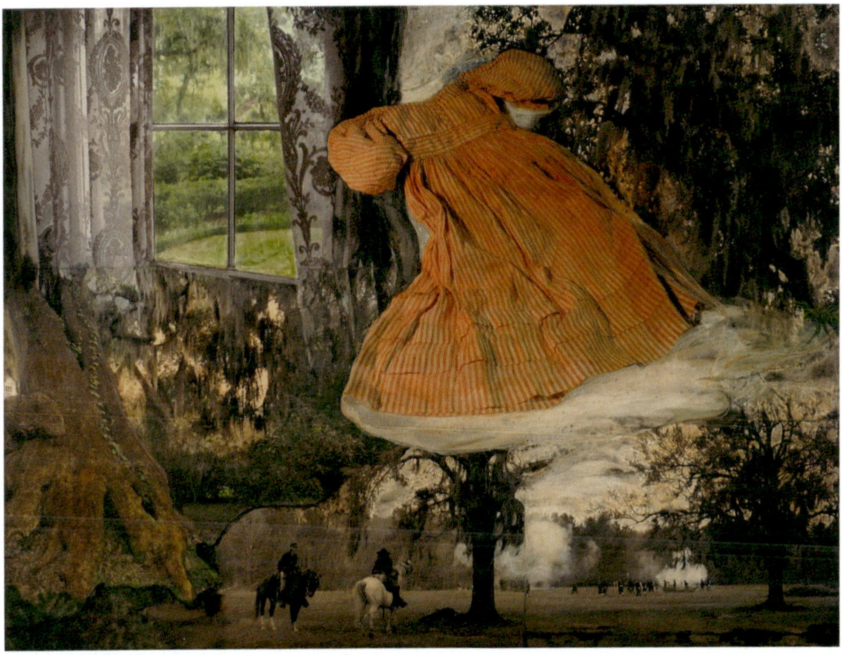

Re-enactment (right side)

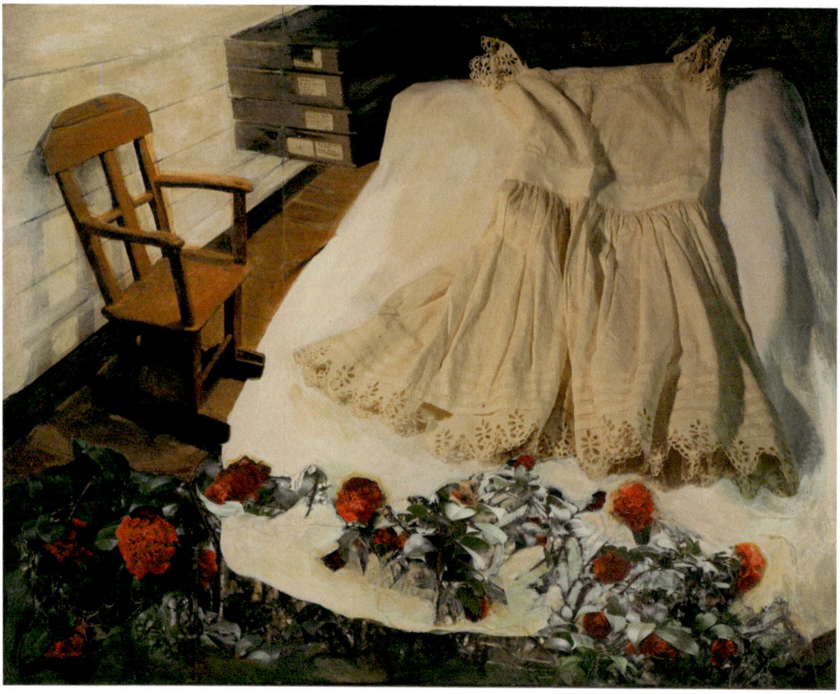

The Rocking Chair

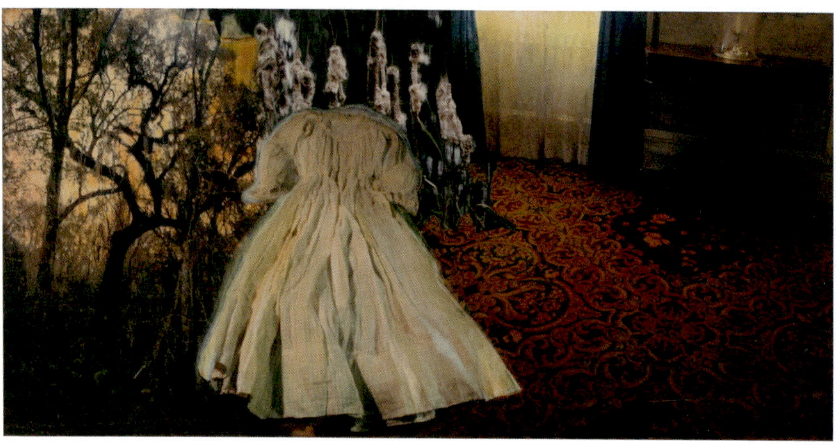

Her Other Dress

Mountain Matriarch
Dr. Mary Martin Sloop's Reform Work in the North Carolina Mountains, 1909–1953

Natasha Thompson

Throughout the Progressive Era, many middle-class women reformers strove to help people living in poverty. While some were active in urban environments, others focused on rural areas. One such woman, Dr. Mary Martin Sloop, spent almost fifty years of her life engaged in reform work in the North Carolina mountains. In May of 1951, the Golden Rule Foundation named her as the recipient of its national Mother of the Year Award. Sloop, who was seventy-eight at the time, had raised two adult children, both of whom had followed in their parents' footsteps by pursuing careers in medicine. The Golden Rule Foundation chose to honor Sloop, though, not for her role as a parent but instead because of her work transforming the small North Carolina mountain community of Crossnore. She gained the most notoriety for establishing and managing a school there that served local children. She once referred to it as "my third child, my other self."[1] Mary Sloop's efforts in reforming education, securing funding for better roads, combating illegal moonshiners, and acquiring assistance for economic development in Crossnore made her a matriarch of the community. Once Sloop decided to implement a change, she advocated tirelessly for it, often challenging existing authority figures to accomplish her goals.

Sloop's Mother of the Year award led to a book deal. She detailed her experiences in her 1953 memoir, *Miracle in the Hills*, written with assistance from North Carolina journalist LeGette Blythe. The book, with editions printed in Spanish, French, Japanese, Arabic, and Bengali, garnered praise in national newspapers, such as the *New York Herald Tribune* and the *Boston Post*. The United States Information Agency funded and distributed translations as

1. Mary T. M. Sloop and LeGette Blythe, *Miracle in the Hills* (New York: McGraw-Hill, 1953), 226.

part of its mission to bolster the image of the nation abroad during the Cold War.[2] So much of the book's popularity stemmed from Sloop's life story and her style of narration. Unlike many other memoirs of women reformers in the first half of the twentieth century, Sloop heavily stressed her personal role in transforming Crossnore, accurately depicting herself as vital to reforms taking place in the community. Her overt ownership of the importance of her work in *Miracle in the Hills* adds complexity not only to the study of Progressive Era reformers in Appalachia, but also that of women's autobiography.

Miracle in the Hills details Sloop's early life. Born Mary Turpin Martin in 1873, her parents, William and Letitia Martin, held very different visions for her future. A geology and chemistry professor at Davidson College, William believed Mary should have a strong academic background. Letitia, however, wanted fifteen-year-old Mary to attend a finishing school for young women. William ultimately won the debate, and at age eighteen, Mary graduated from Statesville Female College for Women. Unbeknownst to Letitia, Mary had planned since age thirteen to become a doctor and pursue a career as a medical missionary abroad. When she made this decision, Mary confided in her family's minister, begging him to keep her plans secret as she feared a negative reaction from her mother.[3]

Mary delayed entering medical school for twelve years, remaining in Davidson, North Carolina, nursing an ailing Letitia until her death. During this time, Mary attended Davidson College, often as the only female student. Despite her mother's illness, the two women clashed over Mary's coursework, with Letitia forbidding Mary from taking certain classes, such as an advanced math course. Mary attempted to negotiate, offering to study French language courses, a subject Letitia viewed as more feminine, if Letitia would permit her to take science courses as well. While Mary's memoir briefly addressed this period of her life, her descriptions suggest considerable tension between the two women as she pushed the boundaries of "ladylike" behavior through her studies, while also serving as her mother's nursemaid. According to Mary,

2. Lois Dann, "The Enclosed Advertisement on Miracle in the Hills," Box 6, Folder 95, LeGette Blythe Papers (#4852), Southern Historical Collection, Wilson Library, University of North Carolina at Chapel Hill; David Scott to LeGette Blythe, December 9, 1965, Box 6, Folder 95, LeGette Blythe Papers (#4852); Wilson P. Dizard, Jr., *Inventing Public Diplomacy: The Story of the U.S. Information Agency* (Boulder: Lynne Rienner Publishers, 2004), 4.

3. Sloop and Blythe, *Miracle in the Hills,* 12, 15–16.

"these twelve years gave me all I could do at home."[4] These battles with Letitia likely helped prepare Mary for conflicts she would later encounter in her work in Crossnore.

After Letitia's death, Mary resumed progress toward her dream of missionary work, completing her medical degree at the Woman's Medical College of Pennsylvania in 1906. No North Carolina college allowed women to enroll in anatomy courses with cadavers, a prohibition Mary attributed to societal views about inappropriate female behavior in the era. Offering insight into Letitia's opposition to science courses, Mary stated, "The neighbors would never have recovered from the shock of hearing about [her attending a lab] with all those naked cadavers lying about on dissecting tables."[5] After an internship at the New England Hospital for Women and Children in Boston and a residency at Agnes Scott College in Georgia, she married Dr. Eustace Sloop in 1908. The two had met while attending Davidson College.[6]

Mary Sloop's struggle to attain her medical degree reflects the challenges faced by women physicians in the late nineteenth and early twentieth centuries. Despite increasing numbers of women entering medicine, many colleges refused to accept female students, leading to the creation of institutions like the Woman's Medical College of Pennsylvania. Just as Mary battled with Letitia, aspiring women physicians regularly faced family opposition, with relatives emphasizing marriage and motherhood instead. Like several other women doctors of the era, Sloop married a fellow physician and remained employed throughout their marriage, though her professional focus shifted from medicine to education upon arriving in Crossnore.[7] Sloop's educational and medical achievements stand as remarkable in their own right.

Mary Sloop gained national notoriety, though, because of her work in Crossnore. She and Eustace began their marriage in an area that would become Avery County.[8] Though they had planned to serve abroad as medical missionaries, the Presbyterian Church rejected them because they were in their thirties. According to Mary, the missionary board deemed them too old

4. Sloop and Blythe, *Miracle in the Hills,* 16.

5. Sloop and Blythe, *Miracle in the Hills,* 16.

6. Sloop and Blythe, *Miracle in the Hills,* 16, 19.

7. Regina Morantz-Sanchez, *Sympathy and Science: Women Physicians in American Medicine* (Chapel Hill: University of North Carolina Press, 2000), 48–49, 65, 88–89, 99–100, 135.

8. The Sloops moved to Cranberry, North Carolina, in 1909, but Avery County was not formed until 1911.

to master learning new languages or cope with a tropical climate. Reflecting on this rejection, Mary contended, "I wonder what those Presbyterian brethren would think if they knew that fifty years later this old woman could still tramp over the mountains around Crossnore!"[9] Mary and Eustace shifted their focus to providing medical care in less affluent areas of the North Carolina mountains. They first settled in the town of Plumtree, practicing medicine with limited facilities, performing surgeries in private homes and even outdoors. The arrival of their first child, Emma, in 1909 kept Mary in their home office while Eustace made the majority of house calls. In 1911, they moved five miles east to Crossnore, where they remained for the rest of their lives and where Mary would rise to prominence.[10]

Sloop's work in many ways fits within the larger context of Progressive Era reformers active in the South and in Appalachia. Inspired by the settlement house work of urban Progressives like Jane Addams, some mountain reformers established schools throughout Appalachia, including Hindman Settlement School and Pine Mountain Settlement School in Kentucky, and the John C. Campbell Folk School in Brasstown, North Carolina. Such institutions provided education to local children and vocational training to adults.[11] Settlements "offered careers and leadership roles to Social Gospel Protestants and college-educated, middle-class women."[12] While Sloop engaged in similar work in Crossnore, she did not reference the larger settlement movement in accounts of her own work. Like many other Progressive women in Appalachia and beyond, Sloop's work focused heavily on assisting children. Early twentieth-century American society was more accepting of women whose career choices fit within the "selfless and nurturing vein of motherhood."[13]

As Appalachian scholar David Whisnant has noted, this period "witnessed the founding of countless schools, academies, and institutes in the

9. Sloop and Blythe, *Miracle in the Hills,* 19.

10. Sloop and Blythe, *Miracle in the Hills,* 19, 21.

11. Jess Stoddart, *Challenge and Change in Appalachia: The Story of Hindman Settlement School* (Lexington: University Press of Kentucky, 2002), 17, 47, 67 70; David E. Whisnant, *All That is Native and Fine: The Politics of Culture in an American Region* (Chapel Hill: University of North Carolina Press, 1983), 38–39, 134–35, 143, 151.

12. William A. Link, *The Paradox of Southern Progressivism, 1890–1930* (Chapel Hill: University of North Carolina Press, 1992), 81.

13. Mina Carson, *Settlement Folk: Social Thought and the American Settlement Movement, 1885–1930* (Chicago: University of Chicago Press, 1990), 25.

mountains," many of which were established by people from outside the region with the goal of improving the lives of mountaineers, often influenced from a perspective dominated by local color stereotypes.[14] Outside reformers often believed that Appalachian people lagged behind the rest of the United States, assuming that mountain inhabitants were an ignorant, impoverished, stagnant, and unsophisticated segment of the American population, prone to alcoholism and violence.[15] Reformers contended, though, that Appalachian people deserved help, portraying mountaineers as racially pure descendants of early British colonists who had preserved elements of traditional English folk culture through ballads, storytelling, handicrafts, and speech patterns. Concerns over twentieth-century immigration fueled a desire to promote this idealized British heritage.[16] Outsiders entered the mountains seeking to correct the perceived ills of the inhabitants, while preserving what they felt were desirable elements of mountain culture, and even introducing to communities what they believed were authentic mountain traditions.[17]

Mary Sloop frequently espoused some of these views of Appalachian people. Throughout her book, Sloop emphasized the English heritage of Crossnore's residents, arguing that local practices like quilting, square dancing, and bear hunting confirmed this connection. She asserted that the region's "ballads are as English as Churchill and plum pudding."[18] Sloop viewed this British connection as a positive trait, even referencing it when she experienced hurdles to her work. She contended that the "English ancestry" of Crossnore's residents caused them to "have a strong feeling for the rights of the individual," which she believed fueled local resistance to compulsory school attendance laws.[19] When seeking financial assistance for her school from the Daughters of the American Revolution (DAR), Sloop encouraged local families to engage in genealogical research to uncover ancestors who served in the Revolutionary War. Sloop repeatedly stressed the English heritage

14. Whisnant, *All That is Native and Fine,* 7–8.

15. Whisnant, *All That is Native and Fine,* 41–42.

16. Jane S. Becker, *Selling Tradition: Appalachia and the Construction of an American Folk, 1930–1940* (Chapel Hill: University of North Carolina Press, 1998), 59–61.

17. Henry Shapiro, *Appalachia on Our Mind: The Southern Mountains and Mountaineers in the American Consciousness, 1870–1920* (Chapel Hill: University of North Carolina Press, 1978), 63–64, 80–81.

18. Sloop and Blythe, *Miracle in the Hills,* 205.

19. Sloop and Blythe, *Miracle in the Hills,* 150.

of Crossnore families in newsletters sent to potential donors.[20] She did the same at speaking engagements.[21] To further supplement local incomes and fund the school, Sloop organized classes in "native mountain weaving," with the pieces created and sold for profit. Sloop acknowledged that this skill had declined in Crossnore as the residents, perhaps not as isolated as she initially assumed, "sought different things from what they had had in the earlier days."[22]

Mary Sloop injected herself into the affairs of Crossnore not long after moving there. On her first Sunday in the community, she offered church attendees the opportunity to earn Bibles she would provide by memorizing and reciting a total of 200 Bible verses. That same Sunday, she observed the poor state of the common building that functioned as a church, magistrate's office, and school, remarking that "its appearance indicated that it had been built from materials of [Noah's] Ark."[23] Her professional focus then shifted from medicine to improving Crossnore's educational facilities and quality of instruction. She recalled early challenges ranging from a lack of funding from the county to reluctance on the part of some Crossnore residents to embrace change. Through a variety of fundraising and construction initiatives, many of which Mary personally launched, Crossnore gained a multi-building campus where college-educated instructors taught elementary through high school grades to both day and residential students.[24]

From the 1910s through the 1950s, Mary Sloop labored extensively to secure money and resources needed to support Crossnore, remarking that such work required "letter writing, speechmaking, travel, and—above all—faith in your cause."[25] She wrote a quarterly newsletter updating readers on successes at Crossnore, as well as the school's needs, a practice she did not stop until 1960 when her health declined.[26] In these newsletters, Sloop expressed

20. Mary M. Sloop, *Crossnore Bulletin* VI, no. 3 (April–June 1939), North Carolina Collection, Wilson Library, University of North Carolina at Chapel Hill.

21. "Dr. Mary Martin Sloop Speaks at Chapel," *Salemite* (Winston-Salem), May 25, 1934, accessed April 29, 2018, http://newspapers.digitalnc.org/lccn/2015236777/1934-05-25/ed-1/seq-1/.

22. Sloop and Blythe, *Miracle in the Hills,* 150, 155, 205, 171–73.

23. Sloop and Blythe, *Miracle in the Hills,* 48.

24. Sloop and Blythe, *Miracle in the Hills,* 51, 56–57.

25. Sloop and Blythe, *Miracle in the Hills,* 185.

26. Mary M. Sloop, *Crossnore Bulletin* XXXIV, no. 4 (October–December 1960), North Carolina Collection, Wilson Library.

pride in student accomplishments. For instance, in 1939, she described how a former male student, referred to as "our boy," had walked five miles each day to Crossnore's high school to learn Latin, then majored in Latin at North Carolina State College, and finally joined the Marines. Similarly, Sloop recounted the ecstatic phone call she received from a young woman who had attended school at Crossnore and then completed a college degree in home economics, noting that the former student chose to return to the mountains to teach. Sloop emphasized these accomplishments and argued that Crossnore could help others attain similar successes, provided that donations kept arriving.[27]

In numerous instances, Mary Sloop's appeals to donors revealed how the school fulfilled a parental role for some of its students. In 1934, she recounted a Crossnore mother who, unable to afford Christmas presents, told her children that "Santa was dead." Sloop contended that donations could ensure the children received gifts.[28] A 1943 call for funds to support residential students stated that parents had temporarily left for war industries jobs. Boarding at Crossnore provided their children with a safe place to stay.[29] Sloop's pleas referenced poverty, indifference, and abuse. She described a seventeen-year-old girl whose physically abusive father was incarcerated and asked readers to send funds to support that student and others in need, contending that scholarships not only provided material support but were "proof to the children that somebody is interested and expects them to measure up to the best that is in them."[30] Sloop strove to prevent teenage marriages, asserting in a newsletter that the school helped to "delay [Cupid's] operations while Crossnore trains his targets."[31] In these ways, Sloop and her school provided forms of parental support that some children might have lacked at home.

27. Mary M. Sloop, *Crossnore Bulletin* VI, no. 4 (July–September 1939), North Carolina Collection, Wilson Library.

28. Mary Martin Sloop, "A Christmas Wish," *Franklin Press and the Highlands Maconian*, December 20, 1934, accessed April 29, 2018, http://newspapers.digitalnc.org/lccn/sn92073966/1934-12-20/ed-1/seq-2/.

29. Mary M. Sloop, *Crossnore Bulletin* X, no. 3 (July–September 1943), North Carolina Collection, Wilson Library.

30. Mary M. Sloop, *Crossnore Bulletin* VIII, no. 4 (July–September 1941), North Carolina Collection, Wilson Library.

31. Mary M. Sloop, *Crossnore Bulletin* X, no. 3 (July–September 1943), North Carolina Collection, Wilson Library.

Similarly, Sloop's school played a role in student development, providing education but also shaping character and preparing youth for adulthood. During World War II, newsletters often referenced Crossnore alumni serving in the military, praising those who volunteered for service. Sloop contended that experiences at the school helped to "build citizens," describing how students, especially those from disadvantaged families, grew into well-rounded individuals.[32] She argued that improvements to a boys' dormitory would not only provide a place for students to comfortably sleep, but also prepare them for adulthood, stating, "When a boy does not experience the satisfaction and influence of living in a home of comfort and attractiveness, he will rarely make the effort necessary to provide such a home for his own family."[33] She relayed the anecdote of a girl who, frustrated with owning a single old dress, damaged the garment in the hopes of getting another one. Rather than punishing the child, Sloop gave the girl two replacement dresses, "not to reward her for tearing but to soothe the suffering that had driven her to tearing." Sloop reported that in adulthood, the girl became a mother with "such neat, attractive children."[34] When appealing for funds to complete a recreation building in 1958, Sloop asserted that play and exercise would help students physically as well as morally.[35] She clearly believed education should extend beyond academic training to cultivate a sense of self within Crossnore's students.

Some fundraising strategies, like appeals for cash or calls for tax increases, were more traditional, but others revealed how Sloop innovated when facing adversity. Sloop often recounted the story of how, during her early years in Crossnore, she saved thirteen-year-old Hepsy from an early marriage by arranging for the girl to attend high school in the nearby town of Banner Elk.[36] Sloop secured Hepsy's tuition money through donations from friends, but

32. Mary M. Sloop, *Crossnore Bulletin* VI, no. 4 (July–September 1939), North Carolina Collection, Wilson Library; Mary M. Sloop, *Crossnore Bulletin* X, no. 2 (January–March 1943), North Carolina Collection, Wilson Library; Mary M. Sloop, *Crossnore Bulletin* X, no. 3 (July–September 1943), North Carolina Collection, Wilson Library.

33. Mary M. Sloop, *Crossnore Bulletin* VIII, no. 4 (July–September 1941), North Carolina Collection, Wilson Library.

34. Mary M. Sloop, *Crossnore Bulletin* IX, no. 1 (September–December 1941), North Carolina Collection, Wilson Library.

35. Mary M. Sloop, *Crossnore Bulletin* XXXII, no. 1 (January–March 1958), North Carolina Collection, Wilson Library.

36. This was before Crossnore's high school had been completed.

Hepsy's widowed father, struggling to support her eight siblings, could not afford new clothes for his daughter. Sloop appealed for used clothing from relatives, only to receive black mourning dresses. Though the clothes were too somber for a teenager, local women expressed interest in them and Sloop sold them to purchase more appropriate clothes for Hepsy.[37] Even into the 1950s, Sloop continued asking donors throughout North Carolina to send contributions of used clothing to stock a second-hand shop.[38] Clothing sales increased the school's revenue. Sloop allowed customers who could not afford to pay cash for the used garments to barter vegetables, which lowered the school's grocery expenditures. In 1940, Sloop discovered that a music school in New York was replacing some of its pianos. She arranged for the school to send two discarded ones to Crossnore for music lessons.[39] Sloop appealed to newsletter readers to send in old sewing machines, scrap fabric, and typewriters for sewing and typing lessons and to produce needed clothing for students.[40]

When donations failed to provide enough resources to address Crossnore's challenges, Mary Sloop sought creative ways to keep her school functioning and took pride in her innovative solutions. When early school construction funds were depleted in the 1910s, she had workers hang large sheets of unbleached muslin fabric over window openings until windowpanes could be purchased. As the local men working on the building lamented the lack of funding for a "store-boughten" door for the school's exterior, Sloop instructed them to move a manufactured interior door to the outside and hang homemade doors inside the school.[41] She sometimes creatively skirted safety regulations. In 1927 an inspector found that individual bedrooms in a boys' dormitory were too small, so Sloop had the doors removed and sold, creating one large room that complied with regulations.[42] To save on labor costs when constructing a new kitchen in 1941, the school employed older boys to complete part of the work, only paying them $1 of the promised wage of $3 per week. Part of their earnings contributed to their boarding fees at the school.

37. Sloop and Blythe, *Miracle in the Hills,* 71–74.

38. Mary M. Sloop, *Crossnore Bulletin* XXX, no. 2 (April–June 1956), North Carolina Collection, Wilson Library.

39. Mary M. Sloop, *Crossnore Bulletin* IX, no. 1 (September–December 1941), North Carolina Collection, Wilson Library.

40. Mary M. Sloop, *Crossnore Bulletin* IX, no. 2 (April–June 1942), North Carolina Collection, Wilson Library.

41. Sloop and Blythe, *Miracle in the Hills,* 65–67.

42. Sloop and Blythe, *Miracle in the Hills,* 216.

The remainder went into savings. Sloop contended that this practice helped the boys develop financial responsibility.[43] She regularly enlisted the assistance of supportive local men and women, who, when they could afford to do so, volunteered their own supplies and labor to construct school facilities.[44]

In conducting her work, Mary Sloop frequently challenged existing forms of male authority, emphasizing the good of the community over deference to traditional, submissive roles for women, even within her own marriage. Sloop endeavored to stop the practice of moonshining, as she believed alcohol led to poverty and violence in the area. In one instance she needed Eustace, who was in the nearby town of Newland examining military recruits for World War I, to drive their car to Crossnore to haul a seized moonshine still back to the courthouse in Newland. Behind with his medical exams, Eustace wanted to delay the trip until the following day. In response, Mary threatened to roll the still six miles from Crossnore to Newland, ending the discussion by hanging up on her husband. Perhaps fearing the public embarrassment that he would endure from having his wife walk into town pushing a wheelbarrow, as well as the possible unpleasant repercussions at home, Eustace postponed his work to transport Mary and the still.[45]

Though she often praised the people of Crossnore for being proud and self-reliant, Mary Sloop sometimes found herself at odds with locals questioning and resisting her efforts toward change. She recalled that in her first year there, a small minority objected to her desire to replace the old, shared building that had initially housed the school. Others in the 1910s balked at her efforts to implement performance and attendance requirements for promotion to higher grades, instead preferring the traditional method of advancement based on student age. After North Carolina enacted compulsory attendance laws in 1913, Sloop became a truancy officer in Avery County and swore warrants against parents who kept their children out of school, despite her fears of retaliatory violence. In response to drunken men disrupting community meetings, Mary had the sheriff deputize Eustace and another male supporter. She and the two men carried visible pistols to a meeting and she instructed her deputies to shoot anyone who caused disorder.[46]

43. Mary M. Sloop, *Crossnore Bulletin* VIII, no. 2 (April–June 1941), North Carolina Collection, Wilson Library.

44. Sloop and Blythe, *Miracle in the Hills,* 62–63.

45. Sloop and Blythe, *Miracle in the Hills,* 113–15.

46. Sloop and Blythe, *Miracle in the Hills,* 57, 95, 97–100, 103–4.

Mary Sloop clashed with the county school board which, in her view, provided inadequate funding to Crossnore. In the early 1920s, the county refused her request to borrow $10,000 to complete the construction of Crossnore's high school. Undeterred, Sloop secured a personal loan for the amount at a local bank even though she lacked the financial resources to repay it on her own. To put pressure on the county to assume the debt, Sloop traveled to the state capital, Raleigh, on the same day that county school board members were attending a gathering there. She met with State Superintendent of Public Instruction Eugene C. Brooks to explain the situation and convinced him to support her cause. According to Sloop, Brooks "laid down the law" to the Avery County School Board delegation. The county assumed responsibility for repayment of the loan.[47]

Challenging authority sometimes incurred consequences for Sloop. One Sunday in the 1910s, a local minister devoted much of his sermon to berating Sloop for allowing recreational square dancing at the school, labeling her and her supporters "Sinful Mary and her band of devil-workers." The outburst stunned the congregation and humiliated Sloop, who had visiting relatives in attendance with her for the service.[48] In other cases, though, she made peace with her opponents. In the 1920s, one adversary, who she had jailed for truancy violations, ended up casting the deciding vote in favor of imposing a local property tax needed to secure state funding for the high school. Uncle Abe, as she called him,[49] only grunted at her when he arrived at the poll, but voted to break the tie in her favor.[50] Even with fame and acclaim, deviating from societal expectations of female submissiveness brought criticism. When reviewing a draft of her memoir, book editor Ed Kuhn cut a passage on Sloop's Mother of the Year Award, due to "a rather unbecoming, boastful tone in Mrs. Sloop's account."[51]

Sloop successfully secured other forms of support from the state to benefit the adults of Crossnore. Recognizing that poor roads held back Crossnore's

47. Sloop and Blythe, *Miracle in the Hills,* 132–35.

48. John Maloney, "Grand Lady of the Blue Ridge," Box 7, Folder 98, in the LeGette Blythe Papers (#4852).

49. Perhaps fearing social ramifications, Sloop opted to use "bogus names" for some Crossnore residents when narrating her memoir. The editorial staff at McGraw-Hill were aware and accepted this. Ed Kuhn to LeGette Blythe, August 6, 1952, Box 6, Folder 95, in the LeGette Blythe Papers (#4852).

50. Sloop and Blythe, *Miracle in the Hills,* 104–7.

51. Ed Kuhn to LeGette Blythe, December 18, 1952, Box 6, Folder 95, in the LeGette Blythe Papers (#4852).

economy, she campaigned throughout the 1920s to obtain funding from the state legislature and the Good Roads Committee for the construction of a road connecting Crossnore to other parts of the county. Tied to that endeavor, Sloop contacted the North Carolina Extension Service, which provided farm agents to work with Crossnore residents on improving incomes through the cultivation of commercial potato crops and home demonstration agents to help families extend budgets through efficient food preparation and preservation.[52]

As a result of her continuous efforts to support Crossnore, Mary Sloop gained notoriety throughout the state and, eventually, the nation. In addition to directly contacting state officials for help with her school, she also participated in speaking engagements throughout North Carolina, such as at Kiwanis Club and DAR meetings.[53] She gave an address at the 1931 North Carolina Farmers' Convention.[54] Governor Angus McClean appointed her in 1926 to the state's sesquicentennial committee.[55] Her quarterly newsletters kept people in the state and beyond abreast of her work at Crossnore. Recognition for her efforts culminated in the 1951 Mother of the Year Award, which she received in New York City. Recalling the ceremony, Sloop remarked with pride on praise she received for her outfit, purchased second-hand in Crossnore.[56]

After hearing Sloop speak on television about the award, Ed Aswell, a vice president from the McGraw-Hill Book Company, contacted LeGette Blythe about working with Sloop to publish her story. An author and playwright,

52. Sloop and Blythe, *Miracle in the Hills,* 69–70, 97, 109–12, 125–28, 209–10.

53. "Alfred Moore Chapter, D.A.R. Held Its Closing Meeting for the Season," *The Pilot* (Southern Pines, NC), May 15, 1925, accessed April 25, 2018, http://newspapers.digitalnc.org/lccn/sn92073968/1925-05-15/ed-1/seq-1/; "Kiwanians Hear of Crossnore School," *The Pilot* (Southern Pines, NC), May 16, 1930, accessed April 25, 2018, http://newspapers.digitalnc.org/lccn/sn92073968/1930-05-16/ed-1/seq-1/; "Hostesses to D.A.R.," *The Pilot* (Southern Pines, NC), December 9, 1938, accessed April 25, 2018, http://newspapers.digitalnc.org/lccn/sn92073968/1938-12-09/ed-1/seq-6/.

54. "National Speakers at Farm Convention," *Forest City Courier*, July 16, 1931, accessed April 29, 2018, http://newspapers.digitalnc.org/lccn/sn91068175/1931-07-16/ed-1/seq-8/.

55. "Governor Appoints Sixty-Four Women," *Daily Advance* (Elizabeth City, NC), April 5, 1926, accessed April 29, 2018, http://newspapers.digitalnc.org/lccn/sn92074042/1926-04-05/ed-1/seq-6/.

56. Sloop and Blythe, *Miracle in the Hills,* 222.

Blythe worked as a journalist for several North Carolina newspapers. Sloop agreed to collaborate and she and Blythe met throughout 1952, mainly in Crossnore, as health problems prevented her from traveling. She narrated stories to Blythe, who took notes and made audio recordings. He then edited and arranged them into a manuscript.[57]

This collaboration raises questions about the degree to which *Miracle in the Hills* is Mary Sloop's work and the degree to which it is LeGette Blythe's creation. According to Blythe, Sloop felt she did not know how to write a book. He added several "passages of sound homey philosophy."[58] However, most of the book's wording came from Sloop. She told Blythe many of the same anecdotes that she had included over several decades in speeches and newsletters. Blythe sometimes spread single stories over several chapters, but the wording remained essentially identical to Sloop's narration. Blythe did condense some of her accounts and also spoke with people who had known and worked with Sloop to fill in details.[59]

The McGraw-Hill editorial staff shaped the final format of the book. Editor Ed Kuhn trimmed sections on "mountain social customs" that he believed were excessive and pushed for more anecdotes about Eustace's work as a physician, arguing that medical stories would increase sales. McGraw-Hill wanted the book written in first-person perspective, perhaps deviating from what Mary Sloop had envisioned, as in some of the audio recordings she alternated between first and third person. The company chose the book's title and pushed Sloop to include a dedication, which she inscribed to Eustace.[60] Though he did contribute to the book, Mary Sloop helped Blythe achieve success with McGraw-Hill that he would be unable to duplicate on his own. The publisher rejected additional projects he submitted. While Blythe later

57. LeGette Blythe, "This One Was Fun," Box 7, Folder 98, in the LeGette Blythe Papers (#4852); "LeGette Blythe," Box 7, Folder 98, in the LeGette Blythe Papers (#4852); Tom Fesperman "It Took Three to Write this Book: Blythe, Sloop, Recorder Great Team," *Charlotte News,* March 7, 1953, Box 7, Folder 98, in the LeGette Blythe Papers (#4852).

58. Fesperman, "It Took Three to Write this Book."

59. Sloop/Blythe Tapes: Cassette 5, in the LeGette Blythe Papers (#4852); Sloop and Blythe, 92, 102, 126–28, 155, 172, 209–11; Ed Kuhn to LeGette Blythe, August 6, 1952, Box 6, Folder 95, in the LeGette Blythe Papers (#4852).

60. Ed Kuhn to LeGette Blythe, September 29, 1952, Box 6, Folder 95, in the LeGette Blythe Papers (#4852); Ed Kuhn to LeGette Blythe, July 12, 1951, Box 6, Folder 95, in the LeGette Blythe Papers (#4852).

published other books with different companies, McGraw-Hill had no interest in him without Mary Sloop.[61]

Miracle in the Hills differs from memoirs of other of women reformers active in the first half of the twentieth century, most notably because of Sloop's tone. Scholars of women's autobiography, such as Jill Conway, argue that women autobiographers of this era tended to downplay accomplishments. Rather than stressing their personal roles in implementing change, notable reformers portrayed themselves having simply been lucky or as passive observers of the actual results of their own hard work. Conway asserts that such passivity is even present in Jane Addams's *Twenty Years at Hull House*, which documents the experiences of one of the most well-known women involved in Progressive reform.[62] In her analysis of Helen Keller's *The Story of My Life,* Peggy Prenshaw contended that the book contained "stories of agency and courage but still deflect[ed] acceptance and recognition of [Keller's] personal power."[63] Jane Simpson McKimmon, who built North Carolina's home demonstration program during the same time period that Sloop was active in Crossnore, took a similar approach to that of Addams. Despite years of hard work developing a program to serve farm women and youth, McKimmon's 1943 *When We're Green We Grow* largely downplays her involvement, instead detailing the actions of others who worked with her. Even McKimmon's description of being hired, coincidentally living next door to the state's director of extension work, minimized her own accomplishments that led him to approach her about the position.[64]

In *Miracle in the Hills*, however, Mary Sloop maintained a more assertive voice in describing her efforts. She deliberately decided to move to the mountains. After the rejection for missionary work, Sloop remarked that she and Eustace "made a momentous decision to marry and move" to Avery County

61. Ed Kuhn to LeGette Blythe, March 23, 1955, Box 6, Folder 95, in the LeGette Blythe Papers (#4852); Ed Kuhn to LeGette Blythe, July 5, 1955, Box 6, Folder 95, in the LeGette Blythe Papers (#4852); Ed Aswell to LeGette Blythe, November 15, 1955, Box 6, Folder 95, in the LeGette Blythe Papers (#4852); "LeGette Blythe," Box 18, Folder 215, in the LeGette Blythe Papers (#4852); "LeGette Blythe Will Publish New Book," Box 18, Folder 215, in the LeGette Blythe Papers (#4852).

62. Jill Ker Conway, *When Memory Speaks: Reflections on Autobiography* (New York: Alfred A. Knopf, 1998), 48–50.

63. Peggy Whitman Prenshaw, *Composing Selves: Southern Women and Autobiography* (Baton Rouge: Louisiana State University Press, 2011), 67, 68.

64. Jane S. McKimmon, *When We're Green We Grow: The Story of Home Demonstration Work in North Carolina* (Chapel Hill: University of North Carolina Press, 1945), 5.

because they "had wanted to be missionaries," a desire Mary had long before she met Eustace.[65] In describing her experiences in Crossnore, Sloop clearly depicted herself as a primary catalyst behind the changes taking place in the community. Though she credited the work of local people, outside donors and supporters, and divine intervention, Mary Sloop heavily and repeatedly emphasized her own role in Crossnore's transformation.

The 1953 publication of *Miracle in the Hills* and its strong sales caused Mary Sloop to gain further acclaim, nationally and abroad. The University of North Carolina awarded her two honorary degrees.[66] Representative Charles Jonas presented President Eisenhower with a signed copy of the book.[67] Into the 1960s, the United States Information Agency commissioned numerous foreign language translations.[68] Despite the book's popularity, Sloop never actually read it. She experienced declining health throughout the 1950s, suffering a major heart attack in 1959 that left her hospitalized until her death in 1962. Eustace passed away a year prior and her children, Emma Fink and William Sloop, assumed work at her school while also practicing medicine and dentistry, respectively.[69]

Work to fully tell the story of Mary Sloop's time in Crossnore still remains, including the need to locate more unfiltered reactions from local people to her efforts. However, she made a significant positive impact on Crossnore in the fifty-one years she lived there, improving education, economics, and healthcare. The school she founded still operates in the present, funded partially by the sale of used clothing.[70] At the time of her death, numerous tributes were offered, but perhaps the most appropriate was the Crossnore newsletter that recounted and praised her life's work, while also reminding readers to continue sending in financial donations to fund the school.[71]

65. Sloop and Blythe, *Miracle in the Hills,* 15, 20–21.

66. "Dr. Sloop Dies; Wrought Miracle in the Hills," *Watauga Democrat* (Boone, NC), January 18, 1962, accessed April 29, 2018, http://newspapers.digitalnc.org/lccn/sn82007642/1962-01-18/ed-1/seq-6/.

67. "'Miracle in the Hills' Lady is Honored at 80," *Charlotte Daily News*, March 10, 1953, Box 7, Folder 99, in the LeGette Blythe Papers (#4852).

68. David Scott to LeGette Blythe.

69. "Dr. Sloop Dies; Wrought Miracle in the Hills," *Crossnore Bulletin* XXXVII, no. 2 (April–June 1962), North Carolina Collection, Wilson Library, University of North Carolina at Chapel Hill.

70. "Sales Store," Crossnore School & Children's Home, accessed May 23, 2018, https://www.crossnore.org/sales-store/.

71. *Crossnore Bulletin* XXXVII, no. 2 (April–June 1962), North Carolina Collection, Wilson Library, University of North Carolina at Chapel Hill.

Bibliography

Primary Sources

Blythe, LeGette Papers (#4852). Southern Historical Collection, Wilson Library, University of North Carolina at Chapel Hill. Chapel Hill, North Carolina.

Crossnore School Bulletin. North Carolina Collection, Wilson Library, University of North Carolina at Chapel Hill. Chapel Hill, North Carolina.

McKimmon, Jane S. *When We're Green We Grow: The Story of Home Demonstration Work in North Carolina*. Chapel Hill: University of North Carolina Press, 1945.

Sloop, Mary T. M. and LeGette Blythe, *Miracle in the Hills*. New York: McGraw-Hill, 1953.

Secondary Sources

Becker, Jane S. *Selling Tradition: Appalachia and the Construction of an American Folk, 1930–1940*. Chapel Hill: University of North Carolina Press, 1998.

Carson, Mina. *Settlement Folk: Social Thought and the American Settlement Movement, 1885–1930*. Chicago: University of Chicago Press, 1990.

Conway, Jill Ker. *When Memory Speaks: Reflections on Autobiography*. New York: Alfred A. Knopf, 1998.

Dizard, Wilson P. Jr. *Inventing Public Diplomacy: The Story of the U.S. Information Agency*. Boulder: Lynne Rienner Publishers, 2004.

Link, William A. *The Paradox of Southern Progressivism, 1890–1930*. Chapel Hill: University of North Carolina Press, 1992.

Morantz-Sanchez, Regina. *Sympathy and Science: Women Physicians in American Medicine*. Chapel Hill: University of North Carolina Press, 2000.

Prenshaw, Peggy Whitman. *Composing Selves: Southern Women and Autobiography*. Baton Rouge: Louisiana State University Press, 2011.

"Sales Store." Crossnore School & Children's Home. Accessed May 23, 2018. https://www.crossnore.org/sales-store/.

Shapiro, Henry. *Appalachia on Our Mind: The Southern Mountains and Mountaineers in the American Consciousness, 1870–1920*. Chapel Hill: University of North Carolina Press, 1978.

Stoddart, Jess. *Challenge and Change in Appalachia: The Story of Hindman Settlement School.* Lexington: The University Press of Kentucky, 2002.

Whisnant, David E. *All That is Native and Fine: The Politics of Culture in an American Region*. Chapel Hill: University of North Carolina Press, 1983.

Natasha Thompson is a history instructor at Vance-Granville Community College. She holds a PhD in US history from UNC-Greensboro and her research focuses on the twentieth-century South, especially the efforts social reformers who worked with young people.

Impact of the Southern Women Dataset on Social Network Analysis

Taniecea A. Mallery

In the 1940s, three researchers observed the social activities of over four hundred women to study the impact of caste and class on daily life in a typical southern community.[1] By examining interviews, guest lists, newspapers, and records of participant observers, they sought to understand the position of southern women based on their social relationships with other members of their own caste. One particular collection of data describing the interaction of eighteen women over a series of fourteen informal events has become known as the "Southern Women dataset," and it has been used extensively by social network analysts as a source for testing new methods of mathematical and computational analysis. However, many of the subsequent analyses have not focused on the context of the original study and the resulting potential for further understanding these social structures.

Social Network Analysis

The field of social network analysis focuses on patterns of relationships that exist between individuals within a group. Beginning in the 1930s, the earliest social network analysis applications were in fields such as psychology, applied mathematics, and anthropology. In the earliest days of network analysis,[2] Jacob Moreno first utilized the sociogram (a diagram with individuals represented as points and relationships represented as lines connecting those points) as a way to visually represent such relationships. In the 1950s and

1. Allison Davis, Burleigh B. Gardner, and Mary R. Gardner, *Deep South: A Social Anthropological Study of Caste and Class* (Chicago: University of Chicago Press, 1941).

2. Jacob Moreno, *Who Shall Survive? A New Approach to the Problem of Human Interrelations* (Washington, DC: Nervous and Mental Disease Publishing Company, 1934).

beyond, Dorwin Cartwright and Frank Harary built on the concept of sociograms by applying mathematical formulas from the field of graph theory to further understand social structure.[3] By the 1960s, network analysis had become popular in the field of anthropology, as researchers began viewing societies not as monolithic entities but as patterns of relationships between individuals, organized by the roles they played relative to one another.[4]

Most of the early social network studies conducted by mathematicians and graph theorists were based on complicated and complex algorithms; therefore, many of the applications of social network analysis were conducted on small social groups because of the complexity and time-consuming nature of the calculations required to analyze them.[5] With the advancement of computer-based analysis techniques, the focus on social network analysis shifted in the 1970s to involve the analysis of larger groups with more complex social structures. Additionally, the 1970s saw a shift toward a focus in sociology, where researchers began conceptualizing network analysis in terms of describing structural positions and roles rather than individuals themselves. This brought about a broad application of network analysis to other fields such as economics and business.[6]

Social network analysis is a unique method of analysis because it focuses on the patterns of relationships between individuals rather than the characteristics of those individuals. It also encompasses multiple levels of analysis, in which researchers may examine the patterns of relationships between individuals, organizations, or geographic locations. This branch of study allows the examination of relational structure from a qualitative, quantitative, and graphical perspective. Because of its ubiquity, social network analysis has been used to examine a variety of social concepts, such as power, cohesion, cliques, and alliances. Social network analysis can be used to describe the subgroups that exist within a larger community and identify key individuals who serve

3. Dorwin Cartwright and Frank Harary, "Balance and Clusterability: An Overview," *Perspectives on Social Network Research,* eds. Paul W. Holland and Samuel Leinhardt (New York: Academic Press, 1979), 25–50.

4. Harrison C. White, *An Anatomy of Kinship: Mathematical Models for Structures of Cumulated Roles* (Englewood Cliffs: Prentice Hall, 1963).

5. Kimberly A. Fredericks and Maryann M. Durland, "The Historical Evolution and Basic Concepts of Social Network Analysis," *New Directions for Evaluation* 2 (February 2006): 15–23.

6. Ronald S. Burt, *Corporate Profits and Cooptation* (New York: Academic Press, 1983).

as brokers or key influencers in the spread of information. This is especially useful in the examination of social stratification within the informal relational structures that existed in the Deep South in the early 1940s.

Southern Women Dataset

In their groundbreaking book published in 1941, three social anthropologists set out to understand the social structure and customs of Black and White women in the heart of the Deep South, an area defined roughly as the states of South Carolina, Georgia, Florida, Alabama, Mississippi, and Louisiana, overlapping into the adjoining states. In a comprehensive study, Allison Davis, Burleigh B. Gardner, and Mary R. Gardner lived among the people of Natchez, Mississippi, for more than eighteen months to investigate how class and caste informed daily life for women in a typical southern community.[7] One important distinction was the difference between class (an indication of an individual's social behavior) and caste (their social status based on racial identity). In particular, the researchers discovered that the division by caste is directly responsible for the existence of distinct systems of social classes among Black and White women.

One aspect of Davis, Gardner, and Gardner's analysis involved examining the correspondence between southern women's social class levels and their patterns of informal interaction. To measure these patterns, they systematically collected data on the social activities of women observed over a nine-month period. They studied patterns of interaction among groups of White women and groups of Black women to observe similarities and differences in the influence of social class on the stratification of informal group relationships. Their study uncovered several notable observations regarding the perceptions of class stratification among Black and White women.

At the onset of their study, the researchers hypothesized that the informal interactions of southern women were organized by *cliques*, defined as groups of individuals that share a certain range of social characteristics. These groups of individuals, often described by members as "our crowd," consisted of tightly formed relationships based on common experiences and identities. In particular, members often delineated the differences between "our little crowd" (the clique) and "our large crowd" (the extended clique). While the members of any one clique were usually all members of the same social class and exhibited similar class behaviors, this was not a requirement.

7. Davis, Gardner, and Gardner, *Deep South.*

As part of their larger study of forty-three groups representing a total of over four hundred individuals in the Deep South, the researchers examined the social interactions of a group of eighteen White women who interacted over a series of fourteen informal social events. During that period, the researchers recorded the attendance of the women at the events using interviews, guest lists, newspapers, and the records of participant observers.

Through the record of attendance at events and the information gleaned from a series of interviews with the fourteen women, the researchers were able to identify each woman's position within the social structure of the group. By observing women who consistently attended informal events together, the researchers identified two isolated cliques; interviews helped them to determine women's position (core, primary, or secondary) within each clique. Core members were those women who participated most often and at the most intimate affairs. Women who participated with core members on some occasions but never as a group alone were called primary members, and those women who participated only infrequently were considered secondary members. The "boundaries" of the cliques were also determined through interviews. For example, Miss Pearl Oglethorpe was claimed by members of Clique I, Miss Verne Sanderson was claimed by Clique 2, and Miss Ruth DeSand was claimed by members of both cliques.[8]

In addition to their study of social structure among groups of White women, Davis, Gardner, and Gardner examined the social structure of informal groups of Black women to further understand the dynamics of social stratification by class and caste. In contrast to the extensive records of White women's participation in social events, it was considerably more difficult to identify Black women's participation. Records of Black women's participation were collected primarily through newspaper records, lists of church and association memberships, and personal interviews. In contrast to the forty-three groups of White women they identified, the researchers were able to identify twenty-six social groups within the Black community.

Their observations uncovered important distinctions between the relational structure of groups of White women and groups of Black women. Within groups of White women, class distinctions were made primarily along educational and economic lines. Therefore, social mobility among White women largely focused on educational and economic gains. Since most of the educational and economic opportunities available to White people were denied to members of the Black community, social class distinctions among

8. Davis, Gardner, and Gardner, *Deep South.*

Black women relied primarily on differences in skin color, with a high social value placed on light skin color and straight hair. Additionally, the fact that the vast majority of Black women were considered lower class (even by their own standards) indicates that there was a conflict between caste and class within the Black community. Efforts to increase Black women's class status were equated psychologically with an attempt to acquire traits of the White caste—Whiteness of skin and straightness of hair—which often resulted in women who possessed those traits to migrate to the upper class by "passing for white."[9] As the years passed, however, there were increasing numbers of darker women in the upper-class levels due to the growing tendency to emphasize solidarity within the Black community by invoking values of racial pride and loyalty.

Impact of the Southern Women Dataset on Social Network Analysis

The collection of data about the fourteen events attended by the eighteen women has come to be known by social network analysts as the Southern Women dataset. It has become somewhat of a touchstone among social network analysts, with many researchers using the data as a test bed for new models designed to analyze social structure. The Southern Women dataset has garnered popularity and utility for a number of important reasons. It has several noteworthy properties that make it attractive from an analytical perspective. It is small and manageable, with a relatively simple structural pattern of two somewhat distinct social groups. Additionally, it is collected and presented in two-mode form, where women are organized by the events they attended. This provides an opportunity to explore mathematical methods designed for two-mode data. At the same time, the data can be easily transformed into two one-mode matrices (either in terms of linking women by their common attendance at events or by linking events by the number of women who jointly attended them). This transformation of the data can then be examined using mathematical tools for one-mode analysis.

Due to these attractive mathematical properties, the Southern Women dataset has been applied by researchers from a variety of disciplines, in a variety of analytical settings, using a variety of methods. Following the initial analysis by Davis, Gardner, and Gardner (which did not include systematic analytic procedures), many social network analysts have used a wide variety of mathematical tools to glean insights from the Southern

9. Davis, Gardner, and Gardner, *Deep South.*

Women dataset.[10] This has included the use of computational methods such as partitioning,[11] algebraic analyses,[12] and applications of graph theory.[13] The Southern Women dataset has had a fundamental impact on the field of network analysis, leading to new methods and innovative approaches for envisioning social structure. However, much of the subsequent analyses have not focused on highlighting the context of the data and its importance in the study of social structure among Black and White women in the Deep South.

Conclusion

Davis, Gardner, and Gardner observed the informal behaviors of women to complete a thorough examination of caste and class in the Deep South during the 1940s, and the simplicity of the data they collected gave rise to a number of subsequent analyses. Their data describing the interaction of eighteen women over a series of fourteen informal events is of special importance. The Southern Women dataset, as it has come to be known within the field of social network analysis, has been used to validate numerous new methods for understanding social structure by illuminating the roles, alliances, and cliques that exist within larger groups of informal relationships.[14] However, much of the literature exploring social network analysis does not set out to extend the

10. Linton C. Freeman, "Finding Social Groups: A Meta-Analysis of the Southern Women Data," *Dynamic Social Network Modeling and Analysis* (Washington, DC: The National Academies Press, 2003).

11. George C. Homans, *The Human Group* (New York: Harcourt, Brace and Company, 1950); David P. Phillips and Richard H. Conviser, "Measuring the Structure and Boundary Properties of Groups: Some Uses of Information Theory," *Sociometry* 35, no. 2 (1972): 235–54.

12. Ronald L. Breiger, "The Duality of Persons and Groups," *Social Forces* 53, no. 2 (1974): 181–90; Phillip Bonacich, "Using Boolean Algebra to Analyze Overlapping Memberships," *Sociological Methodology* 9 (1978): 101–15; Patrick Doreian, "On the Delineation of Small Group Structure," *Classifying Social Data* (San Francisco: Jossey-Bass, 1979); Linton C. Freeman and Douglas R. White, "Using Galois Lattices to Represent Network Data," *Sociological Methodology* 23 (1993): 127–46.

13. Martin G. Everett and Stephen P. Borgatti, "An Extension of Regular Colouring of Graphs to Digraphs, Networks and Hypergraphs," *Social Networks* 15, no. 3 (September 1993): 237–54.

14. Linton C. Freeman, "Finding Social Groups: A Meta-Analysis of the Southern Women Data," *Dynamic Social Network Modeling and Analysis* (Washington, DC: The National Academies Press, 2003).

analysis of southern women, representing a rich area for future research that will lead to a deeper understanding of the social structure among White and Black women in the Deep South.

Bibliography

Bonacich, Phillip. "Using Boolean Algebra to Analyze Overlapping Memberships." *Sociological Methodology* 9 (1978): 101–15.

Borgatti, Stephen P., et al. "Network Analysis in the Social Sciences." *Science* 323 (February 13, 2009): 892–95.

Breiger, Ronald L. "The Duality of Persons and Groups." *Social Forces* 53, no. 2 (1974): 181–90.

Burt, Ronald S. *Corporate Profits and Cooptation.* New York: Academic Press, 1983.

Cartwright, Dorwin, and Frank Harary. "Balance and Clusterability: An Overview." *Perspectives on Social Network Research*, edited by Paul W. Holland and Samuel Leinhardt. New York: Academic Press, 1979.

Davis, Allison, Burleigh B. Gardner, and Mary R. Gardner. *Deep South: A Social Anthropological Study of Caste and Class.* Chicago: University of Chicago Press, 1941.

Doreian, Patrick. "On the Delineation of Small Group Structure." *Classifying Social Data*, edited by H. C. Hudson. San Francisco: Jossey-Bass, 1979.

Everett, Martin G., and Stephen P. Borgatti. "An Extension of Regular Colouring of Graphs to Digraphs, Networks and Hypergraphs." *Social Networks* 15, no. 3 (September 1993): 237–54.

Fredericks, Kimberly A., and Maryann M. Durland. "The Historical Evolution and Basic Concepts of Social Network Analysis." *New Directions for Evaluation* (February 2, 2006): 15–23.

Freeman, Linton C. "Finding Social Groups: A Meta-Analysis of the Southern Women Data." *Dynamic Social Network Modeling and Analysis*, edited by Ronald Breiger, Kathleen Carley, and Philippa Pattison. Washington, DC: The National Academies Press, 2003.

Freeman, Linton C., and Douglas R. White. "Using Galois Lattices to Represent Network Data." *Sociological Methodology* 23 (1993): 127–46.

Homans, George C. *The Human Group*. New York: Harcourt, Brace and Company, 1950.

Moreno, Jacob. *Who Shall Survive? A New Approach to the Problem of Human Interrelations.* Nervous and Mental Disease Publishing Company, 1934.

Phillips, David P., and Richard H. Conviser. "Measuring the Structure and Boundary Properties of Groups: Some Uses of Information Theory." *Sociometry* 35, no. 2 (1972): 235–54.

White, Harrison C. *An Anatomy of Kinship: Mathematical Models for Structures of Cumulated Roles.* Englewood Cliffs, NJ: Prentice Hall, 1963.

Dr. Taniecea A. Mallery serves as the executive director of Strategic Initiatives and chief diversity officer at the University of Louisiana at Lafayette. She is a member of the graduate faculty, teaching doctoral-level courses in the College of Education. Previously, she worked as a senior diversity research specialist at the Association of American Medical Colleges and a postdoctoral research fellow at the U.S. Census Bureau. Dr. Mallery earned a bachelor's degree in mathematics from Loyola University New Orleans, as well as a master's degree and PhD in applied and computational mathematics from Princeton University.

Building H.E.R. House

Interpreting Gendered Spaces, Visualizing Matriarchal Autonomous Tradition, and the Anecdotal Exploration of Southern Black Female Spatial Misogynoir in Literature

Kiwana T. McClung

Matriarchy, Misogynoir, and Architecture

The introductory chapter to Ernest J. Gaines's book *The Autobiography of Miss Jane Pittman* is a literary exemplar of the spatial experience of women of color in the southern United States. In this brief passage, Miss Jane Pittman suffers an invasion of her space by a willful White male journalist who is adamant that she tell him her life story. Although the passage does not speak to a particular spatial condition, Gaines makes it clear in his notes for the book that he envisions the scene taking place on Miss Jane Pittman's porch.[1] Her dialogue with her friend, Mary Hodges, reveals that Miss Jane knows that her space will continuously be invaded unless she gives in to the teacher's will, and she purposefully ignores her caretaker's more radical suggestion of arming herself to get him to desist, understanding that it is not even an option for her. At the end of the excerpt, the teacher insincerely asks, "You mean it's all right?" which earns him respective blank and damning looks from Miss Jane and Mary, during which they decline to comment on his complete and utter lack of awareness of his encroachment. In the end, Miss Jane confirms his choice of Monday as the day to start, all the while inferring that it is not really a choice for her at all.[2] It is a condition that is

1. Ernest J. Gaines, "Introduction Drafts and Notes, *The Autobiography of Miss Jane Pittman*," Box 5, Collection 115, Ernest J Gaines Papers, Ernest J. Gaines Center, Edith Garland Dupré Library, University of Louisiana at Lafayette, Lafayette, LA.

2. Ernest J. Gaines, *The Autobiography of Miss Jane Pittman* (New York: Bantam, 1978), 2–5.

revealed several times throughout the work; one where the Black female body is inevitably disrespected, intruded upon or posited about in physical space according to the limited worldviews of autocratic individuals. It is the debatably unknowing usurpation of her position of authority, her autonomy over her own body and the space she occupies; her space. This very real condition can be found in numerous literary works that focus on this particular marginalized group; however, this essay explores particular spatial conditions which give the Black matriarch both a power and a vulnerability that is driven by the people she engages with.

It is an interesting concept that architecture intended for a more sociocultural condition with altruistic undertones can facilitate the execution of a racially driven misogyny, and also one that has rarely been explored. There are two significant reasons for this, both of which can be explained best by the concept of intersectionality in the experiences and discrimination of Black women. First, race has historically been excluded from the feminist repertory, therefore negating the experiences of Black women more often than not. In her essay on intersectionality and feminist theory, Kimberle Crenshaw states, "Black women are sometimes excluded from feminist theory and anti-racist policy discourse because both are predicated on a discrete set of experience that often does not accurately reflect the interaction of race and gender."[3] Historically, intersectionality has not been a focus of mainstream feminism and, as such, the plight of Black women being spatially besieged simultaneously by the overbearing quality of masculinity and the discriminatory nuances of race is largely ignored. Sharon Smith, in her article on Black feminism and intersectionality, furthers the understanding of Crenshaw's arguments, "Black women are frequently absent from analyses of either gender oppression or racism since the former focuses primarily on the experiences of white women and the latter on Black men."[4] The point that Crenshaw seeks to make clear is that the racial oppression of Black women occurs under the auspices of patriarchy, and the conditions that dictate the gender oppression of Black women are significantly affected by race dynamics; as Smith states, "A key

3. Kimberle Crenshaw, "Demarginalizing the Intersection of Race and Sex: A Black Feminist Critique of Antidiscrimination Doctrine, Feminist Theory and Antiracist Politics," in *Feminist Legal Theory: Readings in Law and Gender*, eds. Katharine T. Bartlett and Rosanne Kennedy (New York: Routledge, 1991), 58.

4. Sharon Smith, "Black feminism and intersectionality," *International Socialist Review* 91 (Winter 2013–14).

aspect of intersectionality lies in its recognition that multiple oppressions are not each suffered separately, but rather as a single, synthesized experience."[5] In her book *Where We Stand: Class Matters*, bell hooks identifies a key component of feminism that often keeps intersectionality out of the conversation: Classicism.

> Ironically, anti-feminist public policy is steadily undermining the rights gained by feminist struggle so women who have gained class privilege by colluding with white supremacist capitalist patriarchy will lose in the long run. The only genuine hope of feminist liberation lies with a vision of social change that takes into consideration the ways interlocking systems of classism, racism and sexism work to keep women exploited and oppressed.[6]

Speaking to an often-invisible class of women, bell hooks realized that any feminist gains made within a patriarchal system hinged on class and race "required the sustained subordination of working-class women. When privileged women left home to work, someone had to stay in the home and do the dirty work."[4] With patriarchal systems of class and White supremacy left in place, the strides made toward equality under mainstream feminism unfortunately offer no room to consider the plight of Black women. The second reason that architecture as a facilitator of racially driven misogyny has not been considered is because there has been little to no exploration into the role architecture plays in shaping spatial experiences for people of color. Craig Wilkins, in his book *The Aesthetics of Equity*, brilliantly manages to do so using the concept of *spatial membership*, or placed-based identity provided to all members of a society, put forth by Aspa Gospodini and referencing John Locke's fundamental concepts of space. Wilkins asserts that Locke's views on preexisting space and our ability to know and fix the limits of space, as defined by the relationship of bodies to one another, actually identifies the framework for how and why race dynamics occur in physical space:

> When viewed from the dominant spatial perspective, the issue for African Americans becomes this: What happens when the relational foundation of space has to navigate between aspects of identity and rights, or, in other words, when Locke's space is defined by a single white body and a single Black body? What is typically observed is that the white body, while recognizing the Black body because it is necessary—as a relational point—to

5. Smith, "Black feminism and intersectionality."
6. bell hooks, *Where We Stand: Class Matters* (New York: Routledge, 2000), 109.

> define their own (place in) space, at the same time is hostile to the Black body's right to be in the space.[7]

Wilkins posits that it is Locke's own statements, acknowledging the connection between property ownership and physical space yet completely disregarding the role that race plays within the concept and history of ownership, that unequivocally reveal this differential socio-spatial experience of power dynamics in space:

> And it is by this single characteristic that Locke excludes one group from freely accessing space and property while empowering another. African Americans were legally defined as property primarily—if not solely—because they were Black, while whites were not property because they were white.[8]

In his essay on the role race and place in the formation of Whiteness in the Jim Crow South, Steven Hoelscher states,

> Like all social constructions, then, whiteness is both a geographic phenomenon and, as Peter Jackson notes, "an historically specific social formation." Put somewhat differently, what we today identify as whiteness has a temporary trajectory and a spatial context that can—and desperately needs to be investigated.[9]

There is no place more evident of the spatial implications of race and gender than the Jim Crow South, the remnants of which can still be felt, seen, and even more importantly experienced today, and by no other social group more than Black women. It is precisely this aspect of spatial understanding, drawing primarily from the perspectives of Black women, that will be extensively studied in this essay. The concept of architecture as a facilitator of racially driven misogyny is a lived reality for Black women in American society and it is not a surprise that it appears extensively within many literary works; especially those centered on southern Black female matriarchy. A retrospective review of the myriad ways architectural elements and spaces have

7. Craig L. Wilkins, *The Aesthetics of Equity: Notes on Race, Space, Architecture and Music* (Minneapolis: University of Minnesota Press, 2007), 18.

8. Wilkins, *The Aesthetics of Equity*, 15.

9. Steven Hoelscher, "Making Place, Making Race: Performances of Whiteness in the Jim Crow South," *Annals of the Association of American Geographers* 93, no. 3 (2003): 662.

shaped and been shaped by Black matriarchy is both provocative in terms architectural theory and necessary to understanding the unique aspects of Black female oppression. This essay will explore this rarely discussed condition of architecture as a facilitator of misogynoir, as revealed by literary expression and through the detailing of a specific installation project, H.E.R. House, which reinterprets these Black female spaces, allowing these fictional women to symbolically reclaim their power in the name of real-life Black matriarchs.

The Chosen Literary Works and Their Contexts

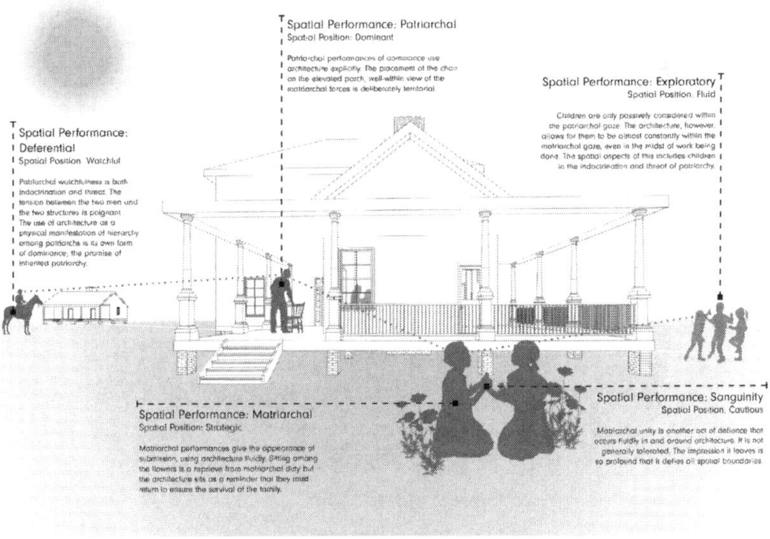

Fig 1: Spatial Analysis of Misogynoir in the Literary and Film-Adapted Work The Color Purple *by Alice Walker*

Diversity and gender disparity are two of the most discussed issues of the current time and, in the architecture profession, these issues extend far beyond gender-discriminatory work cultures and wage gaps. Discrimination against women and the definition of traditional female roles is a spatial problem as well, allowing spaces that are traditionally female to be viewed, considered, and designed through a male lens, without adequate or accurate consideration of their female users. It creates an even more insidious problem for spaces viewed as traditionally male; they typically lack regard for—and in many cases actually create—barriers to female use. To provide an anecdotal example of this, contemporarily over half of architecture students are women but only about 15 percent of architects are women. This disparity is perplexing until one considers the unique social conditions surrounding women entering architectural employment. Most architectural educational attainment usually happens between the ages of twenty-one and twenty-five; for women, this also happens to be the time when women often start families. According to the Center for Disease Control (CDC), the average age for women experiencing their first childbirth in the United States was 26.6 in 2014.[10] It is incredibly difficult to engage in a successful architecture career when spatial allowances, like rooms designed or allocated specifically for mothers who need to periodically pump breast milk for their babies, are still rare in firms today. This is not a surprise, as historically, architecture firms have been largely male in both make-up and leadership; this actually perfectly explains why facilities often lack these sorts of spaces. It does illustrate, however, just how pervasive oppressive systems are; the built environment actively holds together these systems, allowing them to persist even in the face of change. Race provides an additional layer of complexity that defines how these spaces are experienced by different people in the built environment. In contrast to the 15 percent of architects who are women, only 2 percent of architects are Black women. For a Black woman entering the architectural workforce in contemporary times, concerns about accommodations during breastfeeding and career advancement during maternity leave are just as much a worry, but are magnified by race dynamics. The issue of breastfeeding mothers who are invested in their careers can be readily solved by creating a safe, clean space for those mothers to pump, but no space is a guaranteed haven for Black women, for whom spatial occupation is dictated by both the race and the gender of the person sharing a space with them. Furthermore, Black women have always been "working" mothers, yet the adaptation of workspaces for women has not warranted scrutiny until recently. The matriarchal model for Black women, existing for over two hundred years, is essentially predicated on working while also caring for children, even children who are not their

10. Centers for Disease Control and Prevention, T. J. Matthews, and Brady E. Hamilton, *Mean Age of Mothers is on the Rise: United States, 2000–2014* § (2016). https://www.cdc.gov/nchs/data/databriefs/db232.pdf.

own, yet this model has never led to significant spatial consideration for women. The primary directive for Black women engaging any space in the world is adaptation: to the space, the elements, and the people within it. The interpretation of how settings are described in southern Black literature and narratives reveal these gender-driven spatial intricacies. Speaking specifically of the creation of the "Black matriarchy," Smith posits that the unique conditions of their oppression allowed Black women to be blamed for the perceived ills of Black family structure and culture: "The same 'experts' who prescribed a life of happy homemaking for white suburban women, as documented in Betty Freidan's enormously popular *The Feminine Mystique*, reprimanded Black women for their failure to conform to this model."[11] The Black matriarch occupies physical space in a manner that breaks traditional patriarchal edicts but is subject to the whims of supremacy doctrine. In other words, spatial boundaries for Black women are fluid, defined intrinsically both by the races and the genders of the other individuals in that space. A hierarchy emerges in such conditions that reveals the complex ways that Black women navigate everyday life.

When reading the narratives of the works selected for interpretation of the Black woman in architectural space, I was vividly reminded of my own early experiences with Black matriarchy and the dawning realization of its impossible positioning within a patriarchal, racialized societal structure. My grandmother, Ola Mae, was a largely illiterate, spunky, Black woman of Creole ancestry and an outspoken cancer survivor. In our household, the kitchen was understood to be her domain. It was both a place of comfort and power for her, as she had spent her life working in kitchen spaces, having been a cook for White families in south Louisiana for many years, and having conducted most of her interactions with family and visitors in kitchen spaces. Her authority over and in the kitchen was respected by most everyone, even my mother, the rightful lady of the house. Occasionally, however, my father—who envisioned himself quite the cook but was decidedly not—would assert his position in the household and gain unrestricted access to the kitchen; it is only in this condition that her dominance waivers but it does not fully evaporate, only re-forms, becoming more passive-aggressive in its manifestations. She'd wait, often hovering in the kitchen doorway, for the moment my father would leave the space; then she would enter, setting the place to right, subtly tweaking his semi-prepared dishes and adjusting the heat

11. Smith, "Black feminism and intersectionality."

of the cooktop or oven, quietly slipping away as he reentered. Excepting my father, everyone in the family was aware of and had witnessed her actions during these instances, yet we gamely said nothing. I could always sense the resentment Grandmother Ola held inside, knowing she had oftentimes saved these meals from being inedible, but she always maintained her silence; in the kitchen she was queen, but the bounds of the ego-driven male patriarchy ensured that she could not declare it. When containing the dominant male of the household, she is relegated to the interloper role, relying on guerrilla-war-like tactics to assert her authority. She made sure the family could eat, asserted her dominance over that space, and soothed my father's male ego in a delicate dance that reveals the near impossibility of her position. The practiced manner in which she engaged in this performance revealed her experience in this dance, having engaged in it numerous times in the past with the White women that she worked for as a cook and washer. Her efforts were exhausting to watch, yet when I consider them in hindsight, I realize the difficulty of her position. The domestic kitchen has historically been a decidedly feminine space and, due to the legacy of American slavery, one of the primary spaces of dominion and survival for the Black matriarch, yet they were still bound by the patriarchal and racial restriction, forced to maintain authority in more subversive ways to ensure resiliency of the household. Grandmother Ola was a product of a system in which Black female bodies were exploited through the kitchen, for the betterment and survival of *all* families. Grandmother Ola engaged in a spatial performance organized by gender and race, under which her primary objective as a Black matriarch is the continued survival of the family. As Hoelscher states, "Cultural performances invest individuals and social groups with the rhetorical tools necessary to make strategic use of those divisions for their own, political ends."[12] There has been much recent exploration of the complex performances Black women must engage in to navigate a racialized patriarchal society, yet there has not much reflection on how these performances are shaped by defined space and architectural elements. Assuredly, southern spaces, due to their histories being tied intrinsically to Jim Crow spatial politics, offer an uncensored view into architectural space's unique relationship with Black matriarchy.

12. Hoelscher, "Making Place, Making Race," 661.

Interpretation of the Black Female Spatial Experience as Found in African American Literature Narratives

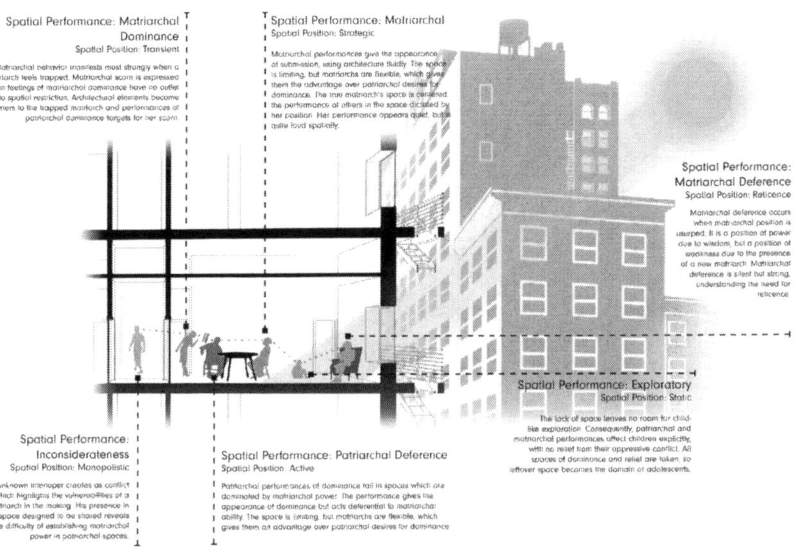

Fig 2: Spatial Analysis of Matriarchal and Patriarchal Conflict in the Literary, Film, and Stage-adapted work A Raisin in the Sun *by Lorraine Hansberry*

There are three architectural elements/spatial conditions that are referenced, both implicitly and explicitly in the chosen passages and narratives selected for interpretation toward the design of H.E.R. House; the porch condition, the kitchen, and the window. The porch is the setting alluded to in the editor's introduction to *The Autobiography of Miss Jane Pittman*; a space where both members of the community and an insistent visitor gains immediate access to Miss Jane, the latter without an invitation. In early drafts of the work, Gaines quite plainly outlines that the introduction setting is a porch, writing, "We were sitting out on the porch—the gall[e]y they call it."[13] A porch condition is also described in the chosen passage from Alice Walker's *The Color Purple*, and windows are referenced, alluding to the fact that these

13. Gaines, "Introduction Drafts and Notes," Ernest J. Gaines Center Archives.

architectural elements were added to make the structure more residential. In the chosen passage, Celie states,

> Harpo fix up the little creek house for him and his family. Mr. _______ daddy used it for a shed. But it sound. Got windows now, a porch, back door. Plus it cool and green by the creek.[14]

The kitchen is a central feature in the passages chosen as well, with Celie describing it as such:

> It not big, but it homey. Got a bed, a dresser, a looking glass, and some chairs. Cookstove for cooking and heating too.[15]

In the passage chosen from *A Raisin in the Sun*, the kitchen is the primary setting for the interactions between the book's characters and is even mentioned as the place of employment for the narrative's young matriarch:

> RUTH: Walter, don't be dragging me in it.
> WALTER: You are in it—Don't you get up and go work in somebody's kitchen for the last three years to help put clothes on her back?[16]

These elements are not referenced arbitrarily in the chosen passages; in every instance of their mention, they bring critical attention to the specific social conditions of Black women, clearly identifying their hierarchy within the social strata of society. Even more, with every mention of these architectural spatial elements, the porch, the kitchen, and the window, it is revealed that with the rise of the Black matriarch their initial or intended uses have been perverted to fit the social constraints of southern life.

14. Alice Walker, *The Color Purple* (New York: Houghton Mifflin Harcourt, 1982), 40.
15. Walker, *The Color Purple*, 40.
16. Lorraine Hansberry, *A Raisin in the Sun* (New York: Random House, 1958), 37.

The Porch

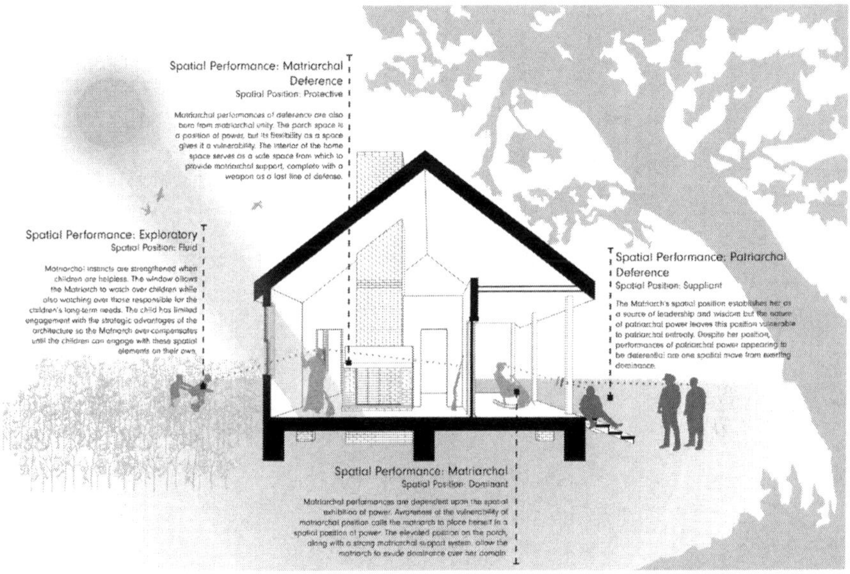

Fig 3: Spatial Analysis of Matriarchal Positioning in the Literary Work
The Autobiography of Miss Jane Pittman *by Ernest J. Gaines*

The word "porch" derives from the Latin word *porticus*, or the Greek word *portico*, both of which define a columned, covered entrance. Historically, the portico denoted entry to Classical temples, structures built to honor Greek deities, not used for formal gathering. The porch presents itself as an extended threshold in its classical examples, spatially preparing the temple patron for the sacred space beyond.[17] American architecture has obvious classical influences; however, the social, political, and economic conditions from the American version of the porch displays a symbolism that seeks to lay purchase to the same stamina boasted by the Greco-Romans, with certain elements changing in their apparent use due to sociocultural state under which it was adopted. The American porch transforms a threshold condition meant to be moved through into a more social condition meant to be occupied as well, giving the porch itself more power in this regard. The porch condition is found in many cultures throughout the world; yet, in America it has

17. Scott Cook, *The Evolution of the American Front Porch*, accessed 2018. http://xroads.virginia.edu/~CLASS/am483_97/projects/cook/first.htm.

been combined with particular architectural, programmatic, and social features that define its use, orientation, and occupation. As a space that is both public and private, that is both leisure space and work space, it is arguably the most versatile, adaptable space in residential structures today, lending itself to a variety of uses. Historically, no other architectural condition resonates more with the Black southern matriarchy than the porch, particularly due to American slavery, under which the American version of the element developed, but perhaps more ironically due to the adaptability of the Black matriarch and the ability of the porch conditions to accept adaptation barring formal use. In the film version of *The Autobiography of Miss Jane Pittman*, the matriarch conducts many conversations and interactions from her porch space, subtly announcing Miss Jane Pittman as an authority on the matters to be presented; the porch in this case acting as a semi-public space in which she could receive the grievances of the community. In *The Color Purple*, the porch space is presented as a necessary architectural feature to rural domestic life and is promptly added to any structure used in this capacity. In the film version, the porch is the scene of some of the most defining and dramatic moments of the film. It is a place of retreat for Celie to read and write when her sister is torn from her arms and ejected from her life by her husband. It is a space of dominion where she watches over her husband's children, prepares meals, and watches as her husband tills the ground. It is space of marginalization when her father-in-law comes over to visit with her husband; Celie subtly undermines this domination of her space and her dismissal within it with a bit of spittle in his drink. The porch is also a space in which Celie displays her resentments concerning her status in life most prominently, where she contemplates murdering her husband, and the space where eventually leaves him standing as she takes her matriarchal support system out of the equation. Celie is simultaneously relegated to this space, defined by it based on who occupies it, and empowered by it. It is implied in both *The Autobiography of Miss Jane Pittman* and *The Color Purple* that the porch is an extended threshold of both the kitchen and the living space, allowing it to be used as a flex space. More importantly, in both works, all that is seen, done, and accessed from the porch is explicitly stated.

The Kitchen

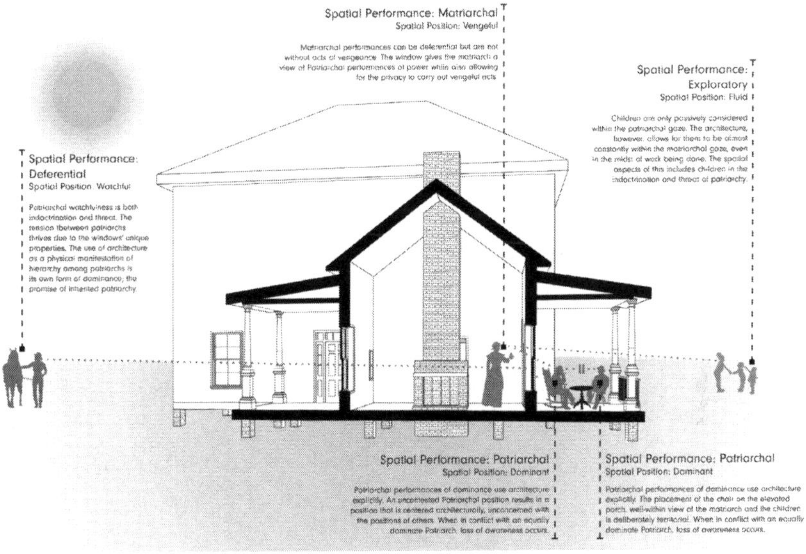

Fig 4: Spatial Analysis of Matriarchal Vengeance in the Literary and Film-Adapted Work The Color Purple *by Alice Walker*

The kitchen is arguably one of the most definitive Black female spaces, existing simultaneously as a place of power and relegation. It is the undisputed domain—and sometime prison—of the Black matriarch, both in its workings and organization; ironically, due to it being the space in which the most basic necessities of human life are assuaged, it is the most powerful space in the home. As evidenced by the passages presented in *A Raisin in the Sun*, the southern kitchen is a space that presents most clearly the complex hierarchy of the household and society. In that space, it is clear that the young matriarch Ruth is the authority, yet her husband Walter postures about the space to assert his dominance over her according to the gaze of society. Ruth does not challenge this display directly, but expresses her dominance in more subtle ways.

> BENEATHA (Turning slowly in her chair): And then there are all those prophets who would lead us out of the wilderness—(WALTER slams out of the house)—into the swamps!

> RUTH: Bennie, why you always gotta be pickin' on your brother? Can't you be a little sweeter sometimes? (Door opens, WALTER walks in)
>
> WALTER: (To RUTH) I need some money for carfare.
>
> RUTH: (Looks at him, then warms; teasing, but tenderly) Fifty cents? (She goes to her bag and gets money) Here, take a taxi.[18]

In this passage, Ruth demonstrates her dominance in the kitchen with her ability to chastise her sister-in-law while ensuring that her husband had a meal to start the day and a means to get to work promptly, thereby ensuring the family's survival. The character Beneatha, Walter's sister, serving as example of the growing opportunities for women of color, boldly challenges her brother's perceived dominance in the space while simultaneously belittling her sister-in-law's and mother's relegation to the space:

> BENEATHA: (Dropping to her knees) Well—I do—all right? —thank everybody. . . and forgive me for ever wanting to be anything at all. . . forgive me, forgive me!
>
> RUTH: Please stop it! Your mama'll hear you.
>
> WALTER: Who the hell told you had to be a doctor? If you so crazy 'bout messing 'round with sick people—then go be a nurse like other women—or just get married and be quiet.[19]

In this passage, Beneatha blithely criticizes her mother's and sister-in-law's existences as matriarchs relegated to the kitchen. Beneatha and Walter's mother, despite the fact that the family discussion taking place for most of the scene concerns a monetary inheritance that is due to her, is silent, contrasting with Ruth and Beneatha's commentary and reflecting the various oppressive experiences and social frameworks of all three women. In that space, Mother is powerless and perhaps feels detached from the power dynamics of the kitchen due to the presence of a new matriarch, yet she remains in the space throughout the argument as if it is the only space for her. Ironically, the kitchen becomes the space where the family receives, from the White insurance agent, devastating news that there is no inheritance to be gained; the power dynamic shifts once again with the entrance of a White male.

18. Hansberry, *A Raisin in the Sun*, 37.
19. Hansberry, *A Raisin in the Sun*, 38.

The Window

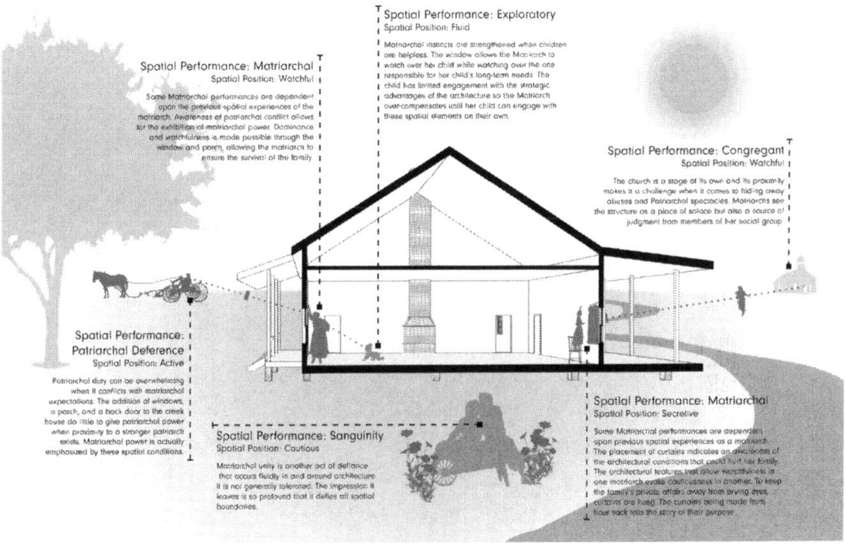

Fig 5: Spatial Analysis of Matriarchal and Patriarchal Conflict in the Literary and Film-Adapted work The Color Purple *by Alice Walker*

The bedroom window is a subtle yet powerful architectural feature of a structure, particularly for the Black matriarch. It simultaneously represents an entry point for light and air into the space, a discreet place from which to observe the outside world, and an instrument of physical and mental escape. It undoubtedly serves as a mechanism that allows the matriarch to complete her duties while also observing the work happening outside and the welfare of playing children. Consideration on the window from another social perspective, however, reveals that, to the Black matriarch, the window is also an element that minimizes privacy. As much as it is a way to see out, get out, and control the light/air of a space, it also provides a way for those outside to see into a space, revealing the private happenings and interactions of an individual or family. In *The Color Purple*, curtains for the window is Celie's contribution to the newlyweds Harpo and Sophia for their new home. Considering Celie's own experiences in her home and marriage, having the option to conceal the abuse and marginalization she suffers in her marriage from the outside world serves as both a survival mechanism and an attempt to exact control over her own narrative in her social group. Celie states the making of the curtains for the couple matter-of-factly and, as Celie economically uses flour sack to make the curtains, it is clear that her choice is not a matter of aesthetics but privacy in the face of limited resources.

In the chosen passage, Celie states,

> But now Sofia coming, he always busy. He chop, he hammer, he plow. He sing and whistle. . . . She tell Harpo, Hold the baby, while she come back in the house with me to git some thread. She making some sheets. He take the baby, give it a kiss, chuck it under the chin. Grin, look up on the porch at his daddy. Mr. ______ blow smoke, look down at him, and say, Yeah, I see now she going to switch the traces on you."[20]

Sofia and Celie both present themselves as matriarchs who ensure the survival of the family, but they each view and treat the window differently based upon their differential experiences with their husbands. While Celie is most concerned with putting up curtains in the window to shield the outside world from the shame of her plight with Mr. _____, Sofia's matriarchal position is established as an overseer for her husband and child, the window allowing her to ensure their safety and the sowing of crops needed for the family's survival. The curtains allow observation by the matriarchs to be discreet, lest they challenge their husband's authority or, in Sofia's case, his ego. The window also serves as a poignant connection between spaces, allowing for the protagonist to blithely gain insights and information from individuals occupying adjacent spaces. Celie's decision to add a bit of her spittle to her father-in-law's drink is made as she observes him through the kitchen window, engaging in a performance of general misogyny and masculine scorn toward his son Mr. _____. In all of these descriptions, it is clear that the window serves these Black matriarchs in ways that go beyond the practical yearning for light and air.

Spaces and Elements Acting in Tandem

Perhaps the most poignant expression is how all of these spaces act in tandem with each other. *The Color Purple* has multiple passages that connect the happenings of the kitchen and porch through the window. *A Raisin in the Sun* has no described porch condition, thus no place of power for the women to occupy, which adds most heavily to the heightened sense of

20. Walker, *The Color Purple*, 40–41.

female oppression in the work. A shared bathroom for all the tenants on their floor of their walk-up, though, becomes a secondary battleground between Beneatha and an unknown tenant, representing Beneatha's desire to advance her life beyond the expectations that society has for her but being unable to do so due to current conditions. The symbolism of the three elements—the porch, the kitchen, and the window—if considered as a whole reveal how the subtleties of spatial power can be engaged as a method of survival. They also reveal the impossibility of the position Black women and matriarchs are asked to fill; if spaces were designed to meet the unique needs of Black matriarchs, they would be as contrasting and unconventional as the spatial conditions found in H.E.R. House.

Design of Installation: H.E.R. House

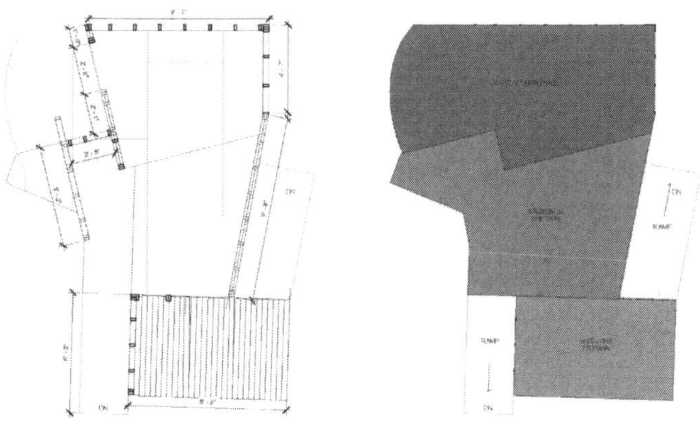

Fig 6: H.E.R. House Floor Plan and Diagram of Literary Spatial Ideas

Considering these three works and the passages chosen from them led to the design and construction of an installation that spatially contextualizes the intricacies of these Black matriarchal characters and their relationships with the people and elements around them. The research project began with a frank and open discussion addressing the students' concerns about diversity within the profession and the little-known stories they are interested in researching. This eventually led to student research into the achievements of Blacks and minority women within the profession of architecture, with a focus on biographical and precedential research. Members in the UL Lafayette chapter of the National Organization of Minority Architecture Students expressed a strong desire to design and build a full-scale installation and after a robust discussion concerning the feasibility of such a venture, the possible themes of the research and design focus of the installation, a collaborative opportunity was suggested. The Gaines Center is a special collection in the University of Louisiana at Lafayette's Edith Garland Dupré Library. Directed by Cheylon Woods, the Gaines Center holds a collection of literature honoring the works of Writer-in-Residence Emeritus Ernest J. Gaines and provides a space for viewing his papers, manuscripts, and relevant works. Gaines's works draws on his life experiences growing up in the South, which were heavily influenced by his own grandmother and other strong matriarchal figures. As the nature of the works found in this collection fit well with the chosen theme, it was decided that a built installation could explore the concept of space from the perspective of Black women, as depicted through literary setting and spatial descriptions in chosen works. Woods was consulted as an expert on the subject and suggested excerpts from several literary works that are explicit in their depiction of physical space and the descriptions of the behaviors and interactions of the women in those spaces. Reading the excerpts as a group revealed incredible insights into the lives of the characters, how their experiences reveal real-life constraints of women in the Reconstruction and Jim Crow eras, and how those experiences are reflected contemporarily. These insights were then employed by the students in the establishment of spatial rules and symbolic architectural artifacts to be used in the design of the installation.

The installation, which interrogated female space as portrayed in southern literature, was designed in three distinct yet intermingled parts, each conveying the differing female perspectives offered in the excerpts from the three chosen works: *The Autobiography of Miss Jane Pittman* by Ernest J. Gaines, *A Raisin in the Sun* by Lorraine Hansberry, and *The Color Purple* by Alice Walker. The students were adamant that the installation be presented as a three-act staging of spatial performance, contextualizing each characters' experience by allowing the user to become the performer, seamlessly interacting with symbolic architectural artifacts. The installation begins with Miss Jane Pittman's space, which is built as a porch condition and represents both the character's described physical setting and implications of the spatial condition, which, in the chosen excerpt, presents a duality in its symbolic meaning. The space is simultaneously a place of power and vulnerability for the aging matriarch. A ramp condition allows for accessible, unrestrained access to Miss Jane Pittman's porch while also allowing visitors to be monitored from the space.

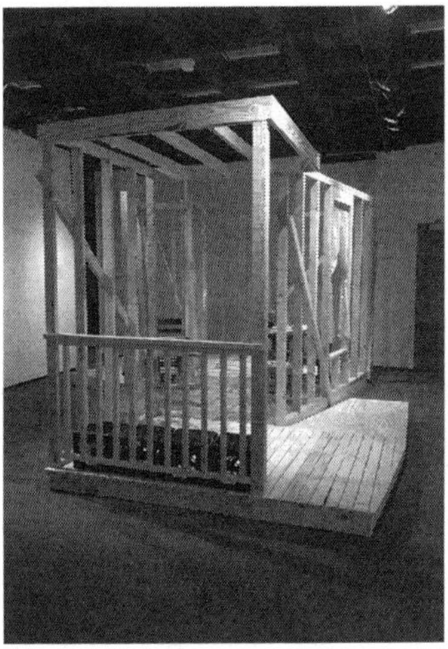

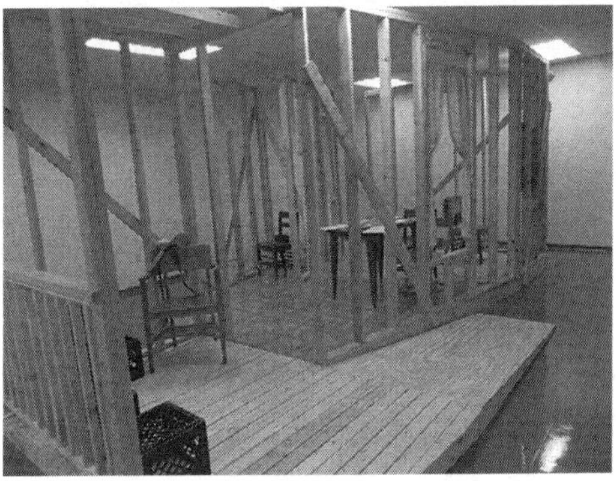

Figs 7 & 8: H.E.R. House in the Fletcher Hall Gallery (Left) and the Gaines Center at the Edith Garland Dupré Library (Above)

The user then crosses a threshold demarking entry into a space representing the characters depicted in an excerpt from *A Raisin in the Sun.* This space is charged with architectural artifacts, juxtaposing spaces in a manner that reveals the differing perspectives of three different generations of women. Ruth occupies the kitchen space with a seat at the table; however, her position is strategically placed next to a curtained window and in full view of all of the spaces within the house. From Ruth's seat, one can monitor visitors using the ramp, see the patrons of the porch space, communicate with occupants in the kitchen, and get an unfettered view into the back bedroom. The character Beneatha, a young medical student, is strikingly, defiantly feminist in her views and spatial movements. Her space sits to the opposite side of the kitchen space, away from the traditionally dressed dining area. Beneatha's space is defined by the kitchen, porch space, and Lena's space on three sides, speaking to her societal condition as a Black woman, bound by expectation, history, and the women who came before her. The fourth side of Beneatha's space lacks a wall and speaks to the opportunities she seeks, while also revealing a level drop that has no ramp or stairs for her to navigate. In her space, Beneatha is allowed to look out of her current condition toward a better future, yet essentially trapped by the lack of societal "structures" that would allow her to secure that future. The third character presented in this setting is that of Lena, the elderly mother of Walter and Beneatha and the matriarch of the family, who remains silent yet watchful throughout the scene. Lena's

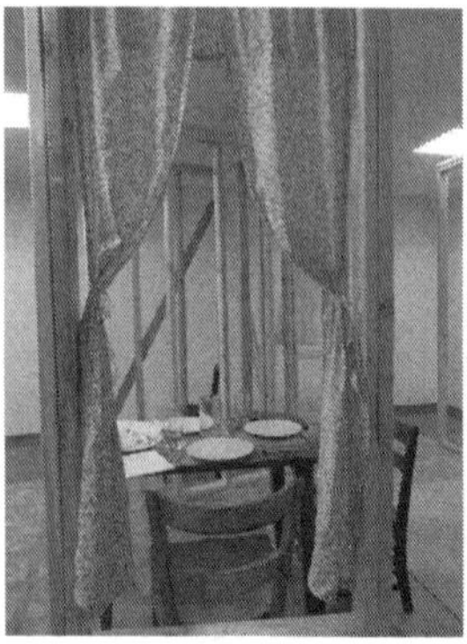 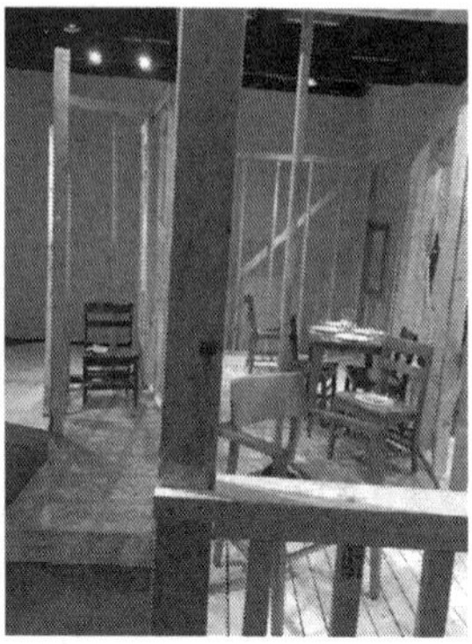 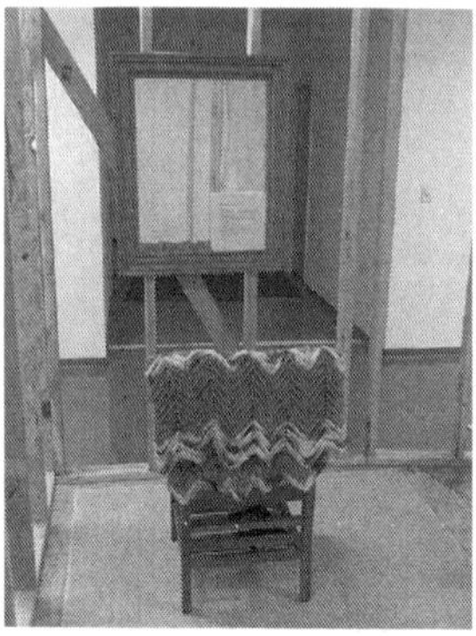

Figs 9, 10, & 11: H.E.R. House in the Gaines Center (left), Fletcher Hall Gallery (center), and the Gaines Center at the Edith Garland Dupré Library (right)

space is its own space within the kitchen, closed-off and confined on three sides, yet angled open toward both the kitchen and Beneatha's space so she can unobtrusively view all characters. Lena's space represents her confinement to a much smaller place within the kitchen as her family grows and due to the usurpation of her matriarchal position. The interactions, or lack thereof, between the women are exacerbated by the design of the spaces, revealing how quickly views on gender shift between generations and also the subtle power dynamics that occur due to race, gender, and age.

Finally, the user moves into Celie's space, which portrays the intricacies found in the excerpt chosen from Walker's *The Color Purple*. Celie's space is a reflective one, a bedroom space, as the protagonist in the chosen passage offers a humorous narrative that cannot hide her abject confusion over the power dynamics exhibited between her stepson Harpo and his new wife Sophia. The space contains a mirror or "looking glass" and forces the user to address their reflection in the same ways that Celie begins to look inward, comparing her observations about the lives and marriages of others to her own situation. Opposite to the mirror, the space opens into another porch condition, signaling Celie's development over time into a matriarch herself, bringing the patron of the installation full-circle. Celie's space is about her beginning to question the implied spatial boundaries that have been defined by her own marriage, as a consequence of witnessing Sophia's total disregard for those same boundaries and, in the face of Sophia's rejection of the gender roles of the time, Harpo's acceptance of Sophia. The walls of the installation were unenclosed, bare, stud walls, representing the inability of Black women to escape scrutiny. There was also no roof, which highlights the striking lack of protection Black women bear. All of these spaces together represent quite the unconventional house, unfinished with sharp corners and strange adjacencies, which I believe perfectly describes the plight of the Black matriarch but only hint at the unique complexity of the Black matriarchal condition.

The students coined the installation H.E.R. House, an acronym for Hope, Empowerment, and Reclamation and representing the intent of the installation. The installation is a "structure in process," exploring the relationship between the portrayal of Black feminine roles in literary space and actual physical space, the unfinished walls symbolizing the work that stills needs to be done in considering the perspectives of Black women. Despite its unconventional design focus, the space was designed using principles of universal design so that users of all physical capacities could have equal access to the spaces. The installation was likewise designed to break down into three distinct parts that could be transported for programming in the Gaines Center, to take place after the minority exhibition during women's history month. The minority exhibition became a central topic of discussion during its tenure in the Fletcher Hall Gallery and the Gaines Center programming that resulted from the research project was highly attended, allowing the installation to serve as a stage for poetry selections, musical selections, and dance performances celebrating the achievements of women.

Conclusion

The impact of the H.E.R. House Installation, both on the students conducting the research and the University of Louisiana at Lafayette School of Architecture and Design as a whole cannot be denied. Furthermore, it revealed that explorations into the unique spatial experiences of those that are *othered* are worthwhile endeavors for understanding the role that architecture plays in societal condition and social life. The research project and resulting discourse also led to the position that discrimination against women, and the definition of traditional female roles, can also be viewed as a spatial problem. Spaces that have traditionally been considered female—predominantly domestic spaces—have been conceived of, designed, and constructed from a male standpoint. Resultantly, spaces occupied by women are created without adequate consideration of their female users. The exploration and re-visioning through the installation allowed the students to address these intricacies, and the minority exhibitions and other resultant programming provided an engaging means of educating a new generation of designers and the public about the importance of diversity and social equity in design. Aside from its facilitation of a diverse discourse and the engaging aspect of undergraduate research, the project highlighted the achievements of women and challenged student ability to visualize experience while also addressing accessibility needs. Additionally, the installation's role in the planned programming created a learning opportunity that explored interplay between design and construction, allowing students to better understand how the decisions they make as designers get executed during construction. As a result of their research, analyses, and work, a shift has been observed within our school, one that identifies the pursuit of diversity and diverse perspectives as progressive and necessary aspects of architectural education. It is my sincere hope that these explorations continue, as they provide a poetic and much-needed insight into differential experience as dictated by race and gender. It is only by understanding these nuances that we begin to reshape the built world to match the highest ideals of human decency.

Bibliography

bell hooks. *Where We Stand: Class Matters.* New York: Routledge, 2000.

Centers for Disease Control and Prevention, T. J. Matthews, and Brady E. Hamilton, *Mean Age of Mothers is on the Rise: United States, 2000–2014* § (2016). https://www.cdc.gov/nchs/data/databriefs/db232.pdf.

Cook, Scott. *The Evolution of the American Front Porch.* Accessed 2018. http://xroads.virginia.edu/~CLASS/am483_97/projects/cook/first.htm.

Crenshaw, Kimberle. "Demarginalizing the Intersection of Race and Sex: A Black Feminist Critique of Antidiscrimination Doctrine, Feminist Theory and Antiracist Politics." In *Feminist Legal Theory: Readings in Law and Gender*, edited by Katharine T. Bartlett and Rosanne Kennedy, 57–80. New York: Routledge, 1991.

Gaines, Ernest J. *The Autobiography of Miss Jane Pittman.* New York: Bantam, 1978.

———. "Introduction Drafts and Notes, *The Autobiography of Miss Jane Pittman.*" Box 5, Collection 115, Ernest J Gaines Papers, Ernest J. Gaines Center, Edith Garland Dupré Library, University of Louisiana at Lafayette, Lafayette, LA.

Hansberry, Lorraine. *A Raisin in the Sun.* New York City: Random House, 1958.

Hoelscher, Steven. "Making Place, Making Race: Perfomances of Whiteness in the Jim Crow South." *Annals of the Association of American Geographers* 93, no. 3 (2003): 657–86. doi:10.1111/1467-8306.9303008.

Korty, John, dir. *The Autobiography of Miss Jane Pittman.* 1974. Universal City, CA: NBCUniversal Television Distribution.

Smith, Sharon. "Black feminism and intersectionality." *International Socialist Review* 91 (Winter 2013–14).

Spielberg, Steven, dir. *The Color Purple.* 1985; Burbank, CA: Warner Bros. Pictures.

Walker, Alice. *The Color Purple.* New York: Houghton Mifflin Harcourt, 1982.

Wilkins, Craig L. *The Aesthetics of Equity: Notes on Race, Space, Architecture and Music.* Minneapolis: University of Minnesota Press, 2007.

Kiwana T. McClung, Assoc. AIA, NOMA is a Baton Rouge, Louisiana, native and an associate professor in the School of Architecture & Design at the University of Louisiana at Lafayette. A graduate of Louisiana State University's Master of Architecture program, Kiwana has worked on a variety of architectural and planning projects, K–12 school renovations, master planning projects, Caribbean resort hotels, and commercial retail and residential projects throughout Louisiana. Kiwana serves as faculty advisor to the UL chapter of NOMAS, the student organization for National Organization of Minority Architects (NOMA). Though heavily involved in service activity, her biggest passion is inspiring and mentoring young student designers, particularly those from minority and disadvantaged backgrounds. Kiwana's research concerns the socio-spatial intricacies of our increasingly globalized and multi-cultural societies and how they affect the built environment, architectural education, and the profession.